DARING
DEEDS
OF
PIONEER
WOMEN

RESCUE OF MISS BOONE—*Page 16*

DARING DEEDS OF PIONEER WOMEN

JOHN FROST

DOVER PUBLICATIONS, INC.
MINEOLA, NEW YORK

Bibliographical Note

This Dover edition, first published in 2020, is an unabridged republication of *Daring and Heroic Deeds of American Women: Comprising Thrilling Examples of Courage, Fortitude, Devotedness, and Self-Sacrifice among the Pioneer Mothers of the Western Country*, originally printed by G. G. Evans, Philadelphia, in 1860. Readers should be forewarned that the text contains racial and cultural references of the era in which it was written and may be deemed offensive by today's standards. Style and punctuation vagaries derive from the original and have been retained for the sake of authenticity.

International Standard Book Number

ISBN-13: 978-0-486-84548-7
ISBN-10: 0-486-84548-6

Manufactured in the United States by LSC Communications
84548601
www.doverpublications.com

2 4 6 8 10 9 7 5 3 1

2020

CONTENTS

Ginny

Ginny

Ginny ML

ML

June

June

LIST OF ILLUSTRATIONS

PREFACE

THE HEROISM OF woman is the heroism of the heart. Her deeds of daring and endurance are prompted by affection. While her husband, her children, and all the other objects of tenderness are safe, her heroic capabilities repose in peace, and external troubles have little power to disturb her serenity. But when danger threatens the household, when the lurking savage is seen near the dwelling, or the war-whoop is heard in the surrounding woods, the matron becomes a heroine, and is ready to peril life, without a moment's hesitation, in the approaching conflict. When the family is overpowered, and the dwelling burnt with all its precious household treasures, she submits without a murmur; but when the life of husband or child is menaced, she throws herself beneath the threatening tomahawk, and is ready to receive the descending blow to save the loved one.

Captured and dragged away from her home, she endures fatigue, braves danger, bears contumely, and sometimes deals the death-blow to the sleeping captors, to save the lives of her children.

Such is woman's heroism. Such heroism it is the purpose of this collection of narratives to illustrate. If the reader will bear in mind, as he peruses these thrilling histories of woman's noble deeds, that affection prompts her daring, this volume will afford him much instruction as to the true character of woman. It will show her noble generosity and self-devotion in their true light; and will prove that chivalrous courtesy, which, by common consent, is always and every where in our noble country, accorded to woman, is no more than her well merited reward.

The Earl of Ellesmere, in his late speech at the Boston School Festival, said that "in America an unprotected woman is unknown." So let it be for ever!

HEROIC WOMEN OF THE WEST

THE DENIZENS OF the Eastern States of our glorious union are accustomed to regard the west as the regions of romance and adventure—a sort of American fairy land, whose people are ennobled by generous and chivalric sentiments, whose history abounds with thrilling adventures, startling incidents, and surprising changes—a land where cities spring up with a celerity which rivals the feats of Aladdin's palace-building Genius—and where fortunes are made with a facility only surpassed by the wonders of Aladdin's Lamp.

But the present security and prosperity of the west have been purchased by the blood of the first settlers. Every inch of their beautiful country had to be won from a cruel and savage foe by unheard-of toils, dangers, and conflicts. In these terrible border wars, which marked the early years of the western settlements, the men signalized themselves by prodigies of valor, enterprise, and endurance; while the women rivalled them in all these virtues, affording often the most splendid examples of that spirit of self-sacrifice and devotion which can only be prompted by disinterested affection.

Of these instances of female heroism, running through the whole period of western history, and coming down to the present time, many have been preserved by historians and annalists; and it is our purpose in the present volume to lay them before the reader in their native, unadorned simplicity. The actions speak for themselves, and require no embellishment of fine writing. We shall, wherever it is practicable, preserve the language of the original narrator with all its racy originality. This course of proceeding we regard as most certain to present a true picture of the persons and events which will illustrate the early history of the west. A single expression, some homely epithet, or household

1

word, often teems with associations, and brings before us the true character of the scene in all its life-like features—all its original vividness of coloring.

The heroic deeds of these noble American women, who first confronted the dangers of the western wilderness are full of instruction. They teach us what women are capable of; they show us how dearly the blessings we now enjoy were purchased by those who went before us in the march of ages, they furnish abundant themes for meditation and study in the mysteries of human character—and they present to us, by the strong contrast of past times with the present, occasion for thankfulness, that in the present age, and in our own quiet homes, the danger of the savage border wars and Indian massacres has passed away never to return.

Our women of the present age may be heroines, no doubt, in another way; and the occasions for self-sacrifice and noble generosity will still present themselves and still be heroically met. But the original Heroines of the West will always maintain their unrivalled place in the annals of our country, illustrious, revered, and "alone in their glory."

MRS. HOWE

THE FOLLOWING NARRATIVE we copy from a periodical. It appears to have been extracted from a biography of General Putnam.

"At the house of Colonel Schuyler, Major Putnam became acquainted with Mrs. Howe, a fair captive, whose history would not be read without emotion, if it could be written in the same manner in which I have often heard it told. She was still young and handsome herself, though she had two daughters of marriageable age. Distress, which had taken somewhat from the original redundancy of her bloom, and added a softening paleness to her cheeks, rendering her appearance the more engaging. Her face, that seemed to have been formed for the assemblage of dimpled smiles, was clouded with care. The natural sweetness was not, however, soured by despondency and petulance, but chastened by humility and resignation. This mild daughter of sorrow looked as if she had known the day of prosperity, when serenity and gladness of soul were the inmates of her bosom. That day was past, and the once lively features now assumed a tender melancholy, which witnessed her irreparable loss. She needed not the customary weeds of mourning, or the fallacious pageantry of woe, to prove her widowed state. She was in that stage of affliction when the excess is so far abated as to permit the subject to be drawn into conversation, without opening the wound afresh. It is then rather a source of pleasure than pain to dwell upon the circumstances in narration. Every thing conspired to make her story interesting. Her first husband had been killed and scalped by the Indians some years before. By an unexpected assault, in 1756, upon Fort Dummer, where she happened to be present with Mr. Howe, her second husband, the savages carried the fort, murdered the greater part of the garrison, mangled in death her husband, and led her away with seven children into captivity. She was for some months kept with them; and during their rambles she was frequently on the point of perishing with hunger, and as often subjected to hardships seemingly intolerable to one of so delicate a frame. Some time after the career of her miseries began, the Indians selected a couple of their young men to marry her daughters. The fright and disgust which the intelligence of this intention occasioned to these poor young creatures, added infinitely to the sorrows and perplexity of the frantic mother. To prevent the hated connection, all the activity of female resource was called into exertion. She found an opportunity of conveying to the governor a petition, that her daughters might be received into a convent for the sake of securing the salvation of their souls. Happily the pious fraud succeeded.

"About the same time the savages separated, and carried off her other five children into different tribes. She was ransomed by an elderly French officer, for four hundred livres. Of no avail were the cries of this tender mother—a mother desolated by the loss of her children, who were thus torn from her fond embraces, and removed many hundred miles from each other, into the utmost recesses of Canada. With them (could they have been kept together) she would most willingly have wandered to the extremities of the world, and accepted as a desirable portion the cruel lot of slavery for life. But she was precluded from the sweet hope of ever beholding them again. The insufferable pang of parting, and the idea of eternal separation, planted the arrows of despair deep in her soul. Though all the world was no better than a desert, and all its inhabitants were then indifferent to her, yet the loveliness of her appearance in sorrow had awakened affections which, in the aggravation of her troubles, were to become a new source of afflictions.

"The officer who bought her of the Indians had a son, who also held a commission, and resided with his father. During her continuance in the same house, at St. John's, the double attachment of the father and son, rendered her situation extremely distressing. It is true, the calmness of age delighted to gaze respectfully on her beauty; but the impetuosity of youth was fired to madness by the sight of her charms. One day, the son, whose attentions had been long lavished upon her in vain, finding her alone in a chamber, forcibly seized her hand, and solemnly declared that he would now satiate the passion which she had so long refused to indulge. She recurred to entreaties, struggles, and tears, those prevalent female weapons which the distraction of danger not less than the promptness of genius is wont to supply; while he in the delirium of vexation and desire, snatched a dagger, and swore he would put an end to her life if she persisted to struggle. Mrs. Howe, assuming the dignity of conscious virtue, told him it was what she most ardently wished, and bade him plunge the weapon through her heart, since the mutual importunities and jealousies of such rivals had rendered her life, though innocent, more irksome and insupportable than death itself. Struck with a momentary compunction, he seemed to relent, and relax his hold; and she, availing herself of his irresolution, or absence of mind, escaped down the stairs. In her disordered state, she told the whole transaction to his father, who directed her, in future, to sleep in a small bed at the foot of that in which his wife lodged. The affair soon reached the governor's ears, and the young officer was, shortly afterwards, sent on a tour of duty to Detroit.

"This gave her a short respite; but she dreaded his return, and the humiliating insults for which she might be reserved. Her children, too, were ever present in her melancholy mind. A stranger, a widow, a captive, she knew not where to apply for relief. She had heard of the name of Schuyler—she was yet to learn that it was only another appellation for the friend of suffering humanity. As that excellent man was on his way from Quebec to the Jerseys, under a parole, for a limited time, she came, with feeble and trembling steps, to him. The same maternal passion which sometimes overcomes the timidity of nature in the birds, when plundered of their callow nestlings, emboldened her, notwithstanding her native diffidence, to disclose those griefs which were ever ready to devour her in silence. While her delicate aspect was heightened to a glowing blush, for fear of offending by an inexcusable importunity, or of transgressing the rules of propriety, by representing herself as being an object of admiration, she told, with artless simplicity, all the story of her woes. Colonel Schuyler, from that moment, became her protector, and endeavoured to procure her liberty. The person who purchased her of the Indians, unwilling to part with so fair a purchase, demanded a thousand livres as her ransom. But Colonel Schuyler, on his return to Quebec, obtained from the governor an order, in consequence of which Mrs. Howe was given up to him for four hundred livres; nor did his active goodness rest until every one of her five sons was restored to her.

"Business having made it necessary that Colonel Schuyler should precede the prisoners who were exchanged, he recommended the fair captive to the protection of his friend Putnam. She had just recovered from the meazles, when the party was preparing to set off for their homes. By this time the young French officer had returned, with his passion rather increased than abated by absence. He pursued her wheresoever she went, and, although he could make no advances in her affection, he seemed resolved, by perseverance, to carry his point. Mrs. Howe, terrified by his treatment, was obliged to keep constantly near Major Putnam, who informed the young officer that he should protect that lady at the risk of his life.

"In the long march from captivity, through an inhospitable wilderness, encumbered with five small children, she suffered incredible hardships. Though endowed with masculine fortitude, she was truly feminine in strength, and must have fainted by the way, had it not been for the assistance of Major Putnam. There were a thousand good offices which the helplessness of her condition demanded, and which the gentleness of his nature delighted to perform. He assisted in leading her little ones, and in carrying them over the swampy grounds and runs of water, with which their course was frequently intersected. He mingled his own mess with that of the widow and the fatherless, and assisted them in supplying and preparing their provisions. Upon arriving within the settlements, they experienced a reciprocal regret at separation, and were only consoled by the expectation of soon mingling in the embraces of their former acquaintances and dearest connections.

"After the conquest of Canada, in 1760, she made a journey to Quebec, in order to bring back her two daughters, whom she had left in a convent. She found one of them married to a French officer. The other having contracted a great fondness for the religious sisterhood, with reluctance consented to leave them and return home."

MRS. NEFF

THE TERRIBLE DEFEAT of the colonial forces under General Braddock, in 1755, was followed by a series of savage depredations unparalleled upon the frontier. The border settlements of Virginia and Pennsylvania, being left completely exposed, were nearly abandoned. The inhabitants fled to the forts and block-houses, leaving their homes, which had cost them much labor and hardship, to the torch of the Indian. Death and desolation visited a great extent of that beautiful region where civilized men had begun to tame the wilderness.

Some of the borderers were not fortunate enough to reach places of security before the bursting of the storm. Among these was a Mrs. Neff, who lived upon the south branch of the Wappatomoca. She was surprised by a party of fourteen savages, who seized and bound her, plundered her house, and then started for their homes by way of Fort Pleasant. On the second night of their journey, they reached the vicinity of the fort, which stood on the south branch of the Potomac, near what is known as "the trough." Mrs. Neff was left in the care of an old Indian. The other warriors separated into parties, that they might better watch the fort.

Mrs. Neff was a woman of cool, determined spirit. She seemed perfectly resigned to her captivity, but was nevertheless eagerly seeking an opportunity to escape, and to give the garrison notice of the enemy being at hand. At a late hour of the night, she discovered that the old warrior was asleep. Noiselessly stealing from his side, she ran off through the woods. Soon after, the old Indian awoke, saw that his prisoner had escaped, and gave the alarm by firing his gun and raising a yell. But the courageous woman had the advantage of a long start, and a thorough knowledge of the ground. She ran between the two parties who were watching for her, and after a short but fearful race, succeeded in reaching

Fort Pleasant. The garrison being aroused, Mrs. Neff communicated information as to the position of the Indians, and a sally was resolved upon the next morning.

After the escape of their captive, the Indians assembled in a deep glen near the fort, where they intended to lie in ambush, for stragglers. Early the next morning, sixteen men, well mounted and armed, left the fort, and after a short search discovered the encampment of the enemy by the smoke of their fire. The whites divided themselves into two parties, intending to inclose the Indians. But a small dog starting a rabbit, gave the red men notice of the approach of danger, and cautiously moving off, they passed between the two parties of white men unobserved, took position between them and their horses, and opened a destructive fire. A desperate battle ensued, both parties displayed the most indomitable courage. The Indians were victorious, chiefly from the slaughter committed by their first fire. Seven of the whites were killed, and four wounded. The remaining five retreated to the fort. The loss of the Indians, however, was so severe that the survivors made an immediate march for home. They had intended to surprise the fort; but the courage of Mrs. Neff frustrated their design, and saved a large number of the garrison from massacre. The heroine survived the perils of the border war, and was held in high esteem for her many good qualities of head and heart.

MRS. PORTER

DURING THE TERRIBLE Indian war, upon the frontier of Pennsylvania and Virginia, instigated by the great Pontiac, a Mr. Porter resided in Sinking Valley, Huntingdon county, Pennsylvania. One day, when he had gone to the mill, leaving Mrs. Porter alone, some Indians approached the house. Mrs. Porter first caught sight of one savage coming towards the door. Her husband being a militia captain, had a sword and a rifle in the house. She boldly took down the sword, and having set the door about half open, waited behind it until the Indian entered, when she split his head open. Another savage then entered, and met the same fate. The third, seeing the slaughter of his comrades, did not attempt to enter at that time. Mrs. Porter then took the gun, and went up stairs, with the hope of finding an opportunity of shooting the savage from the port-holes. But the Indian followed her up stairs. He had no sooner reached the upper floor, than the brave woman turned and shot him dead.

Mrs. Porter now believed that she had slaughtered all her foes. Going down stairs cautiously, she reconnoitred in all directions around the house, and being satisfied that she had a clear field, fled swiftly in the path by which she knew her husband would return. She soon met him, and telling him of the circumstances, mounted the horse, and rode away with him to a neighboring block-house. The next morning, a party of whites was collected, and marching to the scene of Mrs. Porter's heroism, found that other Indians had been there, and had burned the house and barn, partly from revenge, and partly to conceal the evidence of their discomfiture by a woman. The bones of the slain savages however, were found among the ashes.

MRS. CLENDENNIN

THE VERY SIGHT of Indians was terrible to many women on the frontier. The savages could not be looked upon without calling to mind the horrid work of the tomahawk and scalping-knife—the desolated home and the butchered relatives. To rise superior to this feeling of dread was the merit of a large number of bold-spirited daughters of the wilderness. But we question whether any other woman than Mrs. Clendennin would have the courage, amid scenes of blood, to denounce the savages, from chief to squaw, as cowardly and treacherous.

During the year 1763, a party of about fifty Shawanese, under the command of the able chief Cornstalk, made a descent upon the Greenbriar settlements, of Western Virginia. They professed to entertain friendly intentions, and as no hostilities had occurred for some time in that region, the inhabitants were lulled into the belief that there was no danger. The Indians met with every demonstration of a welcome and abundant hospitality. Suddenly they fell upon the people at Muddy Creek, butchered the men, and made captives of the women and children.

A visit was next made to the settlement of Big Levels, where Archibald Clendennin had erected a rude block-house, and where were gathered a considerable number of families. Foolishly unsuspicious, the whites entertained the savages as friends. Mr. Clendennin, a man distinguished for his generosity and hospitality, had just brought in three fine elk, upon which the treacherous Indians feasted. One of the inmates of the house was a decrepit old woman, with an ulcerated limb. She undressed the member, and asked an Indian if he could cure it. "Yes," he replied, and immediately sunk his tomahawk into her head. This was the signal for massacre, and in a few minutes, every man in the house was put to death. The cries of the women and children alarmed a man in the yard, who escaped, and reported the circumstances to the settlement at

Jackson's river. The people would scarcely believe him; but the Indians soon appeared, and massacred the families that attempted to escape.

Flushed with triumph and almost sated with blood, the Indians now marched off in the direction of the Ohio. Mrs. Clendennin was not intimidated by the scenes of horror through which she had passed. She had seen her husband and friends treacherously butchered; but, though a woman of keen sensibility, her spirit was firm. Indignant at the treachery and cruelty of the Indians, she loudly abused them, and taunted them with lacking the hearts of great warriors, who met their foes in fair and open conflict. The savages were astounded. They tried to frighten her by flapping the bloody scalp of her husband in her face, and twirling their tomahawks above her head in a threatening manner. Mrs. Clendennin was undaunted, and continued to express her indignation and detestation. Probably the savages admired her courage; for they did not attempt to inflict any serious injury upon her.

On the day after her capture, Mrs. Clendennin, while marching among the other hapless prisoners, and carrying her child, saw an opportunity, which she instantly resolved to seize. Giving her child to a woman, who promised to take charge of it, the heroic mother slipped unobserved into a dense thicket. After the march had been continued a short distance, the child began to cry. An Indian inquired concerning the mother, but obtained no satisfactory reply. He then swore he would "bring the cow to the calf," and, taking it by the heels, dashed out its brains against a tree.

Mrs. Clendennin succeeded in reaching her desolate home. No sign of life was to be seen there. The mangled bodies of her husband and friends were strewn around, all she could do was to give them decent interment, which she accomplished with the aid of people from neighboring settlements. Throughout the trying scenes of the massacre and the captivity, Mrs. Clendennin acted with extraordinary firmness of spirit, and proved herself worthy to be ranked with the noblest women of history.

THE WIFE AND DAUGHTERS OF
DANIEL BOONE

THE DARING COURAGE of Daniel Boone, the father of Kentucky, has frequently been eulogized. It was certainly a great display of hardihood for him to venture alone in the forests of "the dark and bloody ground," where he was surrounded by swarms of vigilant savages. It seemed like running into the very jaws of death. The manner in which he surmounted all perils and hardships is also worthy of admiration. As bold as he was, no man was possessed of more caution and prudence, and had Kentucky pioneers always submitted to his judicious counsel, many terrible disasters might have been avoided. But whatever praise we concede to Boone, we must remember that his wife and daughters also deserve our eulogy. He was a bold and skilful Indian fighter, and accustomed to scenes of danger and death. They belonged to what is commonly called a "weaker sex," were unaccustomed to the wilderness, and to the constant alarms of savage warfare; yet they ventured to accompany the pioneer far into the forest, hundred of miles from the settlements, with protectors insignificantly weak in comparison with the vast numbers of savages who were known to visit the hunting-grounds of Kentucky. By the journey alone, they proved themselves to possess unusual hardihood.

After his first long hunting expedition in Kentucky, Daniel Boone returned to North Carolina with the determination to sell his farm, and remove, with his family, to the wilderness.

Accordingly, on the 25th of September, 1771, having disposed of all the property which he could not take with him, he took leave of his friends, and commenced his journey to the west. A number of milch cows, and horses, laden with a few necessary utensils, formed the whole of his baggage. His wife and children were mounted on horseback and accompanied him, every one regarding them as devoted to destruction.

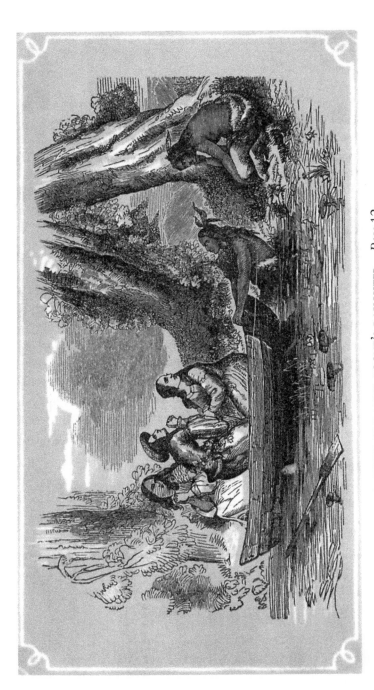

CAPTURE OF DANIEL BOONE'S DAUGHTER—*Page 12*

In Powell's valley they were joined by five more families and forty men well armed. Encouraged by this accession of strength, they advanced with additional confidence, but had soon a severe warning of the future dangers which awaited them. When near Cumberland mountain, their rear was suddenly attacked with great fury by a scouting party of Indians, and thrown into considerable confusion.

The party, however, soon rallied, and being accustomed to Indian warfare, returned the fire with such spirit and effect, that the Indians were repulsed with slaughter. Their own loss, however, had been severe. Six men were killed on the spot, and one wounded. Among the killed was Boone's eldest son, to the unspeakable affliction of his family. The disorder and grief occasioned by this rough reception, seems to have affected the emigrants deeply, as they instantly retraced their steps to settlements on Clinch river, forty miles from the scene of action. Here they remained until June, 1774, probably at the request of the women, who must have been greatly alarmed at the prospect of plunging more deeply into a country, upon the the skirts of which, they had witnessed so keen and bloody a conflict.

At this time, Boone, at the request of Governor Dunmore, of Virginia, conducted a number of surveyors to the falls of Ohio, a distance of eight hundred miles. After his return, he was engaged under Dunmore until 1775 in several affairs with the Indians, and at the solicitation of some gentlemen of North Carolina, he attended at a treaty with the Cherokees, for the purpose of purchasing the lands south of Kentucky.

Boone's next visit to Kentucky was made under the auspices of Colonel Henderson. Leaving his family on Clinch river, he set out at the head of a few men, to mark out a road for the pack horses or wagons of Henderson's party. This laborious and dangerous duty he executed with his usual patient fortitude, until he came within fifteen miles of the spot where Boonesborough now stands. Here, on the 22nd of March, his small party was attacked by the Indians, and suffered a loss of four men killed and wounded. The Indians, although repulsed with loss in this affair, renewed the attack with equal fury on the next day, and killed and wounded five more of the party. On the 1st of April, the survivors began to build a small fort on the Kentucky river, afterwards called Boonesborough, and on the 4th, they were again attacked by the Indians, and lost another man. Notwithstanding the harassing attacks to which they were constantly exposed, for the Indians seemed enraged to madness at the prospect of their building houses on their hunting-ground, the work was prosecuted with indefatigable diligence, and on the 14th was completed.

Boone now returned to Clinch river for his family, determined to bring them with him at every risk. This was done as soon as the journey could be performed, and Mrs. Boone and her daughters were the first white women who stood upon the banks of the Kentucky river, as Boone himself had been the first white man who ever built a cabin upon the borders of the state. The first house, however, which ever stood in the interior of Kentucky, was erected at Harrodsburgh, in the year 1774, by James Harrod, who conducted to this place a party of hunters from the banks of the Monongahela. This place was, therefore, a few months older than Boonesborough. Both soon became distinguished, as the only places in which hunters and surveyors could find security from the fury of the Indians.

Within a few weeks after the arrival of Mrs. Boone and her daughters, the infant colony was reinforced by three more families, at the head of which were Mrs. McGrary, Mrs. Hogan, and Mrs. Denton. Boonesborough, however, was the central object of Indian hostilities, and scarcely had his family become domesticated in their new possession, when they were suddenly attacked by a party of Indians, and lost one of their garrison. This was on the 24th of December, 1775.

In the following July, however, a much more alarming incident occurred. One of the daughters, in company with a Miss Galloway, were amusing themselves in a boat in the immediate neighborhood of the fort, when a party of Indians, suddenly rushed out of a canebrake, and, intercepting their return, took them prisoners.*

The shouts of the girls quickly alarmed the family. The small garrison was dispersed, being engaged in their usual occupations; but Boone hastily collected eight men and pursued the enemy. The Indians had the advantage of a start of several miles. The pursuit, however, was urged through the night by the anxious father, and on the following day, he had the satisfaction of coming up with the Indians. The girls were almost overcome with fatigue; and they expected to be tomahawked every moment; but

---

* McClung's Western Adventure.

they refrained from murmuring, and, by seeming to accompany their captors with a hearty will, were saved from the tomahawk. Boone's attack was sudden and furious, so that the Indians were driven from their ground before they had an opportunity to kill their captives, who were recovered by the victorious party. The Indians lost two men, while Boone's party was entirely uninjured. The happy father then returned to Boonesborough with the girls whom he had saved from a long and dreary captivity, if not from death.

From this time until long after the bloody defeat of the whites at the Blue Licks, Boonesborough was constantly exposed to the harassing attacks of the Indians. The men of the garrison could not venture far from the fort, for savages were lurking around, watching opportunities to pick off stragglers. Mrs. Boone, her daughters, and the other females in the fort, were in a constant state of alarm; and it was truly wonderful that they persuaded themselves to remain amid such perils. They survived all the dangers they had so nobly braved, and lived to see Kentucky, the prosperous home of civilization, where their names will ever be remembered with gratitude and pride.

THE WAR-WOMAN CREEK

In Georgia and North Carolina there is hardly a river, creek, or stream, that has not connected with it some old Indian tradition. The title of the present sketch is taken from one of these—I believe one of the principal tributaries of Natahalee river, in the Cherokee nation, North Carolina. The story, as told by the few Indians remaining since the removal in the fall of 1838, runs thus:

Many years ago, in the first settlement of the country, a wandering party of their tribe attacked the house of a squatter, somewhere upon their borders, during his absence, and massacred all his children, and left his wife covered with the mangled bodies of her butchered offspring; scalped like them and apparently dead. She was not, however, wounded so badly as they had supposed, and no sooner did she hear the sound of their retreating footsteps, than disengaging herself from the heap of slain, haggard, pale, and drenched with her own and the blood of her children, she peered steadily from the door, and finding her enemies no longer in sight, hastily extinguished the fire, which before leaving they had applied to her cabin, but which had, as yet, made very little impression on the green logs of which it was composed.

Wiping from her eyes the warm blood, still reeking from her scalpless head, she directed her agonized gaze to the bleeding and disfigured forms of those who scarce an hour before were playing at the door, and gladdening her maternal heart with their merry laughter, and as she felt, in the full sense of her desolation, the last ray of hope die within her bosom, there stole over her ghostly face an expression as savage as was ever worn by the ruthless slayers of her innocent babes. Her eye gleamed with the wild fury of the tigress robbed of its young, as closing her cabin carefully behind her, with a countenance animated by some desperate purpose, she started off in the same path by which the murderers had

17

departed. Heedless of her wounds and wasting blood, and lost to all sense of hunger and fatigue in the one absorbing and fell purpose which actuated her, she paused not upon the trail of her foes, until at night, she came up with them encamped at the side of the creek, which is indebted to her for its present name.

Emerging from the gloom of the surrounding darkness, on her hands and knees she noiselessly crept towards the fire, the blaze of which, as it flickered upwards, discovered to her the prostrate forms of the Indians, who overcome by an unusually fatiguing day's travel, were wrapt in deep sleep, with their only weapons, their tomahawks, in their belts. Her stealthily advancing figure, as the uncertain light of the burning pine fell upon it with more or less distinctness—now exposing its lineaments clotted with blood, and distorted by an expression, which her wrongs, and the desolaters of her hearthstone, exaggerated to a degree almost fiendish; and now shading all, save two gleaming, spectral eyes—was even more striking than the swarthy faces which she glared upon.

Assuring herself that they were fast asleep she gently removed their tomahawks, and dropped all but one in the creek. With this remaining weapon in her hand, and cool resolution in her heart, she bent over the nearest enemy, and lifting the instrument, to which her own and her children's blood still adhered, with one terrific and unerring blow, buried it into the temple of its owner. The savage moved no more than partly to turn upon his side, gasped a little, quivered a minute like an aspen, and sunk back to his former position, quite dead. Smiling ghastly in his rigid face, the desperate woman left him, and noiselessly as before despatched all the sleepers, but one, to that long rest from which only the last trump can awaken them.

The last devoted victim, however was roused to a consciousness of his situation by the death struggles, of his companions. He sprang to his feet and felt for his weapon. It was not there, and one glance explaining every thing to him, he evaded the blow aimed at him by the brave and revengeful mother, seized from the fire a burning brand, and with it, succeeded partially in warding off the furious attack which followed. In a little time they fell struggling together, the Indian desperately wounded, and the unfortunate woman faint with the loss of blood and her extraordinary exertions. Both were too weak to harm each other now, and the wounded savage only availed himself of his remaining strength to crawl away. In this piteous plight, the poor woman remained until near noon on the following day, when she was accidentally discovered by a straggling party of whites, to whom she told her story, and then died. After burying her on the spot, they made some exertions to overtake the fugitive Indian, but unsuccessfully. He succeeded in reaching his tribe, and from his tale the little stream, before mentioned, was ever afterwards known among the Cherokees, and also by the pale faces, as the "War-Woman Creek."

The instance of intrepidity in a woman, recorded in the above sketch, furnishes a remarkable proof that the heroism of woman, to whatever excesses of daring and even ferocious courage it may lead her, has its foundation in love. It was this "War-Woman's" love for her children, that made her exhaust the last energy of a life, which had lost its motive and its charm, in taking vengeance on their murderers. Under such circumstances, it is difficult to imagine the extent to which a woman's outraged affections will not carry her. Here we see one of the gentle and devoted sex, losing all sense of danger, all feeling of compassion, all regard to her own personal safety, and her ultimate fate, in the desire to avenge the cruel murder of her children. The fact seems startling and almost incredible; but it is corroborated by many other facts illustrating the same principle.

ELIZABETH ZANE

DURING THE HOTTEST part of the revolutionary war, Fort Henry, situated near the site of the present city of Wheeling, was the stronghold of northwestern Virginia. It was a simple stockade fort, and its garrison was exceedingly small. Yet it was twice defended against the furious assaults of large Indian armies, headed by bold and skilful white men. The incidents we are about to relate occurred during the second siege of Fort Henry.

On the night of the 26th of November, 1782, Captain Joseph Ogle, with a small scouting party, while on his return to the fort from an excursion up the Ohio, descried a faint but constant body of smoke rising in the air to the southward of Wheeling. Impressed with the conviction that the smoke was caused by the burning of the block-house at Grave Creek, about twelve miles below, he hastened to the fort and mentioned the circumstance to Colonel Shepherd, the commandant, who lost no time in dispatching two men, in a canoe, down the river to ascertain the truth. In the course of the night all the inhabitants of the village fled to the fort for shelter and safety, and several families residing in the neighborhood were sent for and brought in before the dawn of day.

The garrison numbered only forty-two fighting men. Some of these were far advanced in years, while others were mere boys. A portion of them were skilled in Indian warfare, and all were excellent marksmen. The store-house was well supplied with small-arms, particularly muskets, but was sadly deficient in ammunition.

At the break of day on the 27th, the commandant wishing to dispatch expresses to the nearest settlements, sent a man, accompanied by a negro, out of the fort to bring in some horses, which had been turned loose the day before to graze on the bank of the creek. While these men were passing through the cornfield south of the fort, they encountered a party of six Indians, one of whom raised his firelock and brought the white man to the ground. The negro, seized with alarm, turned about and fled to the fort, which he succeeded in entering without being pursued or molested by the enemy. As soon as the negro related his story, the colonel dispatched Captain Samuel Mason, with fourteen men, to dislodge the Indians from the cornfield. Captain Mason with his party marched through the field, and arrived almost on the bank of the creek without finding the Indians, and had already commenced a retrograde movement when he was suddenly and furiously assailed in front, flank, and rear, by the whole of Girty's army. The captain rallied his men from the confusion produced by this unexpected demonstration of the enemy, and instantly comprehending the situation in which he was placed, gallantly took the lead and hewed a passage through the savage phalanx that opposed him. In this desperate conflict more than half the little band was slain, and their leader severely wounded. Intent on retreating back to the fort, Mason pressed rapidly on with the remnant of his command, the Indians following closely in pursuit. One by one these devoted soldiers fell at the crack of the enemy's rifle. An Indian, who eagerly pursued Captain Mason, at length overtook him; and to make sure of his prey, fired at him from the distance of five paces; but the shot, although it took effect, did not disable the captain, who immediately turned about, and hurling his gun at the head of his pursuer, felled him to the earth. The fearlessness with which this act was performed caused an involuntary dispersion of the gang of Indians who led the pursuit: and Mason, whose extreme exhaustion of physical powers prevented him from reaching the fort, was fortunate enough to hide himself in a pile of fallen timber, where he was compelled to remain to the end of the siege. Only two of his men survived the skirmish, and they, like their leader, owed their safety to the heaps of logs and brush, that abounded in the cornfield.

As soon as the critical situation of Captain Mason became known at the fort, Captain Ogle, with twelve volunteers from the garrison, sallied forth to cover his retreat. This noble, self-devoted band, in their eagerness to press forward to the relief of their suffering fellow-soldiers, fell into an ambuscade, and two-thirds of their number were slain upon the spot. Sergeant Jacob Ogle, though mortally wounded, managed to escape with two soldiers into the woods, while Captain Ogle escaped in another direction, and found a place of concealment, which, like his brother, Captain Mason, he was obliged to keep as long as the siege, continued. Immediately after the departure of Captain Ogle's command, three new volunteers left the garrison to overtake and reinforce him. These men, however, did not reach the cornfield until after the bloody scenes had been enacted, and barely found time to return to the fort before the Indian host appeared before it. The enemy advanced in two ranks, in open order—their left flank reaching to the river bank, and their right extending into the woods as far as the eye could reach. As the three volunteers were about to enter the gate, a few random shots were fired at them, and instantly a loud whoop arose on the enemy's left flank, which passed, as if by concert, along the line to the extreme right, until the welkin was filled with a chorus of the most wild and startling character. This salute was responded to by a few well directed rifle shots from the lower block-houses, which produced a manifest confusion in the ranks of the besiegers. They discontinued their shouting and retired a few paces, probably to await the coming up of their right flank, which, it would seem, had been directed to make a general sweep of the bottom, and then approach the stockade on the eastern side.

At this moment the garrison of Fort Henry numbered no more than twelve men and boys. The fortunes of the day, so far, had been fearfully against them; two of their best officers and more than two-thirds of their original force were missing. The exact fate of their comrades was unknown to them, but they had every reason to apprehend that they had been cut to pieces. Still they were not dismayed—their mothers, sisters, wives and children were assembled around them—they had a sacred charge to protect, and they resolved to fight to the last extremity, and confidently trusted in Heaven for the successful issue of the combat.

When the enemy's right flank came up, Girty changed his order of attack. Parties of Indians were placed in such of the houses as commanded a view of the block-houses; a strong body occupied the yard of Ebenezer Zane, about fifty yards from the fort, using a paling fence as a cover, while the greater part were posted under cover in the edge of the corn-field, to act offensively or serve as a corps of reserve, as occasion might require. These dispositions having been made, with a white flag in his hand, he appeared at the window of a cabin and demanded the surrender of the garrison in the name of his Britannic majesty. He read the proclamation of Governor Hamilton, and promised them protection if they would lay down their arms and swear allegiance to the British crown. He warned them to submit peaceably, and admitted his inability to restrain the passions of his warriors when they once became excited with the strife of battle. Colonel Shepherd promptly told him, in reply, that the garrison would never surrender to *him*, and that he could only obtain possession of the fort when there remained no longer an American soldier to defend it. Girty renewed his proposition, but before he finished his harangue a thoughtless youth in one of the block-houses fired a gun at the speaker, and brought the conference to an abrupt termination. Girty disappeared, and in about fifteen minutes the Indians opened the siege by a general discharge of rifles.

It was yet quite early in the morning, the sun not having appeared above the summit of Wheeling hill, and the day is represented to have been one of surpassing beauty. The Indians not entirely concealed from the view of the garrison, kept up a brisk fire for the space of six hours without much intermission. The little garrison, in spite of its heterogeneous character, was, with scarcely an exception, composed of sharpshooters. Several of them, whose experience in Indian warfare gave them a remarkable degree of coolness and self-possession in the face of danger, infused confidence into the young; and, as they never fired at random, their bullets, in most cases, took effect. The Indians, on the contrary, flushed with their previous success, their tomahawks reeking with the blood of Mason's and Ogle's men, and all of them burning with impatience to rush into the fort and complete their work of butchery, discharged their guns against the pickets, the gate, the logs of the block-houses, and every other object that seemed to shelter a white man. Their fire was thus thrown away. At length some of their most daring warriors rushed up close to the block-houses, and attempted to make more sure work by firing through the logs; but these reckless savages received from the well-directed rifles of the frontiersmen the fearful reward of their temerity. About one o'clock the Indians discontinued their fire and fell back against the base of the hill.

The stock of gunpowder in the fort having been nearly exhausted, it was determined to seize the favorable opportunity offered by the suspension of hostilities, to send for a keg of powder which was known to be in the house of Ebenezer Zane, about sixty yards from the gate of the fort. The person executing this service would necessarily expose himself to the danger of being shot down by the Indians, who were yet sufficiently near to observe every thing that transpired about the works. The colonel explained the matter to his men, and, unwilling to order one of them to undertake such a desperate enterprise, inquired whether any man would volunteer for the service. Three or four young men promptly stepped forward in obedience to the call. The colonel informed them that the weak state of the garrison would not justify the absence of more than one man, and that it was for themselves to decide who that person should be. The eagerness felt by each volunteer to undertake the honorable mission, prevented them from making the arrangement proposed by the commandant; and so much time was consumed in the contention between them that fears began to arise that the Indians would renew the attack before the powder could be procured.

At this moment of indecision, a woman came forward as a volunteer upon the perilous, but necessary service. Elizabeth Zane, the sister of Ebenezer and Silas Zane, a young woman of a calm, determined spirit of heroism, desired that she might be permitted to go for the ammunition. The proposition seemed so extravagant that it was met with a peremptory refusal. But Elizabeth pleaded earnestly, and all the remonstrances and representations of the colonel and her relatives were of no avail. Her purpose was not to be shaken. The colonel said that either of the young men, on account of his superior fleetness and familiarity with scenes of danger, would be more likely than herself to do the work successfully. She replied that the danger attending the errand was the identical reason that induced her to offer her services, for as the garrison was very weak, no soldier's life should be placed in jeopardy needlessly, and if she fell her loss would not be felt. Heroic, but mistaken woman! The world sustains its heaviest loss when such spirits fall. At length, the petition of Miss Zane was granted, her relatives preparing to see her sacrificed. The gate was opened for her to pass out. The opening of the gate attracted the attention of some straggling Indians, and they stopped to gaze at the fearless girl, as she advanced towards the house of her brother. Savages as they were, they were spell-bound by such a display of daring by a woman. They permitted her to enter the house, where she filled her apron with powder. When she reappeared, the Indians, suspecting the character of her burden, and losing their admiration in the desire to cut off supplies from the garrison, they fired a volley at her as she swiftly glided towards the gate; but the balls all flew wide of the mark, and the fearless girl entered the fort, amid the shouts of her friends and relatives. Such an effort of courage, and exhibition of generous devotion was worthy of any heroine of history. Though Elizabeth Zane had no queen's title, she was one of the queens by divine right, to whom all may do homage. The highest effort of heroism is the offer of one's life to save others, and in this kind of nobility, Miss Zane was prominent.

Ammunition being secured, the spirit of the garrison revived; and reinforcements arriving soon after, the assailants were completely baffled, and compelled to a retreat, which they performed with precipitation. Fort Henry and the frontiers were saved. All honor to the gallant garrison. All honor to the wives and daughters there collected; and, above all, a fadeless laurel to Elizabeth Zane.

MRS. CUNNINGHAM

Mrs. Cunningham deserves a share of the praise awarded to Mrs. Clendennin for firmness amid scenes of blood and death. The incidents of her capture, captivity, and release, possess a strong interest, and show the noble character of the heroine.

The house of Edward Cunningham, an enterprising settler, was situated on Bingamon, a branch of West Fork. Thomas Cunningham, a brother of Edward, lived in a house almost adjoining. The two families thus afforded some protection to each other. In the latter part of June, 1785, a small party of Indians approached the houses of the settlers, with designs of plunder and massacre. At that time, Edward and his family were in one cabin, and the wife of Thomas, with four children, were in the other. Thomas Cunningham had gone east on a trading expedition. Both families were eating their dinners, when a huge savage entered the house of Thomas Cunningham, and stood before the astonished mother and her children, with drawn knife, and uplifted tomahawk. Edward Cunningham had seen the entrance of the Indian through a hole in the wall of his house, and he now eagerly watched the movements of the savage. A similar hole being in the wall of Thomas Cunningham's house, the Indian fired through it and shouted for victory. He then commenced cutting an opening in the back wall, with an adze, so that he might pass out without being exposed to a shot from the other house. Edward shot another Indian who appeared in the yard, just after the savage in the house had fired his gun.

In the meantime, Mrs. Cunningham made no attempt to get out, though she retained her presence of mind. She knew that an effort to escape would meet with certain death from those who were watching outside of the house.

She knew, too, it would be impossible to take the children with her. She expected that the Indian inside would withdraw without molesting any of them. A few minutes served to convince her of the hopeless folly of trusting to an Indian's mercy. When the opening had been made sufficiently large, the savage raised his tomahawk, sunk it deep into the brains of one of the children, and throwing the scarcely lifeless body into the back yard, ordered the mother to follow him. There was no alternative but death, and she obeyed his order, stepping over the dead body of one of her children, with an infant in her arms, and two screaming by her side. When all were out he scalped the murdered boy, and setting fire to the house retired to an eminence, where two of the savages were with their wounded companion,—leaving the other two to watch the opening of Edward Cunningham's door, when the burning of the house should force the family from their shelter. They were disappointed in their expectation of that event by the exertions of Cunningham and his son. When the flame from the one house communicated to the roof of the other, they ascended to the loft, threw off the loose boards which covered it, and extinguishing the fire;—the savages shooting at them all the while; their balls frequently striking close by.

Unable to force out the family of Edward Cunningham, and despairing of doing further injury, they beat a speedy retreat.[*]

Before they started, however, they tomahawked and scalped the eldest son of Mrs. Cunningham before her eyes. Her little daughter was next murdered and scalped in the same way. The mother was horror-stricken, but, though in momentary expectation of meeting a similar fate, she remained self-possessed. Carrying her babe, she was led from the scene of bloodshed. The savages carried their wounded companions upon a litter. Crossing a ridge, they found a cave near Bingamon creek, in which they secreted themselves until after night, when some of the party returned to Edward Cunningham's, and finding that the inmates had fled, set fire to the house.

The whole party now took up its march towards the Indian towns. During the journey, Mrs. Cunningham suffered mental and physical pangs not to be described. While weeping for her murdered children she was compelled to be constantly attentive to the helpless babe in her arms. For ten days her only nourishment was the head of a wild turkey and a few paw-paws.

---

[*] De Haas.

After the savages had withdrawn, Edward Cunningham went with his family into the woods, where they remained all night, there being no settlement nearer than ten miles. In the morning, the alarm was given, and a company of men soon collected to go in pursuit of the Indians. When the company arrived at Cunningham's and found both houses heaps of ashes, they buried the remains of the boy who was murdered in the house, with the bodies of his brother and little sister, who were killed in the field; but so cautiously had the savages conducted their retreat, that no traces of them could be found, and the disappointed whites returned to their homes. Subsequently, a second party started in pursuit, and succeeded in tracing the Indians to the cave; but the trail could be followed no further, with certainty, and the pursuit was given up. Mrs. Cunningham afterwards stated, that at the time of the search on the first day, the Indians were in the cave, and that several times the whites approached so near, that she could distinctly hear their voices. Savages stood with their guns ready to fire, in the event of being discovered, and forced the mother to keep her infant to her breast, to prevent its crying. Had the place of concealment been discovered, it is most probable that Mrs. Cunningham and her child would have been tomahawked.

Mrs. Cunningham spent many months in captivity, her husband being ignorant of her fate. At length, that man of bad repute Simon Girty, interfered on her behalf, paid her ransom, and sent her home. This noble act was an atonement for many deeds of darkness, and shows that the renegade was not so destitute of generosity as he is commonly represented to have been. Mrs. Cunningham's claims to the character of a heroine are undeniable. Few women could have passed through such hardships and horrors, with such self-control as she displayed.

MRS. BLAND AND MRS. POLK

AFTER THE FAMOUS battle of Blue Licks, the Indian army, victorious on that fatal field, determined to return home with the scalps. A portion of them, however, passing through Jefferson county, showed a hostile disposition, and were pursued by Colonel Flood, with a party of militiamen. After an unsuccessful pursuit, a portion of this force, at Kincheloe's station, supposing themselves secure, went to sleep at night, without a watch. In the night, the enemy fell upon the place by surprise; and were in the houses before the people were awake. Thus circumstanced, they killed several persons, men, women, and children, and were proceeding to destroy or capture the rest, but the darkness of night favored the escape of a few.

Among them was Mrs. Davis, whose husband was killed—and another woman, who fled to the woods—where they were fortunately joined by a lad, by the name of Ash, who conducted them to Coxe's station.

William Harrison, after placing his wife and a young woman, of the family, under the floor of the cabin, escaped; as they did, after the Indians had retired; and he returned to liberate them. Thompson Randolph stood his ground manfully for awhile, and defended his wife and children like a hero. He killed several Indians—soon, however, his wife, and an infant in her arms, were both murdered by his side—his remaining child, he put into the cabin loft, then mounted himself, and escaped with it through the roof. When he alighted on the ground, he was assailed by two of the savages, whom he had just forced out of the house—one of these he stabbed, the other he struck with his empty gun—they both left him, and he, dragging the child after him, secured his retreat and the safety of both. This representation of facts, obtained full credit in the neighborhood, and with his acquaintances. A signal instance of manly perseverance.

Several women and children were cruelly put to death, after they were made prisoners, and on the route to the towns. But the details of such savage barbarity are omitted, in order to attend the case of Mrs. Bland, who was not killed, probably because she was not a prisoner, after the second day—when she escaped into the bushes—totally unacquainted with the country around her, and destitute of any guide.

For eighteen successive days she rambled through the woods, without seeing a human face; subsisting upon sour grapes, and green walnuts; until she became a mere walking skeleton, without clothes; when she was accidentally found, and taken to Lynn's station. Where kind attention and cautious nursing restored her to life and her friends.

The situation of Mrs. Polk, another prisoner, with four small children, was almost as pitiable as that of Mrs. Bland. She was in a delicate state, and compelled to walk until she became nearly incapable of motion. She was then threatened with death, and the tomahawk brandished over her head by an Indian; when another who saw it begged her life—took her under his care—mounted her on a horse, with her two children—and conducted her safe to Detroit; where those went who had prisoners or scalps to dispose of to purchasers. She was of course purchased, as she was there given up to British authority—well treated—and enabled to write to her husband, who was not at home when she was taken, though a resident of the station. Relying on the letter, which he received after some time, as a passport from the British, and incurring the risk of danger from the Indians, he went for his wife, obtained her, and brought her and five children safe to Kentucky. After the peace of next year, the other prisoners were also liberated, and came home.

MASSY HERBESON

THE CAPTIVITY, SUFFERINGS, and escape of Mrs. Massy Herbeson and her family, occupy a conspicuous place in every history of Indian atrocity. We give her narrative as it was deposed before an alderman of Alleghany county, Pennsylvania. Mrs. Herbeson lived near Reed's block-house, about twenty-five miles from Pittsburg.

Mr. Herbeson, being one of the spies, was from home; two of the scouts had lodged with her that night, but had left her house about sunrise, in order to go to the block-house, and had left the door standing wide open. Shortly after the two scouts went away, a number of Indians came into the house, and drew her, out of bed by the feet; the two eldest children, who also lay in another bed were drawn out in the same manner; a younger child, about one year old, slept with Mrs. Herbeson. The Indians then scrambled about the articles in the house. Whilst they were at this work, Mrs. Herbeson went out of the house, and hallooed to the people in the block-house; one of the Indians then ran up and stopped her mouth, another ran up with his tomahawk drawn, and a third ran and seized the tomahawk and called her his squaw; this last Indian claimed her as his, and continued by her. About fifteen of the Indians then ran down toward the block-house and fired their guns at the store and block-house, in consequence of which one soldier was killed and another wounded, one having been at the spring and the other in coming or looking out of the store-house. On Mrs. Herbeson, telling the Indians there were about forty men in the block-house, and each man had two guns, the Indians went to them that were firing at the block-house, and brought them back. They then began to drive Mrs. Herbeson and her children back; but a boy, about three years old, being unwilling to leave the house, they took it by the heels, and dashed it against the house and then stabbed and scalped it. They then took

31

Mrs. Herbeson and the two other children to the top of the hill, where they stopped until they tied up the plunder they had got. While they were busy about this, Mrs. Herbeson counted them, and the number amounted to thirty-two, including two white men, that were with them, painted like the Indians.

Several of the Indians could speak English, and she knew three or four of them very well, having often seen them go up and down the Alleghany river; two of them she knew to be Senecas, and two Munsees, who had their guns mended by her husband two years ago. They sent two Indians with her, and the others took their course towards Pluckty. The children and the two Indians had not gone above two hundred yards, when the Indians caught two of her uncle's horses, put her and the youngest child upon one, and one of the Indians and the other child upon the other. The two Indians then took her and the children to the Alleghany river, and took them over in bark canoes, as they could not get the horses to swim the river. After they had crossed the river, the oldest child, a boy of about five years of age, began to mourn for his brother, when one of the Indians tomahawked and scalped him. They travelled all day very hard, and that night arrived at a large camp, covered with bark, which, by appearance, might hold fifty men. That night they took her about three hundred yards from the camp, into a large dark bottom, bound her arms, gave her some bed clothes, and lay down on each side of her. The next morning they took her into a thicket on the hill side, and one remained with her till the middle of the day. While the other went to watch the path, lest some white people should follow them. They then exchanged places during the remainder of the day: she got a piece of dry venison, the size of an egg, that day, and a piece about the same size the day they were marching; that evening, (Wednesday 23d) they moved her to a new place, and secured her as the night before. During the day of the 23d, she made several attempts to get the Indian's gun or tomahawk, that was guarding her, and, had she succeeded, she would have put him to death. She was nearly detected in trying to get the tomahawk from his belt.

The next morning (Thursday) one of the Indians went out, as on the day before, to watch the path. The other lay down and fell asleep. When she found he was sleeping, she stole her short gown, handkerchief, a child's frock, and then made her escape;—the sun was then about half an hour high—when she took her course from the Alleghany, in order to deceive the Indians, as they would naturally pursue her that way; that day she travelled along Conequenessing Creek.—The next day she altered her course, and, as she believes, fell upon the waters of Pine Creek, which empties into the Alleghany. Thinking this not her best course, went over some dividing ridges,—lay on a dividing ridge on Friday night, and on Saturday came to Squaw run—continued down the run until an Indian or some other person, shot a deer; she saw the person about one hundred and fifty yards from her.

She then altered her course, but again came to the same run, and continued down it until she got so tired that she was obliged to lie down, it having rained upon her all day and the night before; she remained there that night; it rained constantly. On Sunday she proceeded down the run until she came to the Alleghany river, and continued down the river till she came opposite Carter's house, on the inhabited side, where she made a noise, and James Closier brought her over the river to Carter's house.

MRS. WHITE

AFTER THE DEFEAT of General St. Clair's army, in November, 1791, the frontier on the west was more than ever exposed to the hostilities of the savage foe; and many instances of terrible outrage, on individuals living in exposed situations, are recorded as having taken place at that gloomy period. In April, 1792, information was received, that the Cherokees, of five towns, would join the Shawanese, in a war against Kentucky. One incident of this war was productive of an act of heroism, which Mr. Butler records in his "History of Kentucky," as given below. It is only to be regretted that the historian has not given us more fully the details of the affair. His account is as follows:

"Towards the end of the month, an incident of Indian hostility occurred, which produced more than ordinary interest. A Mrs. White, in the vicinity of Frankfort, defended her house against nine Indians; killed one of them, and scared the others. The facts are these: a few families, forming a small station, were engaged in their usual occupations; some of the men absent, some about the yard; the women, two or three in number, were in Mrs. White's house; when nine of the enemy surprise the place, kill three white men, as many negroes, and make the rest prisoners. The women shut and bar the door. It is immediately assailed by the savages, who attempt, but in vain, to force it. A part of them next try to fire the wall; others mount to the roof, which is of boards, and which must soon have enabled the Indians, by removing them, to enter the house. In this situation, which might have appalled an ordinary hero, Mrs. White seized her husband's rifle, and fired it, with so good an aim, that one of the Indians was killed—and the rest, seeing him fall, instantly fled.

A few days after, one man was killed, and another taken prisoner. By this time the neighboring militia were collected, and pursuing the enemy, killed one of them and rescued the prisoners. About the same time, two men were killed near the upper Blue Licks. Such was the terrible scene exhibited by the war. Of which this seemed but a repetition of others which had preceded.

MRS. DUREE

IN 1779, A settlement was founded at White Oak Spring, about a mile above Boonesborough, and in the same river bottom. It was composed principally of families from York county, Pennsylvania—orderly, respectable people, and the men good soldiers. But they were unaccustomed to Indian warfare, and the consequence was, that of some ten or twelve men, all were killed but two or three. During this period, Peter Duree, the elder, the principal man of the connexion, determined to settle a fort between Estill's station and the mouth of Muddy Creek, directly on the trace between the Cherokee and Shawanese towns. Having erected a cabin, his son-in-law, John Bullock and his family, and his son, Peter Duree, his wife and two children, removed to it, taking a pair of hand mill stones with them. They remained for two or three days shut up in their cabin, but their corn meal being exhausted, they were compelled to venture out to cut a hollow tree in order to adjust their hand mill. They attacked by Indians—Bullock, after running a short distance, fell. Duree reached the cabin, and threw himself upon the bed. Mrs. Bullock ran to the door to ascertain the fate of her husband—received a shot in the breast, and fell across the door sill. Mrs. Duree, not knowing whether her husband had been shot or had fainted, caught her by the feet, pulled her into the house and barred the door. She grasped a rifle, and told her husband she would help him to fight. He replied that he had been wounded and was dying. She then presented the gun through several port-holes in quick succession—then calmly closed his eyes in death. After waiting several hours, and seeing nothing more of the Indians, she sallied out to make her way to the White Oak Spring, with her infant in her arms, and a son three or four years old following. Afraid to pursue the trace, she entered the woods, and after running till she was nearly exhausted, she came at length to the trace. She then determined to to follow it at all hazards, and having advanced a few miles further, she met the elder Mr. Duree with his wife and youngest son, with their baggage, on their way to the new station. The melancholy tidings induced them of course to return. They led their horses into an adjoining canebrake, unloaded them, and regained the White Oak Spring fort before daylight.

It is impossible at this day to make a just impression of the sufferings of the pioneers about the period spoken of. The White Oak Spring fort, in 1782, with perhaps one hundred souls in it, was reduced in August, to three fighting white men—and I can say with truth, (says Captain Nathaniel Hart, of Woodford county, in a letter to Governor Morehead, of Kentucky,) that for two or three weeks, my mother's family never unclothed themselves to sleep, nor were all of them, within the time, at their meals together, nor was any household business attempted. Food was prepared, and placed where those who chose could eat. It was the period when Bryant's station was besieged, and for many days before and after that gloomy event, we were in constant expectation of being made prisoners. We made application to Colonel Logan for a guard, and obtained one, but not until the danger was nearly over. Colonel Logan did every thing in his power, as county lieutenant, to sustain the different forts—but it was not a very easy matter to order a married man from a fort where his family was, to defend some other—when his own was in imminent danger.

I went with my mother in January, 1783, to Logan's station to prove my father's will. He had fallen in the preceding July. Twenty armed men were of the party. Twenty-three widows were in attendance upon the court, to obtain letters of administration on the estates of their husbands who had been killed during the past year. My mother went to Colonel Logan's, who received and treated her like a sister.

The escape of Mrs. Duree may seem the result of her good fortune; but it is more probable that, by her stratagem of presenting the gun through several port-holes in quick succession, as above mentioned, she frightened the foe away, and thus gained a fair field to escape with her children. A heroine was Mrs. Duree.

MRS. ROWAN

IN THE FOLLOWING narrative, communicated by John Rowan, of Kentucky, to Dr. Drake, of Cincinnati, we have an account of a display of cool courage by a woman, in a degree rarely witnessed, even in the west.

In the latter part of April, 1784, my father with his family, and five other families, set out from Louisville, in two flat-bottomed boats, for the Long Falls of Green river. The intention was to descend the Ohio river to the mouth of Green river, and ascend that river to the place of destination. At that time there were no settlements in Kentucky, within one hundred miles of Long Falls of the Green river (afterwards called Vienna.) The families were in one boat and their cattle in the other. When we had descended the river Ohio, about one hundred miles, and were near the middle of it, gliding along very securely, as we thought, about ten o'clock at night, we heard a prodigious yelling, by Indians, some two or three miles below us, on the northern shore. We had floated but a little distance farther down the river, when we saw a number of fires on that shore. The yelling still continued, and we concluded that they had captured a boat which had passed us about midday, and were massacreing their captives. Our two boats were lashed together, and the best practical arrangements were made for defending them. The men were distributed by my father to the best advantage in case of an attack; they were seven in number, including himself. The boats were neared to the Kentucky shore, with as little noise from the oars as possible. We were afraid to approach too near the Kentucky shore, lest there might be Indians on that shore also. We had not yet reached their uppermost fire, (their fires were extended along the bank at intervals for half a mile or more,) and we entertained a faint hope that we might slip by unperceived. But they discovered us when we had got about midway of their fires, and commanded us to come to. We were silent, for my father had given strict orders that no one should utter any sound but that of the rifle: and not that until the Indians should come within powder burning distance. They united in a most terrific yell, and rushed to their canoes, and pursued us. We floated on in silence—not an oar was pulled. They approached us within a hundred yards, with a seeming determination to board us. Just at this moment my mother rose from her seat, collected the axes, and placed one by the side of each man, where he stood with his gun, touching him on the knee with the handle of the axe, as she leaned it up by him against the side of the boat, to let him know it was there, and retired to her seat, retaining a hatchet for herself. The Indians continued hovering on our rear, and yelling, for near three miles, when, awed by the inference which they drew from our silence, they relinquished farther pursuit. None but those who have had a practical acquaintance with Indian warfare, can form a just idea of the terror which this hideous yelling is calculated to inspire. I was then about ten years old, and shall never forget the sensations of that night; nor can I ever cease to admire the fortitude and composure displayed by my mother on that trying occasion. We were saved, I have no doubt, by the judicious system of conduct and defence, which my father had prescribed to our little band. We were seven men and three boys—but nine guns in all. They were more than a hundred. My mother, in speaking of it afterwards, in her calm way, said, "We had made a providential escape, for which we ought to feel grateful."

That mother of the west should have a monument. It would remind her descendants who are accustomed to hearing females designated as the "weaker vessels," that upon trying occasions, the strength of soul, which is beyond that of sinew and muscle, has appeared in woman, and may appear again.

MISS HECKEWELDER

THE FOLLOWING LETTER addressed to the editor of the "American Pioneer," was written by the daughter of the well-known missionary to the Indians, the Rev. John Heckewelder. Miss Heckewelder was the first white child born in Ohio. Her narrative of the toils and sufferings among the Indians is highly interesting.

Bethlehem, Pa., February 24th, 1843.

J. S. WILLIAMS, ESQ.

Dear Sir—Yours of the 31st ult., to Mr. Kummen, post-master at this place, has been handed to me. I have not been in the habit of making much use of my pen for a number of years; I will, however, at your request, endeavor to give you a short account of the first four years of my life, which were all I spent amongst the Indians, having since lived in Bethlehem nearly all the time. My acquaintance or knowledge of them and their history, is chiefly from books, and what I heard from my father and other missionaries.

I was born April 16th, 1781, in Salem, one of the Moravian Indian towns, on the Muskingum river, state of Ohio. Soon after my birth, times becoming very troublesome, the settlements were often in danger from war parties, and from an encampment of warriors near Gnadenhutten; and finally, in the beginning of September of the same year, we were all made prisoners. First, four of the missionaries were seized by a party of Huron warriors, and declared prisoners of war; they were then led into the camp of the Delawares, where the death-song was sung over them. Soon after they had secured them, a number of warriors marched off for Salem and Shoenbrun. About thirty savages arrived at the former place in the dusk of the evening, and broke open the mission house. Here they took my mother and myself prisoners, and having led her into the street and placed guards over her, they plundered the house of every thing they could take with them and destroyed what was left. Then going to take my mother along with them, the savages were prevailed upon through the intercession of the Indian females, to let her remain at Salem till the next morning—the night being dark and rainy and almost impossible for her to travel so far—they at last consented on condition that she should be brought into the camp the next morning, which was accordingly done, and she was safely conducted by our Indians to Gnadenhutten.

After experiencing the cruel treatment of the savages for sometime, they were set at liberty again; but we were obliged to leave their flourishing settlements, and forced to march through a dreary wilderness to Upper Sandusky. We went by land through Goshachguenk to the Walholding, and then partly by water and partly along the banks of the river, to Sandusky creek. All the way I was carried by an Indian woman, carefully wrapped in a blanket, on her back. Our journey was exceedingly tedious and dangerous; some of the canoes sunk, and those that were in them lost all their provisions and every thing they had saved. Those who went by land drove the cattle, a pretty large herd. The savages now drove us along, the missionaries with their families usually in the midst, surrounded by their Indian converts. The roads were exceedingly bad, leading through a continuation of swamps. Having arrived at Upper Sandusky, they built small huts of logs and bark to screen them from the cold, having neither beds or blankets, and being reduced to the greatest poverty and want; for the savages had by degrees stolen almost everything, both from the missionaries and Indians, on the journey. We lived here extremely poor, oftentimes very little or nothing to satisfy the cravings of hunger; and the poorest of the Indians were obliged to live upon their dead cattle, which died for want of pasture.

After living in this dreary wilderness, in danger, poverty, and distress of all sorts, a written order arrived in March, 1782, sent by the governor to the half king of the Hurons and to an English officer in his company, to bring all the missionaries and their families to Detroit, but with a strict order not to plunder nor abuse them in the least. The missionaries were overwhelmed with grief at the idea of being separated from their Indians; but there being no alternative, they were obliged to submit to this, one of the heaviest of their trials. The poor Indians came weeping to bid them farewell, and accompanied them a considerable way, some as far as Lower Sandusky. Here we were obliged to spend several nights in the open air, and suffered great cold besides other hardships. April 14th, we set out and crossed over a part of the lakes Erie and Huron. We were lodged in the barracks by order of the governor. Some weeks after, we left the barracks with his consent and moved into a house at a small distance from the town.

The Indian converts, gathering around their teachers, they resolved with the consent of their governor, to begin the building of a new settlement upon a spot about thirty miles from Detroit, on the river Huron, which they called New Gnadenhutten, and which increased considerably from time to time. Here I lived till the year 1785, when I set out with an aged missionary couple to be educated in the school at Bethlehem. We commenced our journey about the middle May, and arrived at the latter place July 9th, after a very tedious and perilous journey—proceeding down the river Huron into Lake St. Clair, thence to Detroit, and crossing Lake Erie to Niagara and Oswego, thence down Oswego river to Lake Oneida, thence down the Waldbah to Fort Stanwix. We then arrived at a carrying place at the Mohawk river, and proceeded to Schenectady; went by land to Albany, and then by water to New Windsor, and then again by land to Bethlehem.

I fear my account has become rather too long and tedious. I am much obliged to you, sir, for the Pioneer, it is a most interesting work, and I wish I could but gain some patronage for you; but money is so scarce, there is at present no prospect.

MRS. TACKETT, THE CAPTIVE

THE FOLLOWING THRILLING narrative is copied from the Hesperian.

The sufferings endured by the first emigrants to a new country, scarcely admit of description. These have always been greatly multiplied by an encroachment upon the rights and possessions of the aborigines. In reference to this country, where we have long been considered unwelcome intruders, this has been peculiarly the case. The settlement of no part of the world has been more fruitful of incident than that of our own. Although many pens have been employed from time to time, in detailing our wars with the Indians, still many interesting occurrences have escaped the historian's notice. Some of these have appeared in the form of newspaper paragraphs, while others of equal importance have escaped this ephemeral kind of repository.

The writer of this article has several times travelled the road which lies on the banks of the Kenhawa. Although he found mountains whose tops pierced the clouds, and a beautiful river whose margins smoked with salt furnaces, to amuse him by day, his entertainment was not diminished by the approach of darkness. He has usually sought lodgings with some of of the more ancient inhabitants, many of whom accommodate their guests with great hospitality. Like the early adventurers to new settlements, they are social, and delight in the recital of their dangerous enterprises and hair-breadth escapes. Mr. M., at whose comfortable mansion it was the writer's good fortune to tarry one night, the last time he passed through Western Virginia, gave him the following narrative.

Just below the mouth of Cole river, on the farm owned by the heirs of Tays, to insure their safety the early settlers constructed a fortress. It was formed exclusively of timber, without much labor, yet in such a manner as to be deemed adequate to their defence against Indian aggression.

On the apprehension of danger, the gate was closed, and every one prepared for resistance. When the demand for food became imperious, a few of the most skilful hunters would leave this retreat before day, go a few miles distant, return the succeeding night, loaded with game, unnoticed by the skulking savage. These measures of safety were at first considered indispensable. A few weeks of repose, however, seemed to render them inconvenient and unnecessary. Exemption from a morning attack was thought a sufficient pledge of peace through the day. Familiarity with danger, as it always does, relaxed their vigilance and diminished their precaution. Even the women and children, who at first had been frightened by the falling of a tree, or the hooting of an owl, lost their timidity. Indeed, the strife seemed to be, who should be boldest, and the least apprehensive of peril.

On a beautiful morning, in the month of June, 1778, as well as is recollected, the gate was thrown open. Confinement had become painful, nay, insupportable. It was considered rather as a voluntary punishment, than a condition of security. Three of the fearless inhabitants set out on a hunting expedition. Some sought amusement in shooting at a mark; the younger engaged in playing at ball, while the women and children were delighted spectators of the recreation. Scarcely had an hour elapsed in these cheerful relaxations, before some twenty or thirty Indians suddenly ascended the river bank which had concealed their approach, fired upon the whites, and instantly took possession of the fort. Amidst the consternation which ensued, the savages put to death every white man on whom they could lay hands, reserving the women and children for more trying occasions.

The wounded, who were unable to travel, without regard to age or sex, were butchered in the most shocking manner, of which description was James Tackett. The importunities and tears of his interesting wife were wholly unavailing. She was left with two fine boys, the one seven years old, and the other five. Apprehensive of pursuit by the whites, the Indians, after the destruction of every article they could not remove, betook themselves to flight. When a prisoner became too feeble, as was the case with several small children, all entreaties to avert the stroke of the tomahawk were fruitless. Although Mrs. Tackett afforded to her children all the aid which their situation and maternal tenderness could dictate, at the distance of about five miles the youngest became exhausted.

Her extreme anxiety for his safety induced her to take him on her back; but alas! this act of kindness was but the signal for his dispatch.

Two hours afterwards her other child began to fail. He grasped his mother's hand, and said, "I must keep up with you or be killed as poor James was." The exertions which she made for her child were beyond what she could sustain. For a time she inspired him with the hope of relief which the approaching night would bring. Nature, however, became overpowered, and a single blow, sunk him to rest. The distracted parent would cheerfully have submitted to the same fate, but even this barbarous relief was denied her. About dark she lagged behind, regardless of consequences, in charge of a warrior who could speak a little English. He informed her that in the course of an hour they would reach a large encampment, where the prisoners must be divided; that sometimes quarrels ensued on such occasions, and the captives were put to death. He asked her if she could write. An affirmative answer seemed to please him much. He said he would take her to his country in the south, to be his wife and to keep his accounts, as he was a trader. This Indian was a Cherokee, and named Chickahoula; aged about thirty five, and of good appearance.

He soon took the first step necessary for carrying his designs into execution, by making a diversion to the left. After travelling about two miles, the darkness of the night and abruptness of the country forbade their advancing farther. A small fire was made to defend them against the gnats and musqiutoes. After eating a little jerk, Chickahoula told his captive to sleep; that he would watch lest they should be overtaken by pursuers. Early in the morning he directed his course towards the head of the Great Sandy and Kentucky rivers. Until he crossed Guyandotte, Chickahoula was constantly on the lookout, as if he deemed himself exposed to the most imminent danger. After having travelled seven days, the warrior and the captive reached Powell's valley, in Tennessee. By this time they were out of provisions; and the Indian thinking it safer, while passing through a settled district, to steal food than to depend upon his gun, determined to avail himself of the first opportunity of supplying his wants in this manner. It was but a little while till one presented itself. Following the meanderings of a small rivulet, he came suddenly upon a spring-house, or dairy. This was several rods from the dwelling-house of the owner, and so situated that it could be approached unseen from thence. Well satisfied that it contained a rich store of milk, and thinking it probable that other provision was there, the warrior stationed his captive to watch, while he went in to rifle the spring-house. Mrs. Tackett readily and willingly undertook the duty of acting as sentinel; but no sooner was the Indian fairly within the spring-house, than she stole up the slope, and then bounded towards the dwelling. This reached, she instantly gave the alarm; but the Indian escaped.

Mrs. Tackett tarried for some time with her new acquaintances, and spent several months in the different settlements of that section of the west. An opportunity then offering, she returned to Greenbriar. Her feelings on rejoining her friends and listening to the accounts of the massacre at the station,—and those of her relatives on again beholding one whom they considered, if not dead, in hopeless captivity, may be imagined; pen cannot describe them.

MRS. MERRIL

IN THE SUMMER of 1787, the house of John Merril, in Nelson county, Kentucky, was attacked by Indians. The defence was spirited and successful, Mrs. Merril acted with the most determined heroism.

Merril was alarmed by the barking of a dog about midnight, and in opening the door in order to ascertain the cause of the disturbance, he received the fire of six or seven Indians, by which his arm and thigh were both broken. He sank upon the floor and called upon his wife to shut the door. This had scarcely been done when it was violently assailed by the tomahawks of the enemy, and a large breach soon effected. Mrs. Merril, however, being a perfect Amazon, both in strength and courage, guarded it with an axe, and successively killed or badly wounded four of the enemy as they attempted to force their way into the cabin. The Indians then ascended the roof and attempted to enter by way of the chimney, but here, again, they were met by the same determined enemy. Mrs. Merril seized the only feather-bed which the cabin afforded, and hastily ripping it open, poured its contents upon the fire. A furious blaze and stifling smoke ascended the chimney, and quickly brought down two of the enemy, who lay for a few moments at the mercy of the lady. Seizing the axe, she despatched them, and was instantly afterwards summoned to the door, where the only remaining savage now appeared, endeavoring to effect an entrance, while Mrs. Merril was engaged at the chimney. He soon received a gash in the cheek, which compelled him with a loud yell to relinquish his purpose, and return hastily to Chillicothe, where, from the report of a prisoner, he gave an exaggerated account of the fierceness, strength, and courage of the "long knife squaw!"

THE ESCAPE OF MRS. COLEMAN

THE SCENERY OF the Ohio, between Columbia and Cincinnati, was truly romantic in the pioneer days of 1792. Scarcely a tree had been cut on either side, between the mouth of Crawfish and that of Deer creek, a distance of more than four miles. The sand-bar, now extending from its left bank, opposite to Sportsman's Hall, was then a small island, between which and the Kentucky shore was a narrow channel, with sufficient depth of water for the passage of boats. The upper and lower points of this island were bare, but its centre, embracing about four acres, was covered with small cotton wood, and surrounded by willows extending along its sides almost down to the water's edge. The right bank of the river crowned with its lofty hills, now gradually ascending, and now rising abruptly to their summits, and forming a vast amphitheatre, was from Columbia, extending down about two miles, very steep, and covered with trees quite down to the beach. From thence, nearly opposite the foot of the island, its ascent became more gradual, and for two miles farther down, bordering the tall trees with which it was covered, was a thick growth of willows, through which in many places it was difficult to penetrate. Below this, the beach was wide and stony, with only here and there a small tuft of willows, while the wood on the side and on the top of the bank was more open. Not far from this bank and near the line of the present turnpike, was a narrow road leading from Columbia to Cincinnati, just wide enough for the passage of a wagon, which, winding round the point of the hill above Deer creek, descended northwardly about four hundred feet, and crossing that creek, and in a southerly direction ascending gradually its western bank, led along the ground, now Symmes street, directly towards Fort Washington, and diverging at the intersection of Lawrence street to the right and left of the fort, entered the town. The river between Columbia and Cincinnati is thus minutely described to enable the reader to gain a clear idea of the following adventure.

On the afternoon of the 7th of July, 1792, a Mr. Oliver M. Spencer and a few friends, embarked in a canoe, at Fort Washington, to go to Columbia. It was a small craft, and hardly fit to accommodate the party, which thus consisted of a Mr. Jacob Light, a Mr. Clayton, Mrs. Coleman, young Spencer, a boy of thirteen, and one of the garrison soldiers, which last individual being much intoxicated, lurched from one side of the canoe to the other, and finally by the time they had got up a short distance above Deer creek, tumbled out, nearly upsetting the whole party. He then reached the shore, the water not being very deep at the spot. Spencer did not know how to swim, and had become afraid to continue in the canoe, and was therefore at his own request put on shore, where they left the soldier, and the party in the boat and Spencer on shore, proceeded side by side. Light propelled the boat forward with a pole, while Clayton sat at the stern with a paddle, which he sometimes used as an oar, and sometimes as a rudder, and Mrs. Coleman, a woman of fifty years, sat in the middle of the boat. One mile above Deer creek, a party of market people, with a woman and child, on board a canoe, passed them on their way to Cincinnati. Light and the others had rounded a small point in the cove less than a mile below the foot of the island, and proceeded a few hundred yards along the close willows here bordering the beach, at about two rods distance from the water, when Clayton looking back, discovered the drunken man staggering along the shore, and remarked that he would be "bait for Indians." Hardly had he passed the remark, when two rifle-shots from the rear of the willow struck Light and his comrade, causing the latter to fall towards the shore, and wounding the other by the ball glancing from the oar. The two Indians who had fired instantly rushed from their concealment, to scalp the dead, and impede the escape of the living. Clayton was scalped, and Spencer, in spite of all his efforts to get off, was made prisoner, but Light swam out of reach of his pursuers, and Mrs. Coleman, who had also jumped out, preferring to be drowned to falling into the hands of the Indians, and floated some distance off. The Indians would probably have reloaded and fired, but the report of their rifles brought persons to the opposite shore, which forced them to decamp with their young prisoner, saying, "squaw must drown." Light first made for the Kentucky shore, but finding he could not reach it in his crippled state, directed his way out on the Ohio side. Mrs. Coleman followed, using her hands as paddles, and they both got to shore some distance below the scene of these events. Light had barely got out when he fell, but after vomiting blood at length came to.

Mrs. Coleman floated nearly a mile, and when she reached the shore, walked down the path to Cincinnati, crossed Deer creek at its mouth, holding on to the willows which overhung its banks—the water there in those days flowing in a narrow current that might almost be cleared by a spring from one bank to the other. She went direct to Captain Thorp, at the artificer's yard, with whose lady she was acquainted, and from whom she obtained a change of clothes, and rested a day or two to recover from her fatigue. Mrs. Coleman died a few years since, at a very advanced age, at Versailles, Ripley county, Indiana.

THE SISTERS FLEMING

IN FEBRUARY, 1790, a Mr. John May, surveyor of the Kentucky lands, determined to proceed from Virginia to his field of labor by descending the Great Kenawha and the Ohio. He was accompanied by a young clerk, named Charles Johnston; Mr. Jacob Skyles, who had a lot of dry goods intended for Lexington; a hardy borderer named Flinn; and two sisters, named Fleming, who had been accustomed to the dangers of a frontier life.

During their short stay at Point Pleasant, they learned that roving bands of Indians were constantly hovering upon either bank of the Ohio, and were in the habit of decoying boats ashore under various pretences, and murdering or taking captives, all who were on board, so that, upon leaving Point Pleasant, they determined that no considerations should induce them to approach either shore, but steeling their hearts against every entreaty, that they would resolutely keep the middle of the current, and leave distressed individuals to shift for themselves. How firmly this resolution was maintained the sequel will show. The spring freshet was in its height at the time of their embarkation, and their boat was wafted rapidly down the stream. There was no occasion to use the side oars, and it was only necessary for one individual at a time to watch throughout the night, at the steering oar, in order to keep the boat in the current. So long as this could be done, they entertained no dread of any number of Indians on either shore, as boarding had hitherto formed no part of their plans, and was supposed to be impracticable, so long as arms were on board of the boat.

On the morning of the 20th of March, when near the junction of the Scioto, they were awakened at daylight by Flinn, whose turn it was to watch, and informed that danger was at hand. All sprung to their feet, and hastened upon deck without removing their night caps or completing their dress. The cause of Flinn's alarm was quickly evident. Far down the river a smoke was seen, ascending in thick wreaths above the trees, and floating in thinner masses over the bed of the river. All at once perceived that it could only proceed from a large fire—and who was there to kindle a fire in the wilderness which surrounded them? No one doubted that Indians were in front, and the only question to be decided was, upon which shore they lay, for the winding of the river, and their distance from the smoke, rendered it impossible at first to ascertain this point. As the boat drifted on, however, it became evident that the fire was upon the Ohio shore, and it was determined to put over to the opposite side of the river. Before this could be done, however, two white men ran down upon the beach, and clasping their hands in the most earnest manner, implored the crew to take them on board. They declared that they had been taken by a party of Indians in Kennedy's bottom a few days before— had been conducted across the Ohio, and had just effected their escape. They added, that the enemy was in close pursuit of them, and that their death was certain, unless admitted on board. Resolute in their purpose, on no account to leave the middle of the stream, and strongly suspecting the suppliants of treachery, the party paid no attention to their entreaties, but steadily pursued their course down the river, and were soon considerably ahead of them. The two white men ran down the bank in a line parallel with the course of the boat, and their entreaties were changed into the most piercing cries and lamentations upon perceiving the obstinacy with which their request was disregarded. The obduracy of the crew soon began to relax. Flinn and the two females, accustomed from their youth to undervalue danger from the Indians, earnestly insisted upon going ashore, and relieving the white men, and even the incredulity of May began to yield to the persevering importunity of the suppliants.

A parley took place. May called them from the deck of the boat where he stood in his night-cap and drawers, and demanded the cause of the large fire and smoke of which had caused so much alarm. The white men positively denied that there was any fire near them. The falsehood was so palpable, that May's former suspicion returned with additional force, and he positively insisted upon continuing their course without paying the slightest attention to the request of the men. This resolution was firmly seconded by Johnston and Skyles, and as vehemently opposed by Flinn and Miss Flemings, for, the females were allowed an equal vote with the males on board of the boat. Flinn urged that the men gave every evidence of real distress which could be required, and recounted too many particular circumstances attending their capture and escape, to give color to the suspicion that their story was invented for the occasion, and added, that it would be a burning shame to them and theirs forever, if they should permit two countrymen to fall a sacrifice to the savages when so slight a risk on their part would suffice to relieve them. He acknowledged that they had lied in relation to the fire, but declared himself satisfied that it was only because they were fearful of acknowledging the truth, least the crew should suspect that Indians were concealed in the vicinity. The controversy became warm, and during its progress, the boat drifted so far below the men, that they appeared to relinquish their pursuit in despair.

Flinn then made a second proposal, which, according to his method of reasoning, could be carried into effect without the slightest risk to any one but himself. They were now more than a mile below the pursuers. He proposed that May should only touch the hostile shore long enough to permit him to jump out. That it was impossible for Indians, (even admitting that they were at hand,) to arrive in time to arrest the boat, and even should any appear, they could immediately put off from shore and abandon him to his fate. That he was confident of being able to outrun the red devils, if they saw him first, and was equally confident of being able to see them as soon as they could see him. May remonstrated upon so unnecessary an exposure—but Flinn was inflexible, and in an evil hour, the boat was directed to the shore. They quickly discovered, what ought to have been known before, that they could not float as swiftly after leaving the current as while borne along by it, and they were nearly double the time in making the shore, that they had calculated upon. When within reach Flinn leaped fearlessly upon the hostile bank, and the boat grated upon the sand. At that moment, five or six savages, ran up out of breath, from the adjoining wood, and seizing Flinn, began to fire upon the boat's crew. Johnston and Skyles sprang to their arms, in order to return the fire, while May, seizing an oar attempted to regain the current. Fresh Indians arrived, however, in such rapid succession, that the beach was quickly crowded by them, and May called out to his companions to cease firing and come to the oars. This was done, but it was too late.

The river, as we have already observed, was very high, and their clumsy and unwieldy boat, had become entangled in the boughs of the trees which hung over the water, so that after the most desperate efforts to get her off, they were compelled to relinquish the attempt in despair. During the whole of this time the Indians were pouring a heavy fire into the boat, at a distance not exceeding ten paces. Their horses, of which they had a great number on board, had broken their halters, and mad with terror were plunging so furiously as to expose them to danger scarcely less dreadful than that which menaced them from shore. In addition to this, none of them had, ever beheld a hostile Indian before, (with the exception of May,) and the furious gestures and appalling yells of the enemy, struck a terror in their hearts which had almost deprived them of their faculties. Seeing it impossible to extricate themselves, they all lay down upon their faces, in such parts of the boat, as would best protect them from the horses, and awaited in passive helplessness, the approach of the conquerors. The enemy, however, still declined boarding, and contented themselves with pouring in an incessant fire, by which all the horses were killed, and which at length began to grow fatal to the crew. One of the females received a ball in her mouth, which had passed immediately over Johnston's head, and almost immediately expired. Skyles, immediately afterwards, was severely wounded in both shoulders, the ball striking the right shoulder blade, and ranging transversely along his back. The fire seemed to grow hotter every moment, when, at length May arose and waved his night-cap above his head as a signal of surrender. He instantly received a ball in the middle of the forehead and fell perfectly dead by the side of Johnston, covering him with blood.

Now, at last, the enemy ventured to board. Throwing themselves into the water, with their tomahawks in their hands, a dozen or twenty swam to the boat, and began to climb the sides. Johnston stood ready to do the honors of the boat, and presenting his hand to each Indian in succession, he helped them over the side to the number of twenty. Nothing could appear more cordial than the meeting. Each Indian shook him by the hand, with the usual salutation of "How de do?" in passable English, whilst Johnston encountered every visiter with an affectionate squeeze, and a forced smile, in which terror struggled with civility. The Indians then passed on to Skyles and the surviving Miss Fleming, where the demonstrations of mutual joy were not quite so lively. Skyles was writhing under a painful wound, and the girl was sitting by the dead body of her sister. Having shaken hands with all their captives, the Indians proceeded to scalp the dead, which was done with great coolness, and the reeking scalps were stretched and prepared for the usual process of drying, immediately before the eyes of the survivors. The boat was then drawn ashore, and its contents examined with great greediness. Poor Skyles, in addition to the pain of his wounds, was compelled to witness the total destruction of his property, by the hands of these greedy spoilers, who tossed his silks, cambric, and broadcloth into the dirt, with the most reckless indifference. At length they stumbled upon a keg of whiskey. The prize was eagerly seized, and every thing else abandoned. The Indian who had found it, carried it ashore and was followed by the rest with tumultuous delight. A large fire nearly fifty feet long was kindled, and victors and vanquished indiscriminately huddled around it.

The two white men who had decoyed them ashore, and whose names were Divine and Thomas, now appeared and took their seats beside the captives. Sensible of the reproach to which they had exposed themselves, they hastened to offer an excuse for their conduct. They declared that they really had been taken in Kennedy's bottom a few days before, and that the Indians had compelled them, by threats of instant death in case of refusal, to act as they had done. They concluded by some common place expressions of regret for the calamity which they had occasioned, and declared that their own misery was aggravated at beholding that of their countrymen! In short, words were cheap with them, and they showered them out in profusion. But Johnston and Skyles's sufferings had been and still were too severe, to permit their resentment to be appeased by such light atonement. Their suspicions of the existence of wilful and malignant treachery on the part of the white men, at least one of them, were confirmed by the report of a negro, who quickly made his appearance, and who, as it appeared, had been taken in Kentucky a few days before. He declared that Thomas had been extremely averse to having any share in the treachery, but had been overruled by Divine, who alone had planned, and was most active in the execution of the project, having received a promise from the Indians, that, in case of success, his own liberty should be restored to him.

In a few minutes, six squaws, most of them very old, together with two white children, a girl and a boy, came down to the fire, and seated themselves. The children had lately been taken from Kentucky. Skyles's wound now became excessively painful, and Flinn, who, in the course of his adventurous life, had picked up some knowledge of surgery, was permitted to examine it. He soon found it necessary to make an incision, which was done very neatly with a razor. An old squaw then washed the wound, and having caught the bloody water in a tin cup, presented it to Skyles, and requested him to drink it, assuring him that it would greatly hasten the cure. He thought it most prudent to comply.

During the whole of this time, the Indians remained silently smoking or lounging around the fire. No sentinels were posted in order to prevent a surprise, but each man's gun stood immediately behind him, with the breech resting upon the ground, and the barrel supported against a small pole, placed horizontally upon two forks. Upon the slightest alarm, every man could have laid his hand upon his own gun. Their captors were composed of small detachments from several tribes. Much the greater portion belonged to the Shawanese, but there were several Delawares, Wyandottes, and a few wandering Cherokees.

After smoking, they proceeded to the division of of their prisoners. Flinn was given to a Shawanese warrior—Skyles to an old, crabbed, ferocious Indian of the same tribe, whose temper was sufficiently expressed in his countenance, while Johnston was assigned to a young Shawanese chief, whom he represents as possessed of a disposition which would have done him honor in any age or in any nation. The surviving Miss Fleming was given to the Cherokees, while the Wyandottes and the Delawares were allowed no share in the distribution.

The next day, the Indians attacked the boats, and obtained a large amount of booty. Another keg of whiskey was found. A grand drinking frolic was then held, during which the prisoners were bound, to guard against their escape. After this drunken revel, the march commenced. The party having Flinn in charge, left the rest of the band, and took a different route. Leaving the male prisoners to their fate, we will merely narrate what befell Miss Fleming.

Johnston had been much surprised at the levity of her conduct, when first taken. Instead of appearing dejected at the dreadful death of her sister, and the still more terrible fate of her friends, she never appeared more lively or better reconciled to her fate than while her captors lingered upon the banks of the Ohio. Upon the breaking up of the party, the

Cherokees conducted their prisoner towards the Miami villages, and Johnston saw nothing more of her until after his own liberation. While he remained at the house of Mr. Duchouquet, the small party of Cherokees to whom she belonged suddenly made their appearance in the village in a condition so tattered and dilapidated, as to satisfy every one that all their booty had been wasted with their usual improvidence. Miss Fleming's appearance, particularly, had been entirely changed. All the levity which had astonished Johnston so much on the banks of the Ohio, was completely gone. Her dress was tattered, her cheeks sunken, her eyes discolored by weeping, and her whole manner expressive of the most heartfelt wretchedness. Johnston addressed her with kindness, and inquired the cause of so great a change, but she only replied by wringing her hands and bursting into tears. Her master quickly summoned her away, and on the morning of her arrival she was compelled to leave the village, and accompany them to Lower Sandusky. Within a few days, Johnston, in company with his friend Duchouquet, followed them to that place, partly upon business, and partly with the hope of effecting her liberation. He found the town thronged with Indians of various tribes, and there, for the first time, he learned that his friend Skyles had effected his escape. Upon inquiring for the Cherokees he learned that they were encamped with their prisoner within a quarter of a mile of the town, holding themselves aloof from the rest, and evincing the most jealous watchfulness over their prisoner.—Johnston applied to the traders of Sandusky for their good offices, and, as usual, the request was promptly complied with. They went out in a body to the Cherokee camp, accompanied by a white man named Whittaker, who had been taken from Virginia when a child, and had become completely naturalized among the Indians.—This Whittaker was personally known to Miss Fleming, having often visited Pittsburg where her father kept a small tavern, much frequented by Indians and traders. As soon as she beheld him, therefore, she ran up to the spot where he stood, and bursting into tears, implored him to save her from the cruel fate which she had no doubt awaited her. He engaged very zealously in her service, and finding that all the offers of the traders were rejected with determined obstinacy, he returned to Detroit, and solicited the intercession of an old chief known among the whites by the name of "Old King Crane," assuring him (a lie which we can scarcely blame) that the woman was his sister.

King Crane listened with gravity to the appeal of Whittaker, acknowledged the propriety of interfering in the case of so near a relative, and very calmly walked out to the Cherokee camp, in order to try the efficacy of his own eloquence in behalf of the white squaw. He found her master, however, perfectly inexorable. The argument gradually waxed warm, till at length the Cherokees became enraged, and told the old man that it was a disgrace to a chief like him, to put himself upon a level with "white people," and that they looked upon him as no better than "dirt."

At this insupportable insult, King Crane became exasperated in turn, and a very edifying scene ensued, in which each bespattered the other with a profusion of abuse for several minutes, until the Old King recollected himself sufficently, to draw off for the present, and concert measures for obtaining redress. He returned to the village in a towering passion, and announced his determination to collect his young men and rescue the white squaw by force, and if the Cherokees dared to resist, he swore that he would take their scalps upon the spot. Whittaker applauded his doughty resolution, but warned him of the necessity of dispatch, as the Cherokees, alarmed at the idea of losing their prisoner, might be tempted to put her to death without further delay. This advice was acknowledged to be of weight, and before daylight on the following morning, King Crane assembled his young men, and advanced cautiously upon the Cherokee encampment. He found all but the miserable prisoner buried in sleep. *She* had been striped naked, her body painted black, and in this condition, had been bound to a stake, around which hickory poles had already been collected, and every other disposition made for burning her alive at day-light. She was moaning in a low tone as her deliverers approached, and was so much exhausted as not to be aware of their approach, until King Crane had actually cut the cords which bound her, with his knife.

He then ordered his young men to assist her in putting on her clothes, which they obeyed with the most stoical indifference. As soon as her toilet had been completed, the King awakened her masters, and informed them that the squaw was his! that if they submitted quietly it was well!—if not, his young men and himself were ready for them. The Cherokees, as may readily be imagined, protested loudly against such unrighteous proceedings, but what could words avail against tomahawks and superior numbers? They then expressed their willingness to resign the squaw—but hoped that King Crane would not be such a "beast" as to refuse them the ransom which he had offered them on the preceding day! The king replied coolly, that the squaw was now in his own hands—and would serve them right if he refused to pay a single broach—but he disdained to receive any thing at their hands, without paying an equivalent! and would give them six hundred broaches. He then returned to Lower Sandusky, accompanied by the liberated prisoner. She was then painted as a squaw by Whittaker, and sent off, under the care of two trusty Indians to Pittsburg, where she arrived in safety in the course of the following week.

Miss Fleming was much exhausted by her sufferings in the trying scenes through which she had passed; but she lived at Pittsburg many years afterwards.

MRS. PARKER AND DAUGHTER

THE FOLLOWING NARRATIVE, told by an old pioneer, called Tim Watkins, to a correspondent of the "Cincinnati Miscellany," contains some noble instances of female determination, and is worthy of a place by the side of the best of those stories we have related. On the Illinois river, near two hundred miles from its junction with the Mississippi, there lived an old pioneer, known in those days as "Old Parker, the squatter." His family consisted of a wife and three children, the oldest a boy of nineteen, a girl of seventeen, and the youngest a boy of fourteen. At the time of which we write, Parker and his oldest boy had gone in company with three Indians on a hunt, expecting to be absent some five or six days. The third day after their departure, one of the Indians returned to Parker's house, came in and sat himself down by the fire, lit his pipe, and commenced smoking in silence. Mrs. Parker thought nothing of this, as it was no uncommon thing for one or sometimes more of a party of Indians to return abruptly from a hunt, at some sign they might consider ominous of bad luck, and in such instances were not very communicative. But at last the Indian broke silence with "ugh! old Parker die." This exclamation immediately drew Mrs. Parker's attention, who directly inquired of the Indian, "What's the matter with Parker?"

The Indian responded, "Parker sick, tree fell on him, you go he die."

Mrs. Parker then asked the Indian if Parker sent for her, and where he was.

The replies of the Indian somewhat aroused her suspicions. She how-ever came to the conclusion to send her son with the Indian to see what was the matter. The boy and Indian started. That night passed, and the next day too, and neither the boy nor Indian returned. This confirmed Mrs. Parker in her opinion that there was foul play on the part of the

Indians. So she and her daughter went to work and barricaded the doors and windows in the best way they could. The youngest boy's rifle was the only one left, he not having taken it with him when he went out after his father. The old lady took the rifle, the daughter the axe, and thus armed they determined to watch through the night, and defend themselves if any Indians should appear.

They had not long to wait after night fall, for soon after that some one commenced knocking at the door, crying out, "Mother, mother!" but Mrs. Parker thought the voice was not exactly like that of her son, and in order to ascertain the fact, she said, "Jake, where are the Indians?" The reply, which was "um gone," satisfied her on that point. She then said, as if speaking to her son, "Put your ear to the latch-hole of the door." The head was placed at the latch-hole, and the old lady fired her rifle through it and killed the Indian. She stepped back from the door instantly, and it was well she did so, for quicker than I have penned the last two words, two rifle-bullets came crashing through the door.

The old lady then said to her daughter, "Thank God, there is but two, I must have killed the one at the door—they must be the three who went on the hunt with your father. If we can only kill or cripple another one of them, we will be safe; now we must both be still after they fire again, and they will then break the door down, and I may be able to shoot another one; but if I miss them when getting in you must use the axe."

The daughter, equally courageous with her mother, assured her she would. Soon after this conversation two more rifle bullets came crashing through the window. A death-like stillness ensued for about five minutes, when two more balls in quick succession were fired through the door, then followed a tremendous punching with a log, the door gave way, and with a fiendish yell, an Indian was about to spring in when the unerring rifle fired by the gallant old lady laid his lifeless body across the threshold of the door. The remaining, or more properly the surviving, Indian fired at random and ran doing no injury. "Now" said the old heroine to her undaunted daughter "we must leave." Accordingly with the rifle and the axe, they went to the river, took the canoe, and without a mouthful of provision, except one wild duck and two black birds which the mother shot, and which were eaten raw, did these two courageous hearts in six days arrive among the old French settlers at St. Louis. A party of about a dozen men crossed over Illinois—and after an unsuccessful search returned without finding either Parker or his boys. They were never found. There are yet some of the old settlers in the neighborhood of Peoria who still point out the spot where "old Parker, the squatter" lived.

EXPERIENCE BOZARTH

THE COURAGE AND prowess of a woman in defence of herself and family were never more gloriously displayed than by Mrs. Experience Bozarth. This lady lived upon Dunkard's creek, in Westmoreland county, Pennsylvania. About the middle of March, 1779, when the neighboring country was infested with war-like Indians, two or three families gathered at Mrs. Bozarth's house for safety. Soon afterwards, some of the children came running in from play, appearing very much frightened, and exclaiming that ugly red men were near the house. There were but two men in the house. One of them stepped to the door, where he received a ball in the side of his breast, which caused him to fall back upon the floor. The Indian who had shot him immediately jumped over the body and engaged in a struggle with the other white man. The savage was overpowered, and his antagonist, tossing him on the bed, called for a knife to dispatch him. Mrs. Bozarth had retained her presence of mind, and was now prepared for the most desperate defence. Not being able to find a knife, she seized an axe, and with one blow clove in the Indian's skull. At that instant a second Indian entered the door, and shot the white man dead, who was holding the Indian on the bed. Mrs. Bozarth, with unflinching boldness, turned to this new foe, and gave him several cuts with the axe, one of which made his entrails appear. He called out murder, whereupon, other Indians who had been killing some children out of doors, came rushing to his relief. The head of one of these was cut in twain by the axe of Mrs. Bozarth. Another Indian snatched him by the feet and pulled him out of doors, when Mrs. Bozarth, with the assistance of the man who was first shot in the door, and who had by this time recovered some degree of self-command, shut the door and fastened it.

The Indians, rendered furious by the desperate resistance they had met, now besieged the house, and for several days, they employed all their arts to enter and slay the weak garrison. But all their efforts were futile. Mrs. Bozarth and her wounded companion, employed themselves so vigorously and vigilantly, that the enemy were completely baffled. During the siege, the dead Indian and the dead white man remained in the house.

At length, a party of white men arrived, put the Indians to flight, and relieved Mrs. Bozarth from her perilous situation. Many were the encomiums lavished upon the heroic woman, who had made such a noble defence of her home; and, indeed, it may be questioned whether any female ever displayed more courage and prowess in combat against superior numbers.

A HEROINE WITHOUT A NAME

Vast is the catalogue of names, fame gives to the world as great and good—heroes and heroines. But, we believe, the unrecorded great are still more numerous. Sometimes there is a want of a timely historian. Often, modest merit seeks concealment, and so is forgotten, amid the trumpetings of noisy fools. Again, as in the present instance, "a deed without a name," is handed down to us, as an example, with no claimant for admiration.

In 1786, an incident happened upon Green river, Kentucky, which not only illustrates the dangers which beset the pioneers of that period, but also the nobility of woman. About twenty young persons, male and female, of a fort, had united in a flax pulling, in one of the most distant fields. In the course of the forenoon two of their mothers made them a visit, and the younger took along her child, about eighteen months old. When the whole party were near the woods, one of the young women climbed over the fence, was fired upon by several Indians concealed in the bushes, who at the same time raised the usual warwhoop. She was wounded, but retreated, as did the whole party; some running with her down the lane, which happened to open near that point, and others across the field. They were hotly pursued by the enemy, who continued to yell and fire upon them.

The older of the two mothers who had gone out, recollecting in her flight, that the younger, a small and feeble woman was burdened with her child, turned back in the face of the enemy, they firing and yelling hideously, took the child from its almost exhausted mother, and ran with it to the fort, a distance of three hundred yards. During the chase she was twice shot at with rifles, when the enemy were so near that the powder burned her, and one arrow passed through her sleeve, but she escaped uninjured. The young woman who was wounded, almost reached the place of safety when she sunk, and her pursuer, who had the hardihood to attempt to scalp her, was killed by a bullet from the fort.

MRS. RUHAMA BUILDERBACK

THE FORTITUDE TO suffer is as noble as the courage to dare. Perhaps, patient endurance is rarer than bold adventure. Mrs. Ruhama Builderback, the heroine of the following sketch, possessed that steady firmness under suffering, which is the chief distinction of the martyr.

She was born and raised in Jefferson county, Virginia. In 1785, she married a Mr. Charles Builderback, and with him crossed the mountains and settled at the mouth of Short creek, on the east bank of the Ohio, a few miles above Wheeling. Her husband a brave man, had on many occasions distinguished himself in repelling the Indians, who had often felt the sure aim of his unerring rifle. They therefore determined at all hazards to kill him.

On a beautiful summer morning in June, 1789, at a time when it was thought the enemy had abandoned the western shores of the Ohio, Captain Charles Builderback, his wife and brother, Jacob Builderback, crossed the Ohio to look after some cattle. On reaching the shore, a party of fifteen or twenty Indians rushed out from an ambush, and firing upon them, wounded Jacob in the shoulder. Charles was taken while he was running to escape. Jacob returned to the canoe and got away. In the mean time, Mrs. Builderback secreted herself in some drift-wood, near the bank of the river. As soon as the Indians had secured and tied her husband, and not being able to discover her hiding-place, they compelled him, with threats of immediate death, to call her to him. With a hope of appeasing their fury, he did so. She heard him, but made no answer. "Here," to use her own words, "a struggle took place in my breast, which I cannot describe. Shall I go to him and become a prisoner, or shall I remain, return to our cabin and provide for and take care of our two children." He shouted to her a second time to come to him, saying, "that if she obeyed, perhaps it would be the means of saving his life." She no longer hesitated, left her place of safety, and surrendered herself to her savage captors. All this took place in full view of their cabin, on the opposite shore, and where they had left their two children, one a son about three years old, and an infant daughter. The Indians knowing that they would be pursued as soon as the news of their visit reached the stockade, at Wheeling, commenced their retreat. Mrs. Builderback and her husband travelled together that day and the following night. The next morning, the Indians separated into two parties, one taking Builderback, and the other his wife, and continued a westward course by different routes.

In a few days, the band having Mrs. Builderback in custody, reached the Tuscarawas river, where they encamped, and were soon rejoined by the band that had had her husband in charge. Here the murderers exhibited his scalp on the top of a pole, and to convince her that they had killed him, pulled it down and threw it into her lap. She recognised it at once by the redness of his hair. She said nothing, and uttered no complaint. It was evening; her ears pained with the terrific yells of the savages, and wearied by constant travelling, she reclined against a tree and fell into a profound sleep, and forgot all her sufferings until morning. When she awoke, the scalp of her murdered husband was gone, and she never learned what became of it. Her husband commanded a company at Crawford's defeat. He was a large, noble looking man, and a bold and intrepid warrior. He was in the bloody Moravian campaign, and took his share in the tragedy, by shedding the first blood on that occasion, when he shot, tomahawked, and scalped Shebosh, a Moravian chief. But retributive justice was meted to him. After being taken prisoner, the Indians inquired his name. "Charles Builderback," replied he, after some little pause. After this revelation, the Indians stared at each other with a malignant triumph. "Ha!" said they, "you kill many Indians—you big captain—you kill Moravians." From that moment, probably, Captain Builderback's death was decreed.

As soon as the capture of Builderback was known, at Wheeling, a party of scouts set off in pursuit, and taking the trail of one of the bands, followed it until they found the body of Builderback. He had been tomahawked and scalped, and apparently suffered a lingering death.

The Indians, on reaching their towns on the Big Miami, adopted Mrs. Builderback into a family, with whom she resided until released from captivity. She remained a prisoner about nine months, performing the labor and drudgery of squaws, such as carrying in meat from the hunting-grounds, preparing and drying it, making moccasins, leggings and other clothing for the family in which she was raised. After her adoption, she suffered much from the rough and filthy manner of Indian living.

In a few months after her capture, some friendly Indians informed the commandant at Fort Washington, that there was a white woman in captivity at the Miami towns. She was ransomed and brought in to the fort, and in a few weeks was sent up the river to her lonely cabin, and to the embrace of her two orphan children. She then recrossed the mountains, and settled in her native county.

In 1791, Mrs. Builderback married Mr. John Green, and in 1798, they emigrated to the Hockhocking valley, and settled about three miles west of Lancaster, where she continued to reside until the time of her death, about the year 1842.

She lived to witness the settlement of the vast wilderness, where her husband had fought and she had suffered; and until her death had maintained a high character among the mothers of the west.

THE WIDOW SCRAGGS

IN THE FOLLOWING account of an attack upon the house of an old widow, we have two instances of female heroism, which are worthy of preservation. The presence of mind displayed by the old lady was admirable, and but for the destruction of the house, might have saved the family, while the desperate, defence made by one of her daughters, with a mere knife, showed an uncommon degree of resolution.

The house of widow Scraggs, in Bourbon county, Kentucky, was attacked on the night of the 11th of April, 1787. She occupied what is generally called a double cabin, in a lonely part of the county, one room of which was tenanted by the old lady herself, together with two grown sons, and a widowed daughter, at that time suckling an infant, while the other was occupied by two unmarried daughters from sixteen to twenty years of age, together with a little girl not more than half grown. The hour was eleven o'clock at night. One of the unmarried daughters was still busily engaged at the loom, but the other members of the family, with the exception of one of the sons, had retired to rest. Some symptoms of an alarming nature had engaged the attention of the young man for an hour before any thing of a decided character took place.

The cry of owls was heard in the adjoining wood, answering each other in rather an unusual manner. The horses, which were inclosed as usual in a pound near the house, were more than commonly excited, and by repeated snorting and galloping, announced the presence of terror. The young man was often upon the point of awaking his brother, but was often restrained by the fear of the reproach of timidity, at that time an unpardonable blemish in the character of a Kentuckian. At length hasty steps were heard in the yard, and quickly afterwards, several loud knocks at the door, accompanied by the usual exclamation, "who keeps house?" in very good English. The young man, supposing from the language, that some benighted settlers were at the door, hastly arose, and was advancing to withdraw the bar which secured it, when his mother who had long lived upon the frontiers, and had probably detected the Indian tone in the demand for admission, instantly sprung out of bed, and ordered her son not to admit them, declaring that they were Indians. She instantly awakened her other son, and the two young men seizing their guns, which were always charged to repel the enemy. The Indians finding it impossible to enter under their assumed characters, began to thunder at the door with great violence, but a single shot from a loop hole, compelled them to shift the attack to some less exposed point; and, unfortunately, they discovered the door of the other cabin, which contained the three daughters. The rifles of the brothers could not be brought to bear upon this point, and by means of several rails taken from the yard fence, the door was forced from its hinges, and the three girls were at the mercy of the savages. One was instantly secured, but the eldest defended herself desperately with a knife which she had been using at the loom, and stabbed one of the Indians to the heart, before she was tomahawked.

In the mean time the little girl, who had been overlooked by the enemy in their eagerness to secure the others, ran out into the yard, and might have effected her escape, had she taken advantage of the darkness and fled, but instead of that the terrified little creature ran around the house wringing her hands, and crying out her sisters were killed. The brothers, unable to hear her cries, without risking every thing for her rescue, rushed to the door and were preparing to sally out to her assistance, when their mother threw herself before them and calmly declared that the child must be abandoned to its fate; that the sally would sacrifice the lives of all the rest without the slightest benefit to the little girl. Just then the child uttered a loud scream, followed by a few faint moans and all was again silent. Presently the crackling of flames was heard, accompanied by a triumphant yell from the Indians, announcing that they had set fire to that division of the house which had been occupied by the daughters, and of which they held undisputed possession.

The fire was quickly communicated to the rest of the building, and it became necessary to abandon it or perish in the flames. In the one case there was a possibility that some might escape, in the other their fate would be equally certain and terrible. The rapid approach of the flames cut short their momentary suspense. The door was thrown open, and the old lady, supported by her eldest son, attempted to cross the fence at one point, while her daughter carrying her child in her arms, and attended by the younger of the brothers, ran in a different direction. The blazing roof shed a light over the yard but little inferior to that of day, and the savages were distinctly seen awaiting the approach of their victims. The old lady was permitted to reach the stile unmolested, but in the act of crossing, received several balls in her breast and fell dead. Her son, fortunately, remained unhurt, and by extraordinary agility, effected his escape.

The other party succeeded also in reaching the fence unhurt, but in the act of crossing was vigorously assailed by several Indians, who throwing down their guns, rushed upon them with their tomahawks. The young man defended his sister gallantly, firing upon the enemy as they approached, and then wielding the butt of his rifle with a fury that drew their whole attention upon himself, and gave his sister an opportunity of effecting her escape. He quickly fell, however, under the tomahawks of his enemies, and was found at day light, scalped and mangled in a shocking manner. Of the whole family, consisting of eight persons, when the attack commenced, only three escaped. Four were killed upon the spot, and one (the second daughter) carried off as a prisoner.

The neighborhood was quickly alarmed, and by daylight, about thirty men were assembled under the command of Colonel Edwards. A light snow had fallen during the latter part of the night, and the Indian trail could be pursued at a gallop. It led directly into the mountainous country bordering upon Licking, and afforded evidences of great hurry and precipitation on the part of the fugitives. Unfortunately, a hound had been permitted to accompany the whites, and as the trial became fresh and the scent warm, she followed it with eagerness, baying loudly and giving the alarm to the Indians. The consequences of this imprudence were soon displayed. The enemy finding the pursuit keen, and perceiving that the strength of the prisoner began to fail, instantly sunk their tomahawks in her head and left her still warm and bleeding upon the snow.

As the whites came up, she retained strength enough to wave her hand in token of recognition, and appeared desirous of giving them some information, with regard to the enemy, but her strength was too far gone. Her brother sprung from his horse and knelt by her side, endeavoring to stop the effusion of blood, but in vain. She gave him her hand, muttered some inarticulate words, and expired within two minutes of the arrival of the party. The pursuit was renewed, and in twenty minutes the enemy was in view. They had taken possession of a steep, narrow ridge, and endeavored to magnify their numbers by rapidly passing from tree to tree, and yelling in appalling tones. The pursuers, however, were satisfied that the enemy were inferior in number to themselves, and dismounting from their horses, rapidly ascended the ridge. The firing soon commenced, when they discovered that only two Indians were opposed to them. They had voluntarily sacrificed themselves for the safety of the main body, and had succeeded in delaying pursuit until their friends could reach the mountains. One of them was instantly shot dead, and the other was badly wounded, as was evident from the blood which filled his tracks in the snow. The pursuit was recommenced, until night, when the trail entered a running stream and was lost. On the following morning the snow had melted, and every trace of the enemy was obliterated.

MRS. WOODS

AMONG THE MANY instances of women successfully defending their homes in the absence of their husbands, the achievement of Mrs. Woods deserves to be remembered. This woman resided in a cabin near the Crab Orchard, Lincoln county, Kentucky. Early one morning, sometime in the year 1784, Mr. Woods being absent from home, and Mrs. Woods a short distance from the cabin, she discovered several Indians advancing towards it. She ran towards the cabin, and reached the door before all the Indians but one, who pursued so closely, that before she could secure the door, he entered. A lame negro in the cabin instantly seized the savage, and, after a short scuffle, they both fell—the negro underneath. The resolute black fellow held his antagonist so tightly that he could not use his knife. Mrs. Woods then seized an axe from under the bed, and, at the request of the negro, struck the savage upon the head. The first blow was not fatal; but the second scattered the brains of the Indian around the cabin. In the meantime, the other Indians were at the door endeavoring to force it open with their tomahawks. The negro arose, and proposed to Mrs. Woods to let another Indian enter, and they could soon dispatch him. In this way they could have disposed of the whole party. But this was rendered unnecessary. The cabin was but a short distance from a station, the occupants of which, having discovered the perilous situation of the Woods family, fired on the Indians, killed one, and put the others to flight.

Throughout this trying time, Mrs. Woods behaved with the courage and devotion of a lioness defending her offspring. Had she not retained her presence of mind, and aided the efforts of the brave negro, a scene of massacre and desolation would have followed the appearance of the savages.

MRS. WOODS AND THE INDIAN—*Page 74*

THE CAPTIVITY OF JANE BROWN
AND HER FAMILY

THE FOLLOWING ROMANTIC and interesting narrative is copied from the Whig Review.

From the year of 1780 to 1790, many of the best families of the Carolinas, Georgia, and Virginia, sought homes beyond the mountains. Many of them, patriotic republicans, who had sacrificed every thing for their country, in the struggle for independence, and hoped to have found, in the secluded vales and thick forests of the west, that peace and quiet which they had not found amid the din of civil and foreign war, soon experienced all the horrors of a savage, marauding, guerilla warfare, which swept away their property, and deprived them of their wives and children, either by a barbarous death, or not less agonizing slavery as captives, dragged into the wild recesses of the Indian borders.

Many fearful tales of these bloody scenes, which would illustrate the early history of Tennessee, are only known to a few, as family traditions, and even among the descendants of the sufferers, are only remembered as stories of the nursery, and not as chapters of the great historic record of the past. "It is not always," says Pluturch, "in the most distinguished achievements that man's virtues or vices may be best discerned; but often an action of small note, or short saying, or a jest, shall distinguish a person's real character more than the greatest sieges or the most important battles." And so it is, in some sort, with the history of a people or a nation. The experiences, the sufferings, and conduct of a single individual of a community, may better illustrate the condition, progress, or character of the people, than whole chapters devoted to a campaign.

In this point of view, the traditional recollections which are detailed in the following sketch of the family of James Brown, connected as they were, so intimately with some of the most important political events of that period, cannot fail to throw new light upon the pioneer history of the country, and inspire our hearts with renewed gratitude to those hardy, but wise men and women, who built up so goodly a state, amid so many troubles, in the dark and bloody valleys of the Shanvanon, Tanasees, and Ho-go-hegee.

The subject of this sketch was born in Pennsylvania, about the year 1740. Her father was a pioneer in the settlement of North Carolina. Her family was one of the most respectable, as well as the most worthy, in the county of Guilford, where they resided during the revolutionary war. Two of her brothers, Colonel and Major Gillespie, were distinguished for their gallantry and devotion to the cause of liberty, and were honored as brave officers. Herself and most of her family were members of the Rev. David Caldwell's church at Guilford, and ardently espoused both his political and religious principles.

About 1761 or 1762, Miss Gillespie became the wife of James Brown, a native of Ireland, whose family settled in Guilford some years before. At the beginning of the revolution, Mrs. Brown had a large family of small children, but she freely gave up her husband when his country demanded his services. During the masterly retreat of General Greene, in the winter of 1781, on Dan and Deep rivers, Mr. Brown was the pilot and guide of Colonels Lee and Washington, and, by his intimate knowledge of the country, its by-paths and fords, contributed not a little to the successful counter-marches of the American army, by which they were enabled to elude and break the spirit of the army under Lord Cornwallis. When the American army assumed the offensive, and, from a retreating, suddenly became a pursuing army, Brown pressed eagerly into the fight with the bold troopers of Lee and Washington.

Being in moderate circumstances, and pressed by the cares of a large and increasing family, Brown's ardent temperament was not satisfied with the prospect of a plodding life of toil in Guilford. For his revolutionary services he had received from the state of North Carolina land-warrants, which entitled him to locate a large quantity of lands in the wilderness beyond the mountains. His neighbors had honored him as the sheriff of the county, and as a justice of the county court, and he was rapidly rising in the estimation of his countrymen, for his patriotism, integrity, and many other virtues of a good citizen. But he readily saw the advantages which he might secure to his rising family by striking out into the deep forests, and securing for them the choicest homes in the Cumberland valleys. He could command only a trifle in money for his land-script, but by exposing himself to a few years of hardship and danger, he could secure independent estates for his numerous children. With him it was but to think and to act; his decision and his action went together. Tearing himself from the bosom of his family, and all the endearments of a happy home circle, he set out on his journey to explore the valley of the Cumberland.

The whole of Tennessee was then a wilderness, except a small spot on the Holston and Watauga, on the east, and a small spot around Nashville and Bledsoe's Lick, on the west of the Cumberland mountains. Taking with him his two oldest sons, William and John, and a few tried friends, he explored the Cumberland valley. He secured lands on the Cumberland river below Nashville, at the place now known as Hyde's Ferry. He also explored the wilderness south, as far as Duck river, and located a large body of land south of Duck river, near Columbia. The whole country was then almost untrod by the foot of the white man. It was the hunting-ground of the Chicasaws, Creeks, and Cherokees, and was full of deer, bear, and buffaloes. The rich uplands, as well as the alluvial bottoms of the rivers, were covered with canebrakes, which were almost impervious to man. Whoever penetrated these regions, did so with knife and hatchet to cut away the cane, and with rifle to oppose the savage beasts and savage men who swarmed through its deep fastnesses. But Brown's heart was a bold one, and his hopes for the future animated his perseverance. Having located by actual survey, several fine tracts of land, he determined to return to Guilford and remove his family to their new home in the west. Leaving William as a deputy surveyor under Colonel Polk, and John to open and cultivate a small field, and build some cabins at the mouth of White's creek, he returned to North Carolina.

In the winter of 1787–88, Brown and his family, having disposed of their property, found themselves on the banks of the French Broad, in what is now Hawkins county, Tennessee, waiting the opening of the spring, before beginning their journey across the mountains to the Cumberland valley.

In 1785, the treaty of Hopewell had been concluded with the Cherokees, guaranteeing reciprocal friendship between that nation and the Americans. At the time Brown arrived on the banks of the French Broad, there was apparent acquiescence in the terms of this treaty, and the Cherokee and the white man seemed, for a time, to have smoked the pipe of peace, and buried the tomahawk for ever.

There were two routes to the Cumberland valley at this time: the one was by land, the other by water. The land route was a long and tedious one; through the Cumberland Gap, across the head-waters of the Cumberland, Green, and Barren rivers, in Kentucky, to Bledsoe's Lick, or Nashville. The other route was easier of accomplishment, and more desirable; because, being by the descent of the river, it admitted of the transportation of goods and aged persons. Brown, on his recent visit to Cumberland, had heard of Colonel Donaldson's voyage down the Tennessee, up the Ohio and Cumberland, to Nashville, and of one or two other parties who had succeeded in making the same voyage. As he had women and small children, and packages of goods, which he was taking to the West, he resolved to hazard the descent of the Tennessee river.

He was not ignorant of the fact that there were many populous Indian towns on the Tennessee river, of both the Cherokee and Chickasaw nations, and that marauding parties of Creeks and Shawanese were often on its shores and towns. He knew the danger of the voyage, on account of the hostile Indians who might be encountered on its waters or its shores; and he also knew its numerous shoals, rapids, and eddies, rendered its navigation perilous to such frail open boats as could then be constructed. But he confided in the honest disposition of the Cherokees to conform to the treaty of Hopewell, and felt that the marauding Creeks and Shawanese would prove less dangerous on the water than on the circuitous land route to the Cumberland. Having been habitually exposed to danger for many years, it is probable he rather sought the most perilous and dangerous route, feeling a sort of manly desire to meet and overcome it.

Having built a boat, after the style of a common flatboat, modeled as much as possible after the style of Noah's ark, (except that it was open at the top,) he prepared to venture the fearful voyage. About the 1st of May, 1788, having on board a large amount of goods suitable for traffic among the Indians and the pioneers in Cumberland, his party embarked upon the bosom of French Broad. The party was a small and weak one, considering the dangers it had to encounter, and the valuable cargo it had to defend. It consisted of Brown, two grown sons, three hired men and a negro man, in all, seven grown men;

Mrs. Brown, three small sons, and four small daughters; an aged woman, the mother of one of the hired men, and two or three negro women, the property of Brown.

To make up for the weakness of his party, Brown had mounted a small cannon upon the prow of his boat, and no doubt relied as much for his security upon the known terror which such guns inspired in the breasts of the savages, as upon any damage which he expected to inflict upon them with it. Thus appointed, and thus equipped, this happy family began its eventful descent of the French Broad and the Tennessee.

All was gladness, all was sunshine. The land of their fathers, of their loving friends and pastor, was behind them; beneath their oars flashed the bright waters of a lovely stream, whose winding channel would soon bear them to the enchanted valley of the fair Cumberland. As they passed rapidly along the current which was to bear them to their new home, the father sat in the midst of his little children, hopefully describing their new home in the deep forests of the west.

They thus descended the French Broad to the Tennessee, and went on merrily down its waters to the Chickamanga, a considerable town of Cherokee Indians, situated not far from the present site of Chattanooga. Here the Indians appeared friendly; the principal chief went on board the boat, and made inquiry for various kinds of goods, prepared to trade, and finally took his leave, with many professions of kindness. Our voyagers continued their descent, rejoicing in the happy omen which the friendship of the Chickamanga chieftain opened for their future.

The next day, the 9th of May, the solitary perogue or flatboat of the pioneer Brown had passed several Indian villages, and had come in view of the towns of Running Water and Nickajack, the last Cherokee towns where there was any considerable body of Indians. The voyagers began to rejoice in their happy deliverance from the principal dangers which had threatened their journey. They would in a few hours be through the passes of the mountain, on the wide bosom of a noble river, where they would be comparatively free from the ambuscade of lurking Indians.

But suddenly four canoes with white flags and naked savages kneeling in them as rowers, glide out into the river and rapidly approach; fearing some mischief, Brown immediately turned his cannon upon the approaching canoes, and, with the lighted match, bade them keep off at the peril of their lives.

Struck with astonishment at the bold threat, they paused, and pulled their frail canoes a little out of range of the big gun. A man by the name of John Vaun, a well-known half-breed, who spoke good English, was the leader of the party, but he was unknown to Brown. Vaun spoke to Brown, and said that his party came in friendship; that, as an evidence of that, they had raised a white flag; that they came as his friends to trade with him. Brown, who was a bold and fearless man, and dared to face a thousand savages, still kept them off; but at last, confiding in the assurance of Vaun that he was a white man, and that the Indians would respect the persons and property of his party, in an unguarded moment consented that a part of the Indians might come on board. A dozen Indians now came on board, and lashed their canoes to the side of the boat. As they came near the town, hundreds of Indians dashed out into the river in their canoes, and came along side of their boat. Having thus secured possession of the boat, the leading men, more especially Vaun, assured Brown that no harm was intended. In the meantime, each Indian seized upon whatever he fancied, and threw it into his canoe. In this way several boxes and trunks were instantly rifled. Vaun pretended to order his fellows to abstain, but they paid no attention to him. A bold warrior now demanded of Brown the key of a large chest, which contained his most valuable stores, which he refused to give, telling the Indians that Mrs. Brown had it. The Indian now demanded it of Mrs. Brown, but she boldly refused to give it up.

The Indian then split the top of the chest open with his tomahawk, and his example was immediately followed by the other Indians, who broke open and rifled every box and package in the boat. While this was going on, an Indian rudely took hold of Joseph Brown, a lad fifteen years old, and the old man seized the Indian and forced him to let the boy go. An instant after, the Indian seized a sword which was lying on the boat, and while old Brown's back was turned to him, struck him on the back of the neck, almost severing his head from his body. Brown turned in the agony of death and seized the Indian, and in the struggle was thrown overboard, where he sank to rise no more. The boat was now turned into the mouth of a little creek, in the town of Nickajack, and the whole party taken on shore, in the midst of several hundred warriors, women, and children. In the meantime, Vaun continued to tell the sons of Brown that all this was a violation of the treaty of

Hopewell, and that Breath, who was the chief of Nickajack and Running Water, who was expected there that night, would punish the marauders, restore their goods, and send them on their voyage. But at this very moment, several leading warriors of the upper towns had seized upon Brown's negroes as lawful spoil, and had dispatched them in canoes to their several homes. Whatever may have been Vaun's true motives, his interference on this occasion had the effect to place the whole party at the mercy of the Indians, without a particle of resistance. If he acted in good faith, he was shamefully deceived by his followers; but if he only used his address to disarm the voyagers, that they might the more easily fall victims to savage ferocity, his conduct exhibits the climax of perfidy.

A party of Creek braves, who were engaged with the men of Nickajack and Running Water in this outrage, having seized upon their share of the plunder, and having taken possession of Mrs. Brown and her son George, ten years old, and three small daughters, immediately began their march to their own nation. While the Cherokees were deliberating upon the fate of the prisoners and a division of the spoils, they adroitly withdrew from the council, on the plea that all this belonged to the head men of Nickajack. Thus, in one short hour, deprived of husband, sons, friends, liberty, and all, this devoted woman, with her five smallest children, began her sad journey on foot, along the rugged, flinty trails that lead to the Creek towns, on the Tallapoosa river.

At the time of this outrage, there was living at or near Nickajack, a French trader, named Thomas Tunbridge, who was married to a white woman, who had been taken prisoner near Mobile, when an infant, and raised by the Indians. After she was grown, she was exchanged, but refused to leave the Indians, distrusting her abilities to adapt her habits to civilized life. She had been married to an Indian brave, by whom she had a son, now twenty-one years old, who was one of the boldest warriors of the Cherokee towns. He had already killed six white men in his forays to the Cumberland settlement. Having all the versatility of his mother's race, as well as the ferocity of his father, he was fast rising into distinction as a warrior, and bade fair to reach the first honors of his nation. His praises for daring and chivalry were in the mouths of all.

His mother was now growing old, and having no young children, her son desired to present to her some bright-eyed boy as a slave; for, according to the savage code of the times, each captive became a slave to its captor. This woman's son, whose name was Kiachatalee, was one of the leaders of the marauding party who had seized upon Brown's boat, and from the first knew the fate of the party. Before the boat landed, he tried to induce Joseph, a boy then fifteen years old, but quite small, to get into his canoe, with the intentions of withdrawing him from the general massacre, that was soon to take place, but the boy would not go with him. When the boat landed, Kiachatalee took Joseph to his step-father, Tunbridge, who in good English told the boy that he lived a mile out of the town, and invited him to go and spend the night with him. This the boy did, after asking the consent of his older brothers. Tunbridge seized the boy by the hand and hurried him away.

They had scarcely gone out of the town before they heard the rifles of the savage braves, who were murdering his brothers and friends. What were the feelings of this poor boy at this moment? His father slain by an Indian brave; his brothers and friends weltering in their blood, amidst the yells of savage assassins; and his mother and brother, and sisters borne off, he knew not whither, by a band of lawless Creek marauders! To add to this agony at such a moment, an aged Indian woman, with hair dishevelled, and her round, fat face discolored, with excitement, followed them to the trader's house, calling upon Tunbridge to produce the white man, exclaiming with a fiendish air of triumph, "All the rest are killed, and he must die also!"

The trader calmly replied to her, "He's only a little boy. It's a shame to kill children. He shall not be killed."

The old hag was excited, and vowed that the boy should be killed. She said, "He was too large to allow him to live. In two or three years he would be a man; he would learn the country, its towns and its rivers; would make his escape, and come back with an army of white men to destroy us all." She said her son, Cutty-a-toy, was a brave chief, and that he would be there in a few minutes to kill the boy.

In a few minutes, Cutty-a-toy, followed by many armed warriors, rushed upon the trader's house, and demanded the white boy. The chief said the boy was too large, that he would soon be grown, would make his escape, and bring back an army to destroy their town.

The trader stood, with cool courage, in the door of his lodge, and refused to surrender the prisoner, saying it was not right to kill children, and also warning the angry chief that the boy was the prisoner of Kiachatalee, his son, and, if he was injured or slain, Kiachatalee would be revenged for it. As Kiachatalee was only a young warrior, and Cutty-a-toy a chief and a gray-beard, this threat of revenge greatly incensed him. In an instant he raised his tomahawk, and, with the air of a man who intends a deed of murder, demanded of the trader, "And are you the friend of the Virginian?"

Answering the look rather than the words, the trader stepped out of his door, and said to the bloody brave, "Take him."

Cutty-a-toy then rushed into the trader's lodge, seized the boy by the throat, and was about to brain him with his tomahawk, when the wife of Tunbridge interposed, in a tone of supplication which at once succeeded.

"Will the brave chieftain kill the boy in my house? Let not the boy's blood stain my floor."

The appeal of the woman reached the savage's heart. He dropped his weapon and slowly dragged the boy out of the lodge into the midst of a crowd of savages, who waved their knives and hatchets in the poor boy's face, in order to enjoy his terror.

In the path which led from the house the boy fell upon his knees while the savages were tearing off his clothes, and asked the trader to request the savages to give him one half hour to pray. The trader roughly replied, "Boy it's not worth while; they'll kill you." As the boy stood in momentary expectation of his fate, the trader's wife again interposed, and begged the savage chief not to kill the boy in her yard, or in the path along which she had to carry water, but to take him out in the mountains, where the birds and wolves might eat up his flesh, where she could not see his blood!"

The appeal of the woman was again heard, and giving the boy his pantaloons, they held a short talk, and agreed to take the boy down to the Running Water, saying to the trader's wife, "We will not spill this boy's blood near your house; but we will take him to the Running Water, where we will have a frolic knocking him in the head."

Having gone about three hundred yards, they halted and formed a circle around the boy, and with their tomahawks seemed to be on the point of killing him. The boy again fell upon his knees, and, with his face upturned towards heaven, and his hands firmly clasped on his breast, remained in prayer, expecting at each moment the fatal blow. At this dreadful moment the boy thought of Stephen, to whose vision the heavens were opened at the moment of his death and was happy. As the savage braves stood around him, young Brown saw their stern brows of revenge suddenly relax, and a smile of sympathy and pity succeed. They called the trader, told him to take the boy, that they would not kill him; and Cutty-a-toy said he loved the boy and would come back in three weeks and make friends with him. It was afterwards ascertained that Cutty- a-toy had taken some of Brown's negroes, and claimed them as his prisoners, and that his fear lest Kiachatalee might retaliate by killing his negro prisoners, was the thought which suddenly turned Cutty-a-toy to mercy and pity. So thought his own followers, for when he said he *loved* the boy, and would not kill him, his savage followers replied:

"No, no, he does not love the boy; it's the boy's negro he loves."

When Cutty-a-toy's mother saw that the boy's life would not be taken, she seemed displeased; went up to the boy and cut off his scalp-lock, and kicked him so rudely in the side as almost to kill him, exclaiming, "I've got the Virginian's scalp."

The Tuskegee chief, Cutty-a-toy, led his party away leaving the boy in the hands of the trader and his wife. In two or three days, the boy was taken into Nickajack, and the kind old chief, Breath, who greatly regretted what had taken place in his absence, took Joseph by the hand, calmly heard a narrative of his situation from the trader's wife, and then told the boy that he must be adopted into his tribe, and become an Indian, if he would save his life; that there was no other way in which his life could be saved. To that end, the chief adopted him into his own family, and told Joseph that he was his uncle, and that Kiachatalee was his brother. His head was then shaved, leaving only a fillet of hair on the top, in which a bunch of feathers was tied, his ears pierced for rings, and his clothes taken off; the flap substituted for trowsers, and a short shirt substituted for a coat, shirt, and vest, and his nether vestments consisting of a pair of deer-skin moccasins. In this condition he was pronounced an Indian, with the exception of a slit in each ear, which the kindness of the chief deferred making until cold weather. The trader's wife took him to see his two sisters, Jane, aged ten, and Polly, aged five years, who had just been brought back to Nickajack; a party of Cherokees having pursued the Creek braves, and recaptured from them these two small girls, after they had been taken some distance towards the Creek towns. From his sister Jane, Joseph learned the destination of the party who had carried off his mother, his brother George, and sister Elizabeth. These children were now in the same town, adopted into different families, and it was a source of consolation to them to be allowed to see each other occasionally. In the various toils which were imposed upon these captive children, such as carrying water and wood, pounding hominy, and working corn in the fields, and, on the part of the boy, in looking after the stock, nearly a year passed off, without many incidents worthy of note. Hostile parties of savages came and went, and tales of barbarous deeds done by them on the distant frontiers were often told in the hearing of these children, but none of them brought deliverance for them. Yet in but few instances did the savage neighbors of these captive children treat them unkindly. Three or four times the boy's life was in danger from lawless braves, whose blood-thirsty natures panted for the blood of the white man. The good old chief, Breath, hearing of these things, caused young Brown to be armed, and declared it should be lawful for him to slay any Indian who should mistreat him.

In a few months Joseph was allowed a rifle and a horse, and permitted to go into the woods to hunt. He might often have availed himself of the kindness of his savage friends, and made his escape to the frontiers, but he loved his little sisters, and his love for them restrained his desire for freedom, least his escape might add to the rigors of their slavery or perhaps for ever prevent their deliverance.

In the meantime, an open war had been going on between the Indians and the people of Cumberland and East Tennessee. Two thousand warriors, principally Cherokees, of whom four or five hundred were horsemen, dressed as white men, made an irruption into East Tennessee, killing every thing before them.

During this invasion, the Indians, sending forward their mounted men, dressed as white men, were enabled to surprise many, and thus to make a havoc which they could not have done otherwise. This irruption of the Indians was caused, they alleged, by the murder of Tassel, their chief, when he had gone under a white flag to General Sevier, to hold a talk. In this foray, the Indians took Fort Gillespie, murdered the garrison, and carried off Mrs. Glass, the sister of Captain Gillespie.

The whole country was aroused. General Joseph Martin and General John Sevier headed a large army, marched into the Indian nation, burnt their towns, and carried off their women and children. Amongst other prisoners taken at this time, was the daughter of Turkey, the chief of the Cherokees.

In the spring of 1789, an exchange of prisoners was agreed upon, at a talk held with General Sevier. It was agreed that the Cherokees should make an absolute surrender of all the white prisoners within their borders, and runners were sent to each of the head men, to send their captives to the Little Turkey for an exchange. When these runners came to Nickajack, young Brown was on a trading trip down the river with his Indian brother, Kiachatalee, and did not return until Mrs. Glass and all the other prisoners had gone up to Running Water, where the chief was awaiting their arrival.

When young Brown got home, he was sent with one of his sisters to Running Water, in order to be sent up to the treaty-grounds to be exchanged. His little sister would not leave her Indian mother, who had ever treated her kindly, but wept and clung to her neck, declaring that it would break her Indian mother's heart if she left her. This tender feeling was a tribute to savage kindness; but young Brown finally took his sister in his arms, and carried her some distance before he could reconcile her to go with him. His eldest sister belonged to a trader, who said he had bought her with his money, and would not let her go. Young Brown had to leave her behind, being wholly unable to redeem her.

At Running Water, young Brown heard Turkey, the head chief, stating to his chiefs around him the terms of the treaty he had made; and in doing so, his followers upbraided him for agreeing to deliver so many prisoners without any ransom.

To this the chief replied, "That Little John, (Governor Sevier) would have it so; that he was a very mean man—a dog; but he had my daughter a prisoner, and he knew I would have to agree to any terms, to get her back."

The next morning, when the Indian chief was about to start his prisoners forward, young Brown refused to go, and was taken to the chief to give his reasons. He then stated that one of his sisters was left in Nickajack, and that he never would consent to be set at liberty without his sister. The savage chief immediately sent for the girl, and, after some delay, Colonel Bench, the chief of the mounted regiment of Indians, went himself, and brought the girl to Running Water. Thus, about the 1st of May, 1789, young Brown and his two sisters were once more restored to liberty. Being reduced to poverty, these now orphan children were sent into South Carolina, to sojourn with some relatives, until their elder brother, who was in Cumberland, could go after them, or until their mother should be released from her captivity amongst the Creeks.

In order to keep up the thread of our narrative, we must now return to the 9th of May, 1788, and continue the narrative of Mrs. Brown's captivity. Having seen her husband fall by the hands of the savages, she was hurried away by her captors, and took the road southward, just as she heard the yells and rifles of the cruel savages, who also murdered her sons and their companions. What must have been the feelings of horror and agony of this poor woman, herself a prisoner in the hands of she knew not whom, and borne she knew not whither! To add to the horror of her situation, she soon saw two of her sweet little daughters torn from her side by a party of Cherokees, and borne back, she knew not whither, nor for what purpose.

Driven forward on foot for many days and nights, she continued to bear up under the bodily fatigues and mental anguish by which she was tortured, her feet blistered and swollen, and driven before the band along a flinty path, every moment expecting death if she failed, and every moment expecting to fail! She yet accomplishes many days' travel, and finally reaches one of the upper Creek towns, on the Tallapoosa, far down in the wilderness, the prisoner and slave of a savage brave. Arrived at the town of her captor, she finds she is a slave, doomed to bear wood and water, and to pound hominy, and to do all the servile offices of her savage mistress. To add to her distress, her son, nine years old, and her daughter, seven, are taken to different towns, and she is left indeed alone in her sorrow.

At the period of Mrs. Brown's captivity, Alexander M'Gillevray, a half-breed Creek, of Scotch descent, was the head chief of the Muscogee Indians, and actually assumed the high-sounding title of commander-in-chief of the Upper and Lower Creeks and Seminoles; being the military as well as the civil governor of all the Indians of Florida, Alabama, and Lower Georgia. He was a man of letters, of keen sagacity, forest-born and forest-bred, combining the shrewdness of the savage with the learning of the civilized man. Fortunately for Mrs. Brown, her cruel captor took her to a town in which lived a sister of M'Gillevray, who was the wife of a French trader by the name of Durant. Her age and dignified bearing under the toils which were imposed upon her, excited the sympathy and compassion of this kind-hearted Indian woman. Several weeks passed before she found an opportunity, but when Mrs. Brown's savage master was absent, the wife of Durant spoke to her kindly, told her that she pitied her for her sorrow, and would, if she could, relieve her. She said that her brother, the chief of the Creeks, did not approve of his people making slaves of the white women; and that he was a liberal, high-minded man, who had a soul of honor, and could never turn away from a helpless woman who flew to him for succor. "Why do you not fly to him?" asked the simple-hearted woman.

Mrs. Brown explained to her her total ignorance of the country, and her inability to reach the residence of Colonel M'Gillevray. The Indian woman listened to her, and then said, "It is true; but if you will, there is my horse, and there is my saddle. You are welcome to them; but you must take them. I cannot give them, but my husband shall never pursue. You can take them without danger." It was arranged. On a certain morning the Indian woman sent an aged Indian to a trader's house, who was to act as the guide of Mrs. Brown that far, and from that point the trader was to procure a guide and a horse.

At the appointed time, Mrs. Brown, mounted upon her friend's horse and saddle, started on in pursuit of her Indian guide, who travelled on as though he was entirely unconscious of her existence. She arrived in safety at the trader's lodge, and was by him furnished with a guide and horse to the chieftain's residence. Full of gratitude for intended kindness, yet she approached the Creek chieftain with many feelings of doubt and misgiving. He received her kindly, heard her story attentively, and, after considering it well, gave Mrs. Brown a cordial welcome to his house, and bade her stay with his wife, as a member of his family. He explained to her that, according to the usage of his people, she belonged to her captor, and that he had no right to take her from him.

He said, however, that he could no doubt reconcile her master by some presents, when he should follow, as he no doubt would before long. He told her she could make shirts or other garments for the traders, and soon provide herself with every thing necessary for her comfort. In the meantime, he would furnish her with whatever she needed. Mrs. Brown accepted the savage chieftain's proffered protection, and took shelter under his roof.

She had been there but a few days when she was startled by the appearance of her savage master, who had followed her to her place of refuge. Fortunately for her, the chieftain was at home, and himself met her pursuer. The savage gruffly demanded of his chieftain the white woman, his prisoner.

Colonel M'Gillevray at once informed him that she was in his house, and that he had promised to protect her. The savage merely replied, "Well, if you do not give me back my prisoner, I'll kill her." The wily chieftain knew his man, and, humoring his temper, replied, "That is true. She is your prisoner, and you can kill her if you choose. I know she is a weak woman and you are a brave warrior. Would you tie the scalp of a squaw about your neck?"

"But she can carry water, and hoe corn, and pound hominy for my wife," said the Creek warrior; "and she's mine; she's my prisoner."

"That's true," said the chieftain; "but if you kill her, will she carry any more water? Can the dead work? If you will consent to leave her with me, so that I can send her back to her people, I will send your wife a new dress, and will give you a rifle, some powder and lead, and some beads and paints; and when you go back to your wife, she will not see the blood of a woman upon your hands!"

Savage cupidity overcame savage revenge, and Mrs. Brown became the ransomed captive of the brave and generous M'Gillevray; a noble instance of chivalry on the part of a savage chieftain, which reflects more honor on his name than the glory of a hundred battles fought by his people during his chieftaincy.

For several months Mrs. Brown plied her needle in the chieftain's lodge, and, by her experience in the craft of needle-work, soon rendered herself useful to her savage friends, and by her dignity and energy commanded their respect.

The chieftain, on his next visit to the upper Creek towns, found Mrs. Brown's daughter, Elizabeth, aged about seven years, and generously purchased her from her master, and upon his return home had the pleasure of restoring the sweet child to her distressed mother; a grateful duty, nobly performed! He also informed Mrs. Brown that he had seen her son, George, and tried to induce his master to part with him, but that he was so much attached to the boy, he would not part with him on any terms. But he assured her that he would not fail, as soon as possible, to ransom her son, and restore him also to her arms.

In November, 1789, Colonel M'Gillevray had appointed to meet commissioners, to arrange terms of peace, at Rock Landing, Georgia. On his departure for the treaty grounds, he took Mrs. Brown and her daughter, and there delivered them to her son, William, who came from South Carolina, and had gone thither in hopes that he might be enabled to hear something of her and her long lost children.

Thus, in November, 1789, after eighteen months captivity, she was at last united with her surviving children. They spent a short time in South Carolina with some relatives, and returned to Guilford, North Carolina, at last restored to her friends, whom she had left but two short years before. But oh! what a change had taken place in her destiny since she had started westward with her husband and sons and neighbors, so full of life and hope! All her captive children were now restored to her arms, except George, who was doomed to a still longer captivity.

Mrs. Brown had two sons, who were in the Cumberland valley on the 9th of May, 1788; William, the surveyor, and Daniel, aged twelve years, who went over the land route with some stock, to the Cumberland valley. During her short stay in Guilford, her benefactor, the Creek chieftain, passed through Guildford, and sent word to Mrs. Brown that he was there. She immediately went with her brother Colonel Gillespie, Rev. Dr. Caldwell, and her son, William, and with them thanked her benefactor.

In addition, her brother offered to pay Colonel M'Gillevray any sum which he might think proper to demand, as the ransom of Mrs. Brown and her daughter, but the generous Creek refused any compensation whatever. He said he owed it to humanity and honor to do as he had done, and that to receive pay for it would deprive him both of the real pleasure and real honor of such a deed. He assured Mrs. Brown that he would not fail to use his best efforts to restore to her her son, and she might rely upon his finding out some means to accomplish so good an object.

Mrs. Brown, with the remnant of her family, again turned her face westward, seeking the new home which the foresight of her husband had prepared for her and to which he was so boldly and so nobly conducting them, when he perished, May 9th, 1788. And now at last, in 1792, this devoted woman and all her surviving children but one, find themselves at their new home, at the mouth of White's Creek, near Nashville. About this time, her son Joseph, while travelling with a small party of friends, was shot through the arm by a party of savages in ambush; a severe wound, from which he did not recover for some time.

In 1792, a formidable body of Creeks, Cherokees, and Shawanese, invaded Cumberland valley, attacked Buchanan's Station, and were repulsed with great loss. Young Joseph Brown came the next morning, with a large party of friends, to the assistance of Buchanan, but the Indians had retreated. Upon approaching the scene of action, what was young Brown's astonishment at finding his Indian brother, Kiachatalee, lying cold in death upon the field, near the walls of the fort against which he had so gallantly led the assault! The next year, Joseph Brown attended a treaty at Tellico, in East Tennessee, where he met a nephew of Kiachatalee, named Charles Butler, with whom he had been well acquainted while a prisoner at Nickajack. Butler gave him the Indian version of the attack on Buchanan's Station, and also the story of Kiachatalee's heroic death. He said the assault was led by Kiachatalee. That he attempted to set fire to the block-house, and was actually blowing it into a flame, when he was mortally wounded. He continued, after receiving his mortal wound, to blow the fire, and to cheer his followers to the assault, calling upon them to fight like brave men, and never give up till they had taken the fort. The incidents connected with the attack on Buchanan's Station can be seen in Mrs. Ellett's "Women of the Revolution," vol. III., Article, *Sarah Buchanan*, in which the Shawanese chief is represented as performing the heroic part which Kiachatalee really performed, and not he.

There are many incidents connected with frontier life, such as Mrs. Brown was now living, which are of every day occurrence, which would be interesting to the present generation, but the length of this sheet will necessarily exclude many of them. On one occasion, her oldest son, William, while in pursuit of a party of Indians near Nashville, was severely wounded in the arm, so that almost every member of her family, herself included, had been captured, wounded, or slain by the hands of the Indians.

These were trials which were hard to bear; yet amidst all her troubles Mrs. Brown bore herself as an humble Christian, devoutly grateful to the Giver of all good, that he had guided her footsteps aright, in the midst of so many sorrows.

In the year 1794, such had been the continued outrages of the savages from the Lower Cherokee towns, in conjunction with Creeks and Shawanese, upon the Cumberland settlements, that the principal pioneers resolved to fit out an expedition at their own expense, and march to Nickajack and Running Water, and to punish these lawless people with fire and sword. The national administration had, by its commissioners, made treaty after treaty with the Cherokees, but still the people of these lower towns continued their depredations, against the wishes of the upper Cherokees; but it was impossible to induce the national government to take those decided steps which these bold pioneers knew were absolutely necessary to check the marauding spirit of the lower Cherokee towns. These towns were far down the Tennessee, in the midst of mountain fastnesses, which the foot of hostile white man had never trod. They felt secure from all aggression, and reposed in full confidence that, whoever might suffer on account of their incursions into Cumberland, their towns were unapproachable.

At this time, young Joseph Brown was living near Nashville with his mother, and had recently gone with General Robertson to attend an Indian council at Tellico block-house. The intimate knowledge which young Brown had obtained of these lower towns and their people, by his residence there, enabled him to communicate to this thoughtful old man a good idea of the country and the people from whom the Cumberland settlements had so long suffered. The death of Kiachatalee at Buchanan's Station, on the 30th of September, 1792; his war-like character, so well known to Brown, and his leadership as a warrior amongst the men of Nickajack and Running Water, all pointed out these towns as the hives from which came forth such swarms of marauding Indians.

Despairing of succor from the national government, General Robertson wrote to Colonel Whitley, of Kentucky, who was a well-known partisan, to be at Nashville, about September, 1794, with as many trusty riflemen as he could bring with him. About the same time, Colonel Mansco, General Johnson, of Robertson, Colonel Montgomery, of Clarksville, and

General Robertson, each quietly raised a few trusty men. Major Ore commanded a squadron of mounted men, who were in the employ of the United States as rangers, to protect the frontiers of Cumberland. At the request of General Robertson, Major Ore arrived at Buchanan's Station just in time to join in the expedition.

In the mean time, boats were made of hides, and tried in the Cumberland river, to ascertain their capacity of transporting the troops across the Tennessee. These boats were made each out of two raw hides, as large as could be got, sewed together, and each was found capable of carrying about fifty guns, and one or two men. They were capable of being rolled up and packed on mules or horses, and could in a few moments be fully equipped and launched.

All the parties being assembled, it was ascertained that there were about six hundred, including Major Ore's Rangers. As all but Ore's command were volunteers, who came out without any authority, it was resolved to give Major Ore the nominal command of the whole party, which would give color of authority to the party to make the campaign, and would save them from the odium of making a lawless invasion of the Indian country. Colonel Whitley and Colonel Mansco were, however, the prime movers of the campaign, and had most of the responsibility of its conduct. But with the troops were more than a dozen leading partisan officers, who had been distinguished in many an Indian battle.

On the 7th of September, 1794, this formidable army of invasion set out for Nickajack; and, although the route had been unexplored, and the mountains and the river lay between them and their enemies, they had counted the cost, fitted out their boats, and had resolved to strike a blow that would teach the lawless Indians a severe lesson.

The troops made a forced march, reached the Tennessee river just after dark on the fourth day, and in thirty minutes had their raw-hide boats afloat in the river, ready to bear over the arms. They immediately began to cross the river, landing a short distance below the town of Nickajack. Most of the men swam over in perfect silence, their arms and clothes being conveyed in the boats, and on rafts rudely constructed of bundles of canes. In order to guide the swimmers, a very small fire was kindled at the water's edge, by the party which first crossed. Out of six hundred, only two hundred and thirty could be induced to cross over; some holding back because they could not swim, and others because they were subject to the cramp; and others, no doubt, reflecting upon the number of the enemy, and the difficulty of a retreat when once across so wide a river, did not feel quite willing "to stand the hazard of the die." But, in the face of appalling dangers, some men showed a stout-heartedness which might have done honor to the bravest of the brave. A young man by the name of Joseph B. Porter, who could not swim at all, tied an armful of dry canes together, and, nothing daunted, plunged into the rapid river, and kicked himself over in safety. Young Brown although still lame in one arm, from the wound he had received in the Indian ambuscade, plunged into the river and swam safely over.

At daylight, there were two hundred and thirty on the south bank of the Tennessee, within half a mile of Nickajack, and yet they were undiscovered.

Leaving young Brown, with twenty picked men, to guard the crossing of the creek, at the lower end of the town, with instructions to meet them in the centre of the town as soon as he heard their fire, the main body turned towards the town, and came down upon it from above.

Although Nickajack contained about three hundred warriors, they were so completely surprised that they made but little resistance; but, flying precipitately, took to their canoes, and attempted to cross the river. Some fled to the Running Water, and others secreted themselves in the thickets. The whole town ran with blood. About seventy warriors were slain, and a large number of women and children taken prisoners. Young Brown carried the lower end of the town manfully, killing several warriors, and taking some prisoners. In one instance, Brown killed an Indian warrior in a single combat, and carried away his scalp.

As soon as Nickajack was taken, a detachment was sent to destroy Running Water. On the way, the Indians met them, and, after an obstinate resistance, gave way, but not till they had wounded three Americans, one of them Joshua Thomas mortally.

Running Water was also taken, and both towns immediately reduced to ashes.

Amongst the dead, Brown recognised the body of Breath, the generous chief who had adopted him into his family when he was a prisoner.

In the towns, many articles of stolen property, which were recognised as belonging to men who had been killed in Cumberland valley, were found. In addition to these, fresh scalps were found in Nickajack, as well as a number of letters, taken by the Indians from mail-bags, after having killed the rider. They also found a quantity of powder and lead, recently sent by the Spanish government to these Indians.

Never was a visitation of this kind so justly merited as it was by these towns. They were the principal crossing-places for the war-parties of Creeks, Shawanese, and Cherokees, who went to harass the Cumberland settlements. But two days before their destruction, a war-dance was held there, at which were several Cherokee chiefs, as well as Creeks, who had resolved to wage a still more relentless war on the frontiers.

While young Brown could not but feel that the hand of Providence had signally punished these towns for their outrage on the 9th of May, 1788, his exultation was prevented by the death of his brother-in-law, Joshua Thomas, a brave soldier, and a kind, generous friend, who was the only one slain by the enemy on this occasion.

The prisoners recognised young Brown, and, alarmed for their safety, pleaded with him to save their lives, saying to him, that his life had once been spared by them. Brown assured them that they were in no danger; that the white people never killed prisoners, women, and children.

This blow was so unexpected and successful, that it inspired the Cherokees with a sincere desire for peace, which they soon after concluded, and never again violated. Soon after this affair, young George Brown was liberated by the Creeks.

Young Brown returned home, and lived some years with his mother. He was devoted to every relation of life. He soon attached himself to Rev. Thomas B. Craighead's congregation, near Hayesboro, and was made an elder in the church.

For several years, young Brown, his mother, and brothers, memorialized the Congress of the United States to reimburse them for the goods and slaves taken from them on the 9th of May, 1788, in violation of the treaty of Hopewell. But their claims were still unregarded and still delayed, year after year, and Congress after Congress, and yet no relief.

In the year 1806, a treaty was finally concluded with the Indians, which opened all the lands on Duck river to the occupation of those who had located their warrants there. Thus Mrs. Brown and her children came into possession of a large and splendid tract of land south of Columbia, to which she soon after removed with her son Joseph.

During the Creek war of 1812–13, a large number of Cherokee Indians offered their services to General Jackson against their red brethern. General Jackson immediately wrote to Joseph Brown, who had lately been elected colonel by his neighbors, requesting him to consent to command a regiment of Cherokee Indians. This Colonel Brown promptly agreed to do, and started to join the army for that purpose. Colonel Brown, however, never took charge of the Indians, but served with the army, as aid to General Robards, as well as interpreter and guide.

Colonel Brown was thus a participant in the battle of Talladega, and had the honor of leading and conducting a charge upon the most hotly contested part of the Indian lines. During this campaign, Colonel Brown again met Charles Butler, the nephew of Kiachatalee, and learned from him that the old Tuskegee chief, Cutty-a-toy, was still alive. Through him, he learned, that he was then living on an island in the Tennessee river, near the mouth of Elle river, and that he had with him several negroes, the descendants of the woman taken by him at Nickajack, on the 9th of May, 1788.

Colonel Brown had, at that time, a claim before Congress for the value of those negroes, but had always been put off by reason of some defect in the proof as to their value, or some other matter of form. He now determined that, as his negroes were still in the hands of the original wrong-doer, the Tuskegee chief, he would get possession of them, and carry them home.

Colonel Brown stated to General Jackson the facts of the case, and demanded of him, and obtained, an order appointing a mixed commission of American and Cherokee officers, to value the negroes of Cutty-a-toy. The Cherokees had long been in peace with the whites, and were now in alliance with them against the Creeks; and under such circumstances there was friendly intercourse between them.

With ten picked men, Brown proceeded to the island, went to the head man's lodge, and exhibited to him General Jackson's order, and demanded that Cutty-a-toy's negroes be immediately sent over to Fort Hampton, to be valued, in pursuance of said order. The head man sent for Cutty-a-toy, and it was immediately agreed that all would go to the fort the next morning.

The next morning, the negroes, Cutty-a-toy and his wife, and some friends, with Colonel Brown went to the fort. In crossing the river,

Colonel Brown and his men took up the negroes, and Cutty-a-toy's wife behind them, to carry them over the water, while the Indian men crossed on a raft higher up.

When he reached the fort he directed his men to proceed with the negroes towards Ditto's landing, and he turned into the fort with Cutty-a-toy's wife, to await the arrival of the Indians. He immediately called on the commandant of the fort, Colonel Williams, stated the history of the case, and the order of General Jackson, and the failure of Congress to pay for these negroes, and the fact that these negroes were now in his possession; and frankly asked him what course he would pursue, under the circumstances. "Take the negroes home with you," said the Colonel; "and if you wish to do it, and have not men enough, I will give you more."

Upon the arrival of Cutty-a-toy and his followers, they were invited into the fort, and Colonel Brown made known to him that he had sent the negroes off, but was willing for the commissioners to proceed to value them. The Indian became enraged. At last, in the midst of the garrison, officers and men, and the Indians, Colonel Brown gave a brief narrative of the murder of his father by Cutty-a-toy's party, the murder of his brothers, and the captivity of his mother, small brother and sisters; of the capture of the slaves by Cutty-a-toy, and his attempt upon Colonel Brown himself, then a boy at the house of the French trader; and of his being saved by the intercession of the trader's wife, and the Indian's desire to save the life of his captive negro woman. "It is now," said Colonel Brown, "nearly twenty-five years, and yet during all that time you have had the negro woman and her children as your slaves, and, they have worked for you; and yet you got them by the murder of my father and brothers? You made me an orphan and a beggar, when, but for you, I had begun the world with the smiles of a father, and the comfort of a home provided by his care. For this wrong, this crime, Cutty-a-toy, you deserve to die!"

Here Cutty-a-toy hung his head, and said, "It is all true: do with me as you please."

The soldiers who stood around, many of them the neighbors of Colonel Brown, said, "Kill him! he ought to die." But Colonel Brown was now a Christian, and had long, long ceased to cherish feelings of revenge against the savage murderer of his father.

"No, no, Cutty-a-toy," proceeded Colonel Brown; "although you deserve to die, and at my hands, yet I will not kill you. If I did not worship the Great Spirit who rules all things, I would slay you; but vengeance is His, and I will leave you to answer to him for your crimes! But I will not stain my hands with your blood; you are now old, and must soon go down to the grave, and answer to that Great Spirit for the life you have led. Live and repent."

Here Cutty-a-toy assumed a bolder front, and said, by certain treaties made in 1794, this property was guaranteed to him, and that he would sue Brown in the Federal Courts, as some other Indians named by him had done, in similar cases; but he finally agreed, if Brown would give him a young negro fellow, he might take the rest, including the two women and some children, which was generously done.

Thus the fortunes of war, controlled by the steady perseverance of her son, at length restored to Mrs. Brown a part of her long-lost property. Many years afterwards, when General Jackson became President, Colonel Brown finally obtained an allowance from Congress for a part of the property lost by his father in 1788. In 1810, Colonel Brown became a member of the Cumberland Presbyterian church, and in 1832, a regularly ordained minister of the church.

Having lived to the advanced age of ninety, and never having re-married, but always making her home with her son, Colonel Joseph Brown, Mrs. Brown left this world of vexation and sorrow, for such it was to her, at her son's residence, in Maury county, Tennessee. Hers was a most eventful life, full of trials, almost beyond human endurance; yet she did not murmur, but tried to see, in all her afflictions, the kind guidance of a wise Providence.

George, soon after his release from captivity, emigrated to the south, and, after nearly fifty years honorable citizenship, near Woodville, Mississippi, died in the bosom of his family.

The captive daughter, Jane, whose release was due to the manly courage of her youthful brother, was married to a Mr. Collingsworth, and became with him, as early as 1819, a citizen of Texas, where her descendants yet reside.

The history of the events connected with the family of Mrs. Brown possesses all the attractions of a romance; yet it is but a plain, sad story of trials and sufferings incident to the period and the border in which she passed her life. She lived to an octogenarian age and yet she often wept, as she told the tale of her captivity and sufferings, and those of her children.

The only survivor of that pioneer family is the Rev. Joseph Brown, of Maury county, Tennessee, better known as Colonel Brown. From notes and memoranda furnished by him, the principal details of this narrative have been written. They cannot fail to be useful to the future historian of Tennessee, yet Heywood, in his history of 500 pages, only contains the following allusion to the facts contained in this narrative. Speaking of the treaty of peace made at Tellico, October 20th, 1795, between the people of Tennessee, the Creeks and Cherokees, they, (the Creeks,) says the historian, "at this time delivered up Brown, son of Mrs. Brown, formerly a prisoner in the Creek nation."—p. 466. Yet how inadequate is such a notice to do justice either to the sufferings of Mrs. Brown and her children, or to the generous protection of the Creek chieftain, to whom they were indebted for their deliverance! For notwithstanding, says another writer, the "obloquy which both history and tradition have thrown upon the characters of the Creek and Cherokee warriors, some bright gleams occasionally break through, which throw a melancholy lustre over their memories." But a large portion of the pioneer history of Tennessee has never been written. Replete with incidents and heroic deeds which might challenge the admiration of the world, yet all that has been written by Heywood and others would scarcely answer as a thread to guide the future historian through the labyrinth of events which crowded upon the infant colonies of the Cumberland and the Holston.

HEROISM OF WOMEN AT BRYANT'S STATION

IN THE SUMMER of 1782, the Indians of Ohio resolved to make a grand effort to drive the whites from Kentucky. An army of six hundred men, under the command of the renegade whites, Simon Girty and M'Kee, was collected at Chillicothe, and early in August they commenced their march. With a secrecy and celerity peculiar to themselves, they advanced through the woods without giving the slightest indications of their approach; and on the night of the 14th of August, they appeared before Bryant's station, as suddenly as if they had risen from the earth, and surrounding it on all sides, calmly awaited the approach of daylight, holding themselves in readiness to rush in upon the inhabitants the moment that the gates were opened in the morning. The supreme influence of fortune in war, was never more strikingly displayed.

The garrison had determined to march at daylight on the following, morning to the assistance of Hoy's station, from which a messenger had arrived the evening before, with the intelligence of Holder's defeat. Had the Indians arrived only a few hours later, they would have found the fort occupied only by old men, women and children, who could not have resisted their attack for a moment. As it was, they found the garrison assembled and under arms, most of them busily engaged throughout the whole night, in preparing for an early march on the following morning. The Indians could distinctly hear the bustle of preparation, and see lights glancing from block-houses and cabins during the night, which must have led them to suspect that their approach had been discovered. All continued tranquil during the night, and Girty silently concerted the plan of attack.

The fort, consisting of about forty cabins placed in parallel lines, stands upon a gentle rise on the southern bank of the Elkhorn, a few paces to

101

the right of the road from Maysville to Lexington. The garrison was supplied with water from a spring at some distance from the fort on its north-western side; a great error, common to most of the stations, which, in a close and continued siege, must have suffered dreadfully for want of water.

The great body of Indians placed themselves in ambush within half rifle-shot of the spring, while one hundred select men were placed near the spot where the road now runs after passing the creek, with orders to open a brisk fire and show themselves to the garrison on that side, for the purpose of driving them out, while the main body held themselves in readiness to rush upon the opposite gate of the fort, hew it down with their tomahawks, and force their way into the midst of the cabins. At dawn of day, the garrison paraded under arms, and were preparing to open their gates and march off as already mentioned, when they were alarmed by a furious discharge of rifles, accompanied with yells and screams, which struck terror to the hearts of the women and children, and startled even the men.

All ran hastily to the picketing, and beheld a small party of Indians, exposed to open view, firing, yelling, and making the most furious gestures. The appearance was so singular, and so different from their usual manner of fighting, that some of the more wary and experienced of the garrison instantly pronounced it a decoy party, and restrained the young men from sallying out and attacking them, as some of them were strongly disposed to do. The opposite side of the fort was instantly manned, and several breaches in the picketing rapidly repaired. Their greatest distress arose from the prospect of suffering for water. The more experienced of the garrison felt satisfied that a powerful party was in ambuscade near the spring, but at the same time they supposed that the Indiana would not unmask themselves, until the firing upon the opposite side of the fort was returned with such warmth, as to induce the belief that the feint had succeeded.

Acting upon this impression, and yielding to the urgent necessity of the case, they summoned all the women, without exception, and explaining to them the circumstances in which they were placed, and the improbability that any injury would be offered them, until the firing had been returned from the opposite side of the fort, they urged them to go in a body to the spring, and each to bring up a bucket full of water

Some of the ladies, as was natural, had no relish for the undertaking, and asked why the men could not bring water as well as themselves? observing that they were not bullet-proof, and that the Indians made no distinction between male and female scalps! To this it was answered, that women were in the habit of bringing water every morning to the fort, and that if the Indians saw them engaged as usual, it would induce them to believe that their ambuscade was undiscovered, and that they would not unmask themselves for the sake of firing at a few women, when they hoped, by remaining concealed a few moments longer, to obtain complete possession of the fort. That if men should go down to the spring, the Indians would immediately suspect that something was wrong, would despair of succeeding by ambuscade, and would instantly rush upon them, follow them into the fort, or shoot them down at the spring. The decision was soon over.

A few of the boldest declared their readiness to brave the danger, and the younger and more timid rallying in the rear of these veterans, they all marched down in a body to the spring, within point blank shot of more than five hundred Indian warriors! Some of the girls could not help betraying symptoms of terror, but the married women, in general, moved with a steadiness and composure, which completely deceived the Indians. Not a shot was fired. The party were permitted to fill their buckets, one after another, without interruption, and although their steps became quicker and quicker, on their return, and when near the gate of the fort, degenerated into a rather un-military celerity, attended with some little crowding in passing the gate, yet not more than one-fifth of the water was spilled, and the eyes of the youngest had not dilated to more than double their ordinary size.

The various attacks upon the fort proving unsuccessful, the Indian army at length retreated. Unfortunately, the whites followed them, with insufficient forces and reckless hardihood. The disastrous battle of the Blue Licks ensued. The whites were completely defeated, and the Indians returned home with a large number of scalps.

MRS. HELM, THE HEROINE OF CHICAGO

THE MASSACRE OF Chicago was one of the most terrible of the events which occurred in the early part of the war of 1812. A fort had been erected upon the site of the present city of Chicago, as early as 1803. Around the fort several families had clustered, built cabins, and began to cultivate the ground. When the war broke out, the garrison of the fort consisted of fifty men, commanded by Captain Heald. As it was remote from the other American posts, and the neighboring country was occupied by the Pottawatomie Indians, whose adherence to the United States was more than doubtful, the garrison should have been withdrawn or strengthened. When it was too late, General Hull ordered the evacuation of the post.

On the 7th of August, (1812,) in the afternoon, Winnemeg, or Catfish, a friendly Indian of the Pottawatomie tribe, arrived at Chicago, and brought dispatches from general Hull, containing the first, and at that time, the only intelligence, of the declaration of war. General Hull's letter announced the capture of Mackinaw, and directed Heald "to evacuate the fort at Chicago, if practicable, and in that event, to distribute all of the United States property contained in the factory, or agency, among the Indians in the neighborhood, and repair to Fort Wayne." Winnemeg having delivered his dispatches to Captain Heald, and, as he was acquainted with the purport of the communication he had brought, urged upon Captain Heald the policy of remaining in the fort, being supplied, as they were, with ammunition and provisions for a considerable time. In case, however, Captain Heald thought proper to evacuate the place, he urged upon him the propriety of doing so immediately, before the Pottawatomies (through whose country they must pass and who were as yet ignorant of the object of his mission,) could collect a force sufficient to oppose them. This advice, though given in great earnestness, was not sufficiently regarded by Captain Heald; who observed, that he should evacuate the fort, but having received orders to distribute the public property among the Indians, he did not feel justified in leaving it, until he had collected the Pottawatomies in its vicinity, and made an equitable distribution among them. Winnemeg then suggested the expediency of marching out, and leaving every thing standing; "while the Indians," said he, "are dividing the spoils, the troops will be able to retreat without molestation." This advice was also unheeded; an order for evacuating the fort was read next morning on parade. Captain Heald, in issuing it, had neglected to consult his junior officers, as it would have been natural for him to do in such an emergency, and as he would have done, had there not been some coolness between him and Ensign Roman.

The lieutenant and ensign, after the promulgation of this order, waited on Captain Heald to learn his intentions; and being apprised, for the first time, of the course he intended to pursue, they remonstrated against it. "We do not," said they to Captain Heald, "believe that our troops can pass in safety through the country of the Pottawatomies, to Fort Wayne. Although a part of their chiefs were opposed to an attack upon us last summer, they were actuated by motives of private friendship for some particular individuals, and not from a regard to the Americans in general; and it can hardly be supposed that, in the present excited state of feeling among the Indians, those chiefs will be able to influence the whole tribe, now thirsting for vengeance. Besides," said they, "our march must be slow, on account of the women and children. Our force, too, is small. Some of our soldiers are superannuated, and some of them are invalids. We think, therefore, as your orders are discretionary, that we had better fortify ourselves as strongly as possible, and remain where we are. Succor may reach us before we shall be attacked from Mackinaw; and, in case of such an event, we had better fall into the hands of the English, than become victims of the savages." Captain Heald replied, that his force was inadequate to contend with the Indians, and that he should be censured were he to continue in garrison, when the prospect of a safe retreat to Fort Wayne was so apparent. He therefore deemed it advisable to assemble the Indians, and distribute the public property among them, and ask of them an escort thither, with the promise of a considerable sum of money to be paid on their safe arrival; adding, that he had perfect confidence in the friendly professions of the Indians, from whom, as well as from the soldiers, the capture of Mackinaw had studiously been concealed.

From this time forward, the junior officers stood aloof from their commander, and, considering his project as little short of madness, conversed as little upon the subject as possible. Dissatisfaction, however, soon filled the camp; the soldiers began to murmur, and insubordination assumed a threatening aspect.

The savages, in the meantime, became more and more troublesome; entered the fort occasionally, in defiance of the sentinels, and even made their way without ceremony into the quarters of its commanding officer. On one occasion an Indian, taking up a rifle, fired it in the parlor of Captain Heald. Some were of opinion that this was intended as the signal for an attack. The old chiefs at this time passed back and forth among the assembled groups, apparently agitated; and the squaws seemed much excited, as though some terrible calamity was impending. No further manifestations, however, of ill feeling were exhibited, and the day passed without bloodshed. So infatuated, at this time, was Captain Heald, that he supposed he had wrought a favorable impression upon the savages, and that the little garrison could now march forth in safety.

From the 8th to the 12th of August, the hostility of the Indians was more and more apparent; and the feelings of the garrison, and of those connected with, and dependent upon it for their safety, more and more intense. Distrust every where at length prevailed, and the want of unanimity among the officers, was appalling. Every inmate retired to rest, expecting to be aroused by the war-whoop; and each returning day was regarded by all as another step on the road to massacre.

The Indians from the adjacent villages having at length arrived, a council was held on the 12th of August. It was attended, however, only by Captain Heald on the part of the military; the other officers refused to attend, having previously learned that a massacre was intended. This fact was communicated to Captain Heald; he insisted, however, on their going, and they resolutely persisted in their refusal. When Captain Heald left the fort, they repaired to the block-house, which overlooked the ground where the council was in session, and opening the port-holes, pointed their cannon in its direction. This circumstance, and their absence, it is supposed, saved the whites from massacre.

Captain Heald informed the Indians in council, that he would, next day, distribute among them all the goods in the United States factory, together with the ammunition and provisions with which the garrison was supplied; and desired of them an escort to Fort Wayne, promising them a reward on their arrival thither, in addition to the presents they were about to receive. The savages assented, with professions of friendship, to all he proposed, and promised all he required. The council was no sooner dismissed, than several, observing the tone of feeling which prevailed, and anticipating from it no good to the garrison, waited on Captain Heald, in order to open his eyes if possible, to their condition.

The impolicy of furnishing the Indians with arms and ammunition, to be used against themselves, struck Captain Heald with so much force, that he resolved, without consulting his officers, to destroy all not required for immediate use.

On the next day, (August 13th,) the goods in the factory were all distributed among the Indians, who had collected near the fort; and in the evening, the ammunition, and also the liquor belonging to the garrison, were carried, the former into the sally-port and thrown into the well, and the latter through the south gate, as silently as possible, to the river bank, where the heads of the barrels were knocked in, and their contents discharged into the stream.

The Indians, however, suspecting the game, approached as near as possible, and witnessed the whole scene. The spare muskets were broken up, and thrown into the well, together with bags of shot, flints, and gun-screws, and other things; all, however, of but little value.

On the 14th, the despondency of the garrison was for a time dispelled by the arrival of Captain Wells, and fifteen friendly Miamies. Having heard at Fort Wayne of the order to evacuate Chicago, and knowing the hostile intentions of the Pottawatomies, he hastened thither, in order to save, if possible, the little garrison from its doom. He was the brother of Mrs. Heald, and having been reared from childhood among the savages, knew their character; and some thing whispered him, "that all was not well."

This intrepid warrior of the woods, hearing that his friends at Chicago were in danger, and chagrined at the obstinacy of Captain Heald, who was thus hazarding their safety, came thither to save his friends or participate in their fate. He arrived, however, too late to effect the former but just in time to effect the latter. Having, on his arrival, learned the ammunition had been destroyed, and the provisions distributed among the Indians, he saw no alternative. Preparations were therefore made for marching on the morrow.

In the afternoon, a second council was held with the Indians, at which they expressed their resentment at the destruction of the ammunition and liquor, in the severest terms. Notwithstanding the precautions which had been observed, the knocking in of the heads of the whiskey barrels had been heard by the Indians, and the river next morning tasted, as some of them expressed it, "like strong grog." Murmurs and threats were every where heard; and nothing, apparently, was wanting but an opportunity for some public manifestation of their resentment.

Among the chiefs, there were several who participated in the general hostility of their tribe, and retained, at the same time, a regard for the few white inhabitants of the place. It was impossible, however, even for them to allay the savage feeling of the warriors, when provocation after provocation had thus been given; and their exertions, therefore, were futile.

Among this class was Black Partridge, a chief of some renown. Soon after the council had adjourned, this magnanimous warrior returned to the head-quarters of Captain Heald, and, taking off a medal he had long worn, said, "Father—I have come to deliver up to you the medal I wear. It was given me by your countrymen, and I have long worn it as a token of our friendship. Our young men are resolved to imbrue their hands in the blood of the whites. I cannot restrain them, and will not wear a token of peace when compelled to act as an enemy."

Had doubts previously existed, they were now at an end. The devoted garrison continued, however, their preparations as before; and, amid the surrounding gloom, a few gallant spirits still cheered their companions with hopes of security.

The ammunition reserved, twenty-five rounds to each soldier, was now distributed. The baggage wagons designed for the sick, the women, and the children, containing also a box of cartridges, were now made ready, and the whole party, anticipating a fatiguing, if not a disastrous march, on the morrow, retired to enjoy a few moments precarious repose.

The morning of the 15th dawned as usual. The sun rose with uncommon splendor, and Lake Michigan "was a sheet of burnished gold." Early in the day a message was received in the American camp, from To-pee-na-bee, a chief of the St. Joseph's band, informing them that mischief was brewing among the Pottawatomies, who had promised them protection.

About nine o'clock the troops left the fort with martial music, and in military array. Captain Wells, at the head of the Miamies, led the van, his face blackened after the manner of the Indians. The garrison, with loaded arms, followed, and the wagons with the baggage, the women and children, the sick, and the lame, closed the rear. The Pottawatomies, about five hundred in number, who had promised to escort them in safety to Fort Wayne, leaving a little space, afterwards followed. The party in advance took the beach road. They had no sooner arrived at the sand-hills, which separate the prairie from the beach, about a mile and a half from the fort, when the Pottawatomies, instead of continuing in rear of the Americans, left the beach and took to the prairie. The sand-hills of course intervened and presented a barrier between the Pottawatomies, and the American and Miami line of march. This divergence had scarcely been effected, when Captain Wells, who, with the Miamies, was considerably in advance, rode back, and exclaimed: "They are about to attack us; form instantly and charge upon them." The word had scarcely been uttered, before a volley of musketry from behind the sand-hills was poured in upon them. The troops were brought immediately into a line, and charged upon the bank. One man, a veteran of seventy, fell as they ascended. The battle at once became general. The Miamies fled in the outset; their chief rode up to the Pottawatomies, charged them with duplicity, and brandishing his tomahawk, said, "he would be the first to head a party of Americans, and return to punish them for their treachery." He then turned his horse and galloped off in pursuit of his companions, who were then scouring across the prairie, and nothing was seen or heard of them more.*

While the battle was raging some incidents occurred, which displayed the calm courage and complete presence of mind of Mrs. Helm, the wife of Lieutenant Helm. That lady was in the action, where death was threatened on every hand. Doctor Voorhes, the surgeon, being badly wounded, approached Mrs. Helm, and said, "Do you think they will take our lives? I am badly wounded, but I think not mortally. Perhaps

---

* Brown's History of Illinois.

we can purchase safety by offering a large reward. Do you think," continued he, "there is any chance?" "Doctor Voorhes," replied Mrs. Helm, "Let us not waste the few moments which yet remain, in idle or ill-founded hopes. Our fate is inevitable. We must soon appear at the bar of God. Let us make such preparations as are yet in our power." "Oh!" said he, "I cannot die. I am unfit to die! If I had a short time to prepare!—Death!—oh, how awful!"

At this moment, Ensign Roman was fighting at a little distance, with a tall and portly Indian; the former, mortally wounded, was nearly down, and struggling desperately upon one knee. Mrs. Helm, pointing her finger, and directing the attention of Doctor Voorhes thither, observed: "Look," said she, "at that young man, he dies like a soldier."

"Yes," said Doctor Voorhes, "but he has no terrors of the future; he is an unbeliever."

A young savage immediately raised his tomahawk to strike Mrs. Helm. She sprang instantly aside, and the blow intended for her head fell upon her shoulder. She thereupon seized him around his neck, and while exerting all her efforts to get possession of his scalping-knife, was seized by another Indian, and dragged, forcibly from his grasp.

The latter bore her, struggling and resisting, towards the lake. Notwithstanding, however, the rapidity with which she was hurried along, she recognised, as she passed, the remains of the unfortunate surgeon, stretched lifeless on the prairie.

She was plunged immediately into the water, and held there, notwithstanding her resistance, with a forcible hand. She shortly, however, perceived that the intention of her captor was not to drown her, as he held her in a position to keep her head above the water. Thus reassured, she looked at him attentively, and, in spite of his disguise, recognised the "white man's friend," Black Partridge.

When the firing had ceased, her preserver bore her from the water and conducted her up the sand-bank. It was a beautiful day in August. The heat, however, of the sun was oppressive; and walking through the sand, exposed to its burning rays, in her drenched condition; weary, and exhausted by efforts beyond her strength; anxious, beyond measure, to learn the fate of her friends, and alarmed for her own, her situation was one of agony.

The troops having fought with desperation till two-thirds of their number were slain, the remainder twenty-seven in all, borne down by an overwhelming force, and exhausted by efforts hitherto unequalled, at length surrendered. They stipulated, however, for their own safety and of their remaining women and children. The wounded prisoners, however, in the hurry of the moment were unfortunately omitted, or rather not particularly maintained, and were therefore regarded by the Indians as having been excluded.

One of the soldiers' wives, having frequently been told that prisoners taken by the Indians were subjected to tortures worse than death, had from the first expressed a resolution never to be taken; and when a party of savages approached to make her their prisoner, she fought with desperation, and though assured of kind treatment and protection, refused to surrender, and was literally cut in pieces, and her mangled remains left on the field.

After the surrender, one of the baggage wagon, containing twelve children, was assailed by a single savage, and the whole number were massacred. All, without distinction of age or sex, fell at once beneath his murderous tomahawk.

Captain Wells, who had as yet escaped unharmed, saw from a distance the whole of this murderous scene, and being apprised of the stipulation, and on seeing it thus violated, exclaimed aloud, so as to be heard by the Pottawatomies around him, whose prisoner he then was: "If this be your game, I will kill too!" and turning his horse's head, instantly started for the Pottawatomy camp, where the squaws and Indian children had been left before the battle began.

He had no sooner started, than several of the Indians followed in his rear and discharged their rifles at him, as he galloped across the prairie. He laid himself flat on the neck of his horse, and was apparently out of their reach, when the ball of one of his pursuers took effect, killing his horse and wounding him severely. He was again a prisoner—as the savages came up, Winnemeg and Wa-ban-see, two of their number, and both his friends, used all their endeavors in order to save him; they had disengaged him already from his horse, and were supporting him along, when Pee-so-tum, a Pottawatomy Indian, drawing his scalping-knife, stabbed him in the back, and thus inflicted a mortal wound. After struggling for a moment, he fell, and breathed his last in the arms of his friends, a victim for those he had sought to save.

The battle having ended, and the prisoners being secured, the latter were conducted to the Pottawatomy camp near the fort. Here the wife of Wau-bee-nee-mah, an Illinois chief, perceiving the exhausted condition of Mrs. Helm, took a kettle, and dipping up some water from the stream, which flowed sluggishly by them, threw into it some maple sugar, and stirring it up with her hand, gave her to drink. "It was," says Mrs. Helm, "the most delicious draught I had ever taken, and her kindness of manner, amid so much atrocity, touched my heart." Her attention, however, was soon directed to other objects. The fort, after the troops had marched out, became a scene of plunder. The cattle were shot down as they ran at large, and lay dead, or were dying around her.

Most of the wounded prisoners were butchered. The unwounded remained in the wigwams of their captors. The work of plunder being complete, the fort next day was set on fire. Captain and Mrs. Heald, after being exposed to many dangers, were taken to Detroit, where they were finally exchanged. Lieutenant Helm was wounded in the action, and made prisoner. He was afterwards taken by some friendly Indians to the Au Sable, and thence to St. Louis, where he was liberated from captivity through the intervention of an Indian trader, named Forsyth. Mrs. Helm, who suffered from a severe wound in the ankle, was taken to Detroit, where she was exchanged. She lived for many years after her thrilling adventures, and was a highly respected lady.

MRS. PURSLEY

THE INSTANCES OF women voluntarily encountering danger, that men shrink from in the greatest dread, are so rare, that every one should be carefully recorded. Mrs. Purley, the heroine of the following sketch, was a woman who only needed a wider field to become as celebrated as Joan of Arc. She must be considered preëminent, even in the west—that region so fertile in daring spirits, and iron nerves.

During the war of 1812, a fort was erected about twenty miles from Vandalia, to protect the frontier settlements from the Indians. Lieutenant Journay and twelve men were assigned for its garrison. On the 30th of August, 1814, Indians were discovered near the fort. The next morning, before dawn, the lieutenant sallied out with his whole force. The party had not proceeded far, before a large body of Indians rose from an ambush, and fired a destructive volley. The commander and three of his men were killed, and one wounded. Six returned in safety to the fort, where Mrs. Pursley had in the meantime remained alone. One indomitable borderer, named Thomas Higgins, lingered outside of the fort to have "one more pull at the enemy." His horse had been shot, and he had dismounted, thinking the animal had been mortally wounded. He discovered his error, but instead of remounting, and making a rapid retreat, sought the shelter of a tree, and resolved to avenge the death of his comrades.

The Indians caught sight of Higgins before he could reach a tree sufficiently large to protect his body, and were advancing to attack him, when he turned and deliberately shot the foremost savage. Somewhat concealed by the smoke, the brave ranger then re-loaded his rifle, mounted his horse, and was about to ride away, when a voice exclaimed, "Tom, you won't leave me, will you?"

Higgins turned immediately around, and seeing a fellow-soldier by the name of Burgess lying on the ground, wounded and gasping for breath, replied: "No I'll not leave you—come along."

"I can't come," said Burgess; "my leg is all smashed to pieces."

Higgins dismounted, and taking up his friend, whose ankle had been broken, was about to lift him on his horse, when the horse taking fright, darted off in an instant, and left Higgins and his friend behind.

"This is too bad," said Higgins; "but don't fear; you hop off on your three legs, and I'll stay behind between you and the Indians, and keep them off. Get into the tallest grass, and crawl as near the ground as possible." Burgess did so, and escaped.

The smoke, which had hitherto concealed Higgins, now cleared away, and he resolved, if possible, to retreat. To follow the track of Burgess was most expedient. It would, however, endanger his friend.

He determined, therefore, to venture boldly forward, and, if discovered, to secure his own safety by the rapidity of his flight. On leaving a small thicket, in which he had sought refuge, he discovered a tall, portly savage near by, and two others in a direction between him and the fort. He paused for a moment, and thought if he could seperate and fight them singly, his case was not so desperate.

He then started for a little run of water which was near, but found one of his limbs failing him—it having been struck by a ball in the first encounter, of which, till now, he was scarcely conscious.

The largest Indian pressed close upon him, and Higgins turned round two or three times in order to fire. The Indian halted and danced about to prevent his taking aim. Higgins saw it was unsafe to fire at random, and perceiving two others approaching, knew he must be overpowered in a moment, unless he could dispose of the forward Indian first. He resolved, therefore, to halt and receive his fire. The Indian raised his rifle; and Higgins, watching his eye, turned suddenly, as his finger pressed the trigger, and received the ball in his thigh.

Higgins fell, but rose immediately, and ran. The foremost Indian, now certain of his prey, loaded again, and with the other two, pressed on. They overtook him—Higgins fell again, and as he rose, the whole three fired, and he received all their balls. He now fell and rose again; and the Indians, throwing away their guns, advanced upon him with spears and knives. As he presented his gun at one or the other, each fell back. At last, the largest Indian, supposing Higgins's gun to be empty, from his fire having been thus reserved, advanced boldly to the charge. Higgins fired, and the savage fell.

He had now four bullets in his body—an empty gun in his hand—two Indians unharmed, as yet, before him—and a whole tribe but a few yards distant. Any other man but Higgins would have despaired. But he had no notion of surrendering yet. He had slain the most dangerous of the three; and having but little to fear from the others, began to load his rifle. They raised a savage whoop, and rushed to the encounter; keeping at a respectful distance when Higgin's rifle was loaded, but when they knew it was empty, "they were better soldiers."

A bloody conflict now ensued. The Indians stabbed him in several places. Their spears, however, were but thin poles, hastily prepared for the occasion, and bent whenever they struck a rib or muscle. The wounds they made were not, therefore, deep, though numerous, as his scars sufficiently testified.

At last one of them threw his tomahawk. It struck him upon the cheek, passed, through his ear, which it severed, laid bare his skull to the back of his head, and stretched him upon the prairie. The Indians again rushed on; but Higgins, recovering his self-possession, kept them off with his feet and hands. Grasping at length one of their spears, the Indian, in attempting to pull it from him, raised Higgins up; who, taking up his rifle, smote the nearest savage, and dashed out his brains. In doing so, however, his rifle broke—the barrel only remaining in his hand.

The other Indian, who had hitherto fought with caution, came now manfully into the battle. His character as a warrior was in jeopardy. To have fled from a man thus wounded and disarmed, or to have suffered his victim to escape, would have tarnished his fame for ever.

Uttering, therefore, a terrific yell, he rushed on, and attempted to stab the exhausted ranger; but the latter warded off his blow with one hand, and brandished his rifle-barrel with the other.

The Indian was as yet unharmed, and under existing circumstances, by far the most powerful man. Higgins's courage, however, was unexhausted. The savage, at last, began to retreat from the glare of his untamed eye, to the spot where he dropped his rifle. Higgins knew that if he recovered that, his own case was desperate; throwing, therefore, his rifle barrel aside, and drawing his hunting-knife, he rushed upon his foe.

A desperate strife ensued—deep gashes were inflicted on both sides. Higgins, fatigued, and exhausted by the loss of blood, was no longer a match for the savage. The latter succeeded in throwing his adversary from him, and went immediately in pursuit of his rifle. Higgins, at the same time, rose and sought for the gun of the other Indian. Both, therefore, bleeding and out of breath, were in search of arms to renew the combat. A party of Indians were in sight.

The smoke had now cleared, and a party of Indians were coming up. Nothing, it seemed, could save the gallant ranger. The little garrison had witnessed the whole combat. Mrs. Pursley urged, with much vehemence, that some of the men should attempt to rescue their brave comrade. To the rangers it seemed too much like rushing in the face of death. They shrank from the task and were deaf to all Mrs. Pursley's entreaties, as well as taunts. The heroic woman was not to be turned from a noble purpose. Finding that the men would not stir from the fort, she seized a rifle, and declaring that "so fine a fellow as Tom Higgins should not be lost for want of help," mounted a horse and rode forth to the rescue. The men were thereby shamed into action. To be outdone by a woman was too great a degradation. They followed Mrs. Pursley at full gallop, reached the spot where Higgins fainted and fell, before the Indians came up; and while the savage with whom he had been contending was looking for his rifle, the wounded ranger was raised upon a horse and carried safely into the fort.

Higgins continued insensible for several days, but his life was saved by constant care and attendance. To the brave woman who preserved him from death, after his own desperate and astonishing efforts had ceased to avail him, he was ever profoundly grateful. Mrs. Pursley deserved a monument, but it is only of late years that justice has been so far awarded to her memory as to record her noble deed.

MARY HART

THE FOLLOWING NARRATIVE is copied from the New York Knickerbocker. It was derived from an officer of General Wellborn's corps, who was in battle with the Creek Indians, as below narrated, and an eyewitness of the remarkable events here recorded. The whole affords but another proof, that truth is indeed often stronger than fiction.

The Creek war of 1836–37 was a most barbarous one, and continued nearly two years. The Creek population comprehended in the treaty for emigration westward, was about twenty-two thousand souls, about two thousand of whom, warriors, broke the treaty, and commenced hostilities in May, 1836, by an attack on the town of Roanoke, in the night, butchering its inhabitants, putting them to flight, and pillaging and setting fire to their habitations. The terrors of an affrighted population, once exposed to Indian barbarities, can hardly be conceived. Rumor follows quick upon the heels of rumor; yet no story can exceed the horrors of Indian warfare, as it is impossible for language adequately to depict its realities. It is stated of a man in flight with his family from a supposed pursuit of Indians in this war, that having got fresh intelligence of alarm by the less hasty flight of others who had overtaken him, he took up his boy from behind his wagon, tossed him in, and ran forward to whip up his team, when lo! at the place of stopping, he found that the violence of his action to save his son had killed him by breaking his neck!

When General Jessup had reported the Creek war at an end, and drawn off his troops into Florida, to act against the Seminoles, contrary to the remonstrances of the inhabitants of the state of Alabama—who assured him that the Indians were not all subdued, but that some hundreds were still lurking in their hiding-places—the war broke out afresh, with increased barbarity; and the Governor of Alabama, the

Hon. Clement C. Clay, was forced to act with great vigor in mustering fresh troops for the exigency, by enlisting the citizens of the state into the service of the United States. General William Wellborn received the command, and acquitted himself with great valor and honor, to the end of the war.

Sometime in the winter of 1836–37, General Wellborn heard of an encampment of Indians on the banks of the Pee river, near its confluence with Pee creek, between the forks. With a company of two hundred mounted men, he set off in search of the foe. Having discovered and reconnoitred their position, from the west bank of the Pee, without being observed, he left one hundred and twenty of his troops on the higher grounds, about half a mile from the river, at a point by which the Indians must retreat, if dislodged, with instructions to cut them off whenever they should be driven in upon them. With the remainder, ninety men, he descended the river a few miles, and crossed on a bridge, below the confluence of the two streams, with the view to come round and attack the Indians by surprise. Having made his way across Pee creek, he found the access greatly impeded by low and wet grounds, it being a time of high water, and several lagoons, or channels, running from one river to the other, and at this time flooded; canebrakes and palmetto thickets were to be broken through, and various obstacles, peculiar to that wild retreat, interposed. Nevertheless, the bravery and determination of the troops surmounted all impediments, and they arrived at last on the bank of a lagoon, on the other side of which was the Indian encampment, themselves screened from observation by a grove of palmettoes, and by favorable grounds.

At this moment a firing was heard in the direction of the place were the one hundred and twenty troops had been left, and it was manifest, as none but women and children were to be seen on the opposite bank of the lagoon, that the Indians had discovered the whites on the west side of the Pee, and had themselves become the assailants. This was the more painful to observe, as the firing grew rapidly more distant, an indication that the Indians were victorious and in pursuit.

General Wellborn instantly conceived the project, as retreat was impossible, of placing his men in line as near the bank of the lagoon as he could, for a desperate onset on the return of the Indians; and having given his orders, he retired to an eminence about a quarter of a mile, and showed himself to the women, who instantly raised the cry of "Esta-Hadka! Esta-Hadka!" "White man! White man!"—pointing to General Wellborn, on the distant eminence. This alarm was rapidly conveyed by runners to the Indians now engaged on the other side of the Pee, and as soon as possible, some three hundred warriors or more came rushing back, flushed with victory, and full of vengeance. They seemed to know that they had routed the largest body of their opponents, and were eager to find the remainder. It was a critical moment when they stood upon the open ground, within gun-shot of General Wellborn's men, on the other bank of the lagoon, demanding of the women where they had seen the white man. The Indians knew that the lagoon was fordable, but their opponents did not. At the moment they were about to rush in, and at a given signal, a well-directed fire was pored in upon them from the whole line, and they fell back, with a shout of terror and discomfiture, into a pine wood, about forty rods distant, leaving a number of their dead upon the field.

It was evident that the fire told well, but no less certain that the foe would soon rally, and return with confidence of victory. They knew there was no escape for the white man, and that they had driven from the field his strongest force. Violent speeches of the chiefs and warriors were heard and understood. In about forty minutes, a hideous yell of onset rang through the forest, and the entire array of the Indian force leaped upon the bank of the lagoon, to cross and drive their assailants by closer fight. At that moment they received a second time the whole fire of General Wellborn's men from behind the palmettoes, halted, staggered, and again fell back into the woods, leaving the ground strewed with their slain. Again the rallying speeches were heard, and General Wellborn saw that he and his men must transfer the action to the other bank, or perish before a superior force. Believing from the demonstrations of the Indians, that the lagoon was fordable, he ordered two men, at different points, to make the attempt, and if they succeeded, the whole corps were to plunge in, form upon the opposite bank, and rush upon the foe.

It was but the work of a moment, and every man was in line. The conflict was desperate and bloody. Women fought and fell with the men. A single white man encounted a warrior and two of his wives, all three of whom were laid dead at his feet, by a necessity which he could not avoid, in self-preservation. The Indians fled across a bridge of trees, which they had thrown over the Pee, fighting and falling in their retreat; and all that could were soon out of the battle, leaving behind them camp and spoils, the wounded, the dying, and the dead. Seventy-three warriors, averaging six feet and two inches in height, were counted among the slain.

An old chief, Apothlo-Oholo, who afterward escaped in the night, being entirely disabled by the shot he had received in various parts of his body, fell into the river, as he was attempting to cross the bridge of trees. He clung to the branches, and buried himself entirely under water, while the victors were crossing and re-crossing during and after the action.

He lived to recover of his wounds, joined his party, and afterwards made the following speech to General Wellborn, at Conchatto-Mecco's Town, when about to emigrate with his people:

"You are a Great Chief. I have fought you as long as I could. You have beaten me. You have killed and taken nearly all my people. I am now ready to go: the farther from you the better. We cannot be friends. I thank you for taking care of my women, children, and wounded warriors, and for sending them back to me. You are a Great Chief!"

In the sleeve of the coat of Apothlo-Oholo, after the battle, were found twenty-eight hundred dollars in gold; and many spoils that had been taken from murdered white families, or pillaged from their deserted homes, were recovered. A roll of bank notes was also found. Most of the Indian ponies were left behind, and the whole of the next day was consumed in making arrangements for a vigorous pursuit of the routed Indians. Nine of the ninety engaged in this attack were killed. The bodies of the Indians, were left without burial. The exasperated troops, themselves citizens of a commonwealth doomed to the horrible atrocities of an Indian war, with their families exposed, many of whom had already suffered, must stand as an apology for not paying to a fallen enemy the usual respect of civilized warfare. It was a scene of carnage, left to the face of the sun, and to the eyes of the stars.

On the morning of the third day, a pursuit of the retreating foe was ordered, the trail of which led them down the Pee, to the plantation of two brothers, Josiah and Robert Hart, about forty miles below the battle-ground. As they approached these settlements, it needed no prophet's ken to anticipate the fate of these unhappy families. The Indians, still counting less than two hundred warriors, came upon them the second night.

Josiah Hart had a wife, a son, and two daughters, the youngest of whom, Mary, was nine years of age. The family of Robert Hart, living about a mile from his brother, consisted of himself, two sons, a married daughter, and son-in-law. The log cabin of Robert, as is usual, in that country, was built in two separate parts with an open space or court between, over which the roof of the building extended, the door of each part being in the middle of this court, opposite to each other. Aware of the dangers to which he was exposed, Mr. Hart had "Chinked" the logs, before open, and admitting of being fired through by the musketry or rifles of an enemy, leaving here and there a port-hole, through which the tenants might be able to repulse assailants. He was also provided with nine pieces of fire-arms, rifles, double-barrel and others, kept constantly charged, and ready for a sudden emergency. In one of these buildings, the whole family slept by their arms and ammunition, while the watch dog kept his post without.

At the mid-hour of this fatal night, they were suddenly awakened by the earnest barking of the dog, and the simultaneous yells of the Indians. The dog was soon silenced by the rifles of the savages; and the subsequent stillness without, except when interrupted by the occasional light tread or sudden bound of the wily foe around the house, reconnoitring, in preparation for the execution of his purpose, was fearful. Having failed in their usual stratagem of driving out the tenants of the house in affright, by the yells of the onset, in an opposite direction, where they would be sure to fall into the hands of a party in ambush, they sought opportunity to make an attack through the crevices of the logs which composed the walls of the building. Not succeeding in this, for the reason before mentioned, and not venturing yet to enter the court, for fear of a fire from within, which had not yet opened upon them, their next device was, to kindle a fire under the side of the dwelling, by which, if successful, they were sure of their prey. This, however, they could not well do in the dark, without becoming marks for an unseen hand. Accordingly, the first attempt proved fatal to those engaged in it, and two or three Indians fell before the sure aim of the rifle from within the walls. Hour after hour, in painful suspense passed away, with now and then a shot from either party, to little or to no purpose, except that a chance ball from an Indian rifle, found its way between the logs, and wounded Mr. Hart's daughter in the arm. Not daring to strike a light, they endeavored as well as they could, to bind it up, and to staunch the blood. At length a lurid light cast upon the clouds, discovered to Mr. Hart his brother's house in flames, and a yell of triumph broke from the horde of savages by whom he and his children were environed, secure, though less successful hitherto, in accomplishing the same object. The flames rose higher, and threw upon his besieged habitation a flood of light, that compelled the besiegers to retire behind the out-houses for protection, as they would otherwise be exposed to the fire of Mr. Hart and his sons.

Day dawned at last, and a desultory fire was commenced, as chance invited, and as an Indian head was exposed to view. Several of the Indians fell. Exasperated by these failures, they resolved to set the house on fire at any hazard. They collected combustibles, chose their position, and rushed with fire and kindling-wood under the stick chimney of the house, where, as it happened the rifles from within could not be brought to bear. The smoke was soon felt in the house, and not a moment was to be lost. Despair finds weapons; and by the concert of an instant, a bold device was projected, to strike the frail chimney-back on the heads of the Indians, and by a sudden sortie, drive them from the field, to purchase to themselves an opportunity of escape to the fort, about seven miles distant. It was done. Three or four Indians were killed, and the rest fled. In some two hours after, Mr. Hart and his children were all safely lodged in the fort, having left their house to pillage and flames, to which it was doomed in the course of the morning, so soon as the Indians had mustered a stronger force, and returned to renew the attack. Plunder was all they bad to enjoy.

About thirty-six hours after the Indians had quitted the plantation of the Harts, which they had left a scene of ruin and of carnage, and descended the river, little dreaming of being pursued by the party whose power they had felt two days before, General Wellborn and his men came in sight of the smoking ruins of Josiah Hart's habitation and out-houses. Not a living creature moved before their eyes, and every aspect was that of desolation. From a party in advance, so soon as they approached the ruins, a cry of horror and vengeance arose, which broke the awful silence of the place; and each one, as he came near, was petrified at the spectacle which was presented.

In the yard, a few rods from the house, lay the mangled and naked bodies of Mr. and Mrs. Hart, their son and eldest daughter; and a little removed from them, the body of Mary, also naked, with her skull broken in apparently by a pine-knot, which lay by her side, covered with hair and blood. She was lying upon her side, her person stabbed in several places, from head to foot; and the blood of each wound extending in unbroken coagulation to the ground, which had drunk the crimson streams. The sight of Mary was not so fearful as that of the rest of family, though sufficiently shocking. It was evident, that she had never struggled or moved, from the moment she was left in that position, thirty-six hours before. With the exception of her wounds, her appearance was that of an innocent, marble repose.

The mutilated and mangled condition of the other members of the family was too horrible to be recorded. Mr. Hart had been pierced with many balls; Mrs. Hart with less; each had been shot, and all were covered and disfigured with ghastly wounds. The spectacle filled the men with absolute madness. They raved, stamped, ran to and fro, struck the trees and stones with their clenched hands, until the blood followed from their blows, without seeming to feel the wounds they had inflicted on themselves; and they cried, "Vengeance! vengeance! vengeance!" till all the region rang with it, and loud enough to awake the sleeping dead.

And it *did* awake the dead! Surrounded at this moment by a throng of these exasperated beholders, who were looking upon her innocent countenance, and raising those fearful cries, but not having yet presumed to touch this relic of mortality, little Mary Hart opened her eyes, turned up her face, and said, audibly and distinctly, "How they did beat us!" and then closed her eyes, and turned back, clasped again in the same silent and death-like repose!

The moment was awful, and the feeling of the spectators entirely changed. The innocent victim was carefully approached, tenderly lifted up, her wounds bathed, and the proper surgical applications applied. On examination, it was found that life was not extinct; but she was so literally drained of her blood, that no symptom of reviving animation could be awakened. She was wrapped in a blanket, and carefully carried on horseback, in the arms of General Wellborn, to the fort, with little more sign of life than when first taken from the ground, and was committed to the charge of her uncle and his family, whose escape has already been narrated.

The troops started off in hot pursuit of the flying foe, and after two days' march, overtook them in Florida. Thirty-nine of them were slain in the engagement that ensued; many prisoners were taken, with the booty from the pillaged houses of the Harts; and the rest took flight to the town of Canchatto-Mecco, were they surrendered for emigration, and the Creek war was ended.

Mary Hart, by means of tender nursing, and the restoring powers of nature, gradually recovered. The indenture in the skull proved not to be a fracture, and she is now as well as if the massacre had never happened.

A YOUNG HEROINE

IN SEPTEMBER, 1840, a small party of Indians appeared in Washington county, Florida, and killed the wife of Mr. Wiley Jones, and two of his children. This gave occasion to a remarkable display of heroism in a very young girl. The affair is narrated as follows in the Tallahassee Floridian.

Mr. Jones, on returning from one of his fields, about ten o'clock in the morning, and when within two hundred yards of the house, heard four or five rifles fired in his yard, he ran for the house, and on rising the hill, found the house surrounded by Indians, and eight or ten in the piazza. The Indians discovered him at that moment, and pursued him, firing and whooping at him like devils. Being entirely unarmed, without even a knife to defend himself, he fled, and escaped in the hammock.

Mr. Jones's daughter, a girl of about thirteen years of age, states that her mother, a negro woman, and four children were in the house when the Indians were discovered in the yard. Mrs. Jones caught up the youngest child, and was shot in attempting to escape out of the door, struck by three balls, one passing through the head of the child in her arms.

The daughter above mentioned took the two children, and, while the Indians were ransacking and plundering the house, passed out unmolested, and hid them in the bushes. The little heroine then returned to the house, in the midst of the Indians, helped her mother up, who was lying in the porch, and assisted her about three hundred yards into the field, when becoming faint from the loss of blood, the little girl left her in search of water. She returned with it, but her mother, after drinking, died in a few moments. She then covered her mother and the dead infant with bushes, and carried the remaining children to the nearest neighbor. The Indians destroyed all the furniture and stole about three hundred dollars.

MRS. DAVIESS

DAVIESS IS A name written boldly in the heroic annals of the west. Noble men and women—chiefly the children of Kentucky—have contributed brave and generous deeds to render it brilliant and undying. The Mrs. Daviess, whose heroic acts we are now about to record, was a glorious example to her sex. Firm, cool, and fertile of resource in the hour of peril, and gentle and amiable by the peaceful fireside.

In the fall of the year 1779, Samuel Daviess, who resided in Bedford county, Virginia, moved with his family to Kentucky, and lived for a time, at Whitley's station, in Lincoln. After residing for some time in the station, he removed with his family to a place called Gilmer's Lick, some six or seven miles distant from said station, where he built a cabin, cleared some land, which he put in corn next season, not apprehending any danger from the Indians, although he was considered a frontier settler. But this imaginary state of security did not last long; for on a morning in the month of August, in the year 1782, having stepped a few paces from his door, he was suddenly surprised by an Indian's appearing between him and the door, with tomahawk uplifted, almost within striking distance. In this unexpected condition, and being entirely unarmed, his first thought was, that by running round the house, he could enter the door in safety, but to his surprise, in attempting to effect this object, as he approached the door he found the house full of Indians. Being closely pursued by the Indian first mentioned, he made his way into the cornfield, where he concealed himself, with much difficulty, until the pursuing Indian had returned to the house.

Unable as he was to render any relief to his family (there being five Indians,) he ran with the utmost speed to the station of his brother James Daviess—a distance of five miles. As he approached the station—his undressed condition told the tale of his distresses, before he was able to

tell it himself. Almost breathless, and with a faltering voice, he could only say, his wife and children were in the hands of the Indians. Scarcely was the communication made when he obtained a spare gun, and the five men in the station, well armed, followed him to his residence. When they arrived at his house, the Indians, as well as the family, were found to be gone, and no evidence appeared that any of the family had been killed. A search was made to find the direction the Indians had taken, but owing to the dryness of the ground, and the adroit manner in which they had departed, no discovery could be made! In this state of perplexity, the party being all good woodsmen, took that direction in pursuit of the Indians, which they thought it most probable, they would take. After going a few miles, their attention was arrested by the howling of a dog, which afterwards turned out to be a house-dog that had followed the family, and which the Indians had undertaken to kill, so as to avoid detection, which might happen from his occasionally barking. In attempting to kill the dog, he was only wounded, which produced the howling that was heard, and satisfied them that they were near the Indians, and enabled them to rush forward with the utmost impetuosity. Two of the Indians being in the rear as spies, discovering the approach of the party, ran forward to where the Indians were with the family—one of them knocked down the oldest boy, about eleven years old, and while in the act of scalping him, was fired at, but without effect. Mrs. Daviess, seeing the agitation and alarm of the Indians, saved herself and sucking child, by jumping into a sink hole. The Indians did not stand to make fight, but fled in the most precipitate manner. In that way the family was rescued by nine o'clock in the morning, without the loss of a single life, and without any injury but that above mentioned. Soon as the boy had risen on his feet, the first word he spoke was, "Curse that Indian he has got my scalp." After the family had been rescued, Mrs. Daviess gave the following account of the manner in which the Indians had acted.

A few minutes after her husband had opened the door and stepped out of the house, four Indians rushed in, whilst the fifth, as she afterwards learned, was in pursuit of her husband. Herself and children were in bed when the Indians entered the house. One of the Indians immediately made signs, by which she understood him to inquire how far it was to the next house. With an unusual presence of mind, knowing how important it would be to make the distance as far as possible, she raised both her hands, first counting the fingers of one hand, then the other—making a distance of eight miles. The Indian then signed to her that she must rise; she immediately got up, and as soon as she could dress herself, commenced showing the Indians one article of clothing after another, which pleased them very much; and in that way, delayed them at the house nearly two hours. In the mean time, the Indian who had been in pursuit of her husband, returned with his hands stained with poke berries, which he held up, and with some violent gestures, and waving of his tomahawk, attempted to induce the belief, that the stain on his hands was the blood of her husband, and that he had killed him. She was enabled at once to discover the deception, and instead of producing any alarm on her part, she was satisfied that her husband had escaped uninjured.

After the savages had plundered the house of every thing that they could conveniently carry off with them, they started, taking Mrs. Daviess and her children—seven in number, as prisoners along with them. Some of the children were too young to travel as fast as the Indians wished, and discovering, as she believed, their intention to kill such of them as could not conveniently travel, she made the two oldest boys carry them on their backs. The Indians, in starting from the house, were very careful to leave no signs of the direction which they had taken, not even permitting the children to break a twig or weed, as they passed along. They had not gone far, before an Indian drew a knife and cut off a few inches of Mrs. Daviess's dress, so that she would not be interrupted in travelling.

Mrs. Daviess was a woman of cool, deliberate courage, and accustomed to handle the gun so that she could shoot well, as many of the women were in the habit of doing in those days. She had contemplated, as a last resort, that if not rescued in the course of the day, when night came and the Indians had fallen asleep, she would rescue herself and children by killing as many of the Indians as she could—thinking in a night attack as many of them as remained, would most probably run off. Such an attempt would now seem a species of madness; but to those who were acquainted with Mrs. Daviess, little doubt was entertained, that if the attempt had been made, it would have proved successful.

The boy who had been scalped, was greatly disfigured, as the hair never after grew upon that part of his head. He often wished for an opportunity to avenge himself upon the Indians for the injury he received. Unfortunately for himself, ten years afterwards, the Indians came to the neighborhood of his father and stole a number of horses. Himself and a party of men went in pursuit of them, and after following them for some days, the Indians finding that they were likely to be overtaken, placed themselves in ambush, and when their pursuers came up, killed young Daviess and one other man; so that he untimely fell into their hands when about twenty-one years old. The next year after the father died; his death being caused, as it was supposed, by the extraordinary efforts he made to release his family from the Indians. We cannot close this account, without noticing an act of courage displayed by Mrs. Daviess, calculated to exhibit her character in its true point of view.

Kentucky, in its early days, like most new countries, was occasionally troubled with men of abandoned character, who lived by stealing the property of others, and after committing their depredations, retired to their hiding places, thereby eluding the operation of the law. One of these marauders, a man of desperate character, who had committed extensive thefts from Mr. Daviess, as well as from his neighbors, was pursued by Daviess and a party whose property he had taken, in order to bring him to justice. While the party were in pursuit, the suspected individual, not knowing any one was pursuing him, came to the house of Daviess, armed with his gun and tomahawk—no person being at home but Mrs. Daviess and her children. After he had stepped into the house, Mrs. Daviess asked him if he would drink something—and having set a bottle of whiskey upon the table, requested him to help himself. The fellow not suspecting any danger, set his gun by the door, and, while he was drinking, Mrs. Daviess picked up his gun, and placed herself in the door, had the gun cocked and levelled upon him by the time he turned around, and in a peremptory manner ordered him to take a seat, or she would shoot him. Struck with terror and alarm, he asked what he had done. She told him, he had stolen her husband's property, and that she intended to take care of him herself. In that condition, she held him a prisoner, until the party of men returned and took him into their possession.

Such deeds procured for Mrs. Daviess a high reputation for courage and determination, among the bold spirits of the frontier, although they were accustomed to expect such qualities in the men and women of that region. All deemed her an extraordinary woman; and when wives and daughters displayed timidity at approaching danger, they were stimulated to daring efforts by being reminded of what Mrs. Daviess had performed.

MARY CHASE

RUXTON, IN HIS inimitable "Life in the Far West," gives a thrilling account of an attack upon a family named Chase, who were crossing the prairies. He has changed the name to Brand, but the incidents are narrated as they actually happened. The courage and devotion of Mary Chase, the Mary Brand of the story, cannot be too much extolled. The narrative is as follows:

One fine sunny evening in April of 1847, when the cotton woods on the banks of the Arkansas began to put forth their buds, and robins and blue-birds—harbingers of spring—were hopping, with gaudy plumage, through the thickets, three white-tilted Conostoga wagons emerged from the timbered bottom of the river, and rumbled slowly over the prairie, in the direction of the Platte's waters. Each wagon was drawn by eight oxen, and contained a portion of the farming implements and household utensils of the Brand family. The teams were driven by the young boys, the men following in rear with shouldered rifles—old Brand himself mounted on an Indian horse, leading the advance. The women were safely housed under the wagon tilts, and out of the first the mild face of Mary Brand smiled adieu to many of her old companions, who had accompanied them thus far, and now wished them "God-speed" on their long journey. Some mountaineers galloped up, dressed in buckskin, and gave them rough greeting—warning the men to keep their "eyes skinned," and look out for the Araphos, who were out on the waters of the Platte. Presently all retired, and then the huge wagons and the little company were rolling on their solitary way through the deserted prairies—passing the first of the many thousand miles which lay between them and the "setting sun," as the Indians style the distant regions of the Far West. And on, without casting a look behind him, doggedly and boldly marched old Brand, followed by his sturdy family.

They made but a few miles that evening, for the first day the *start* is all that is effected; and nearly the whole morning is taken up in getting fairly under weigh. The loose stock had been sent off earlier; for they had been collected and corralled the previous night; and, after a twelve hours' fast, it was necessary they should reach the end of the day's journey betimes. They found the herd grazing in the bottom of the Arkansas, at a point previously fixed upon for their first camp. Here the oxen were unyoked, and the wagons drawn up so as to form the three sides of a small square. The women descended from their seats, and prepared the evening meal. A huge fire was kindled before the wagons, and round this the whole party collected; while large kettles of coffee boiled on it, and hoe-cakes baked upon the embers.

The women were sadly down-hearted, as well they might be, with the dreary prospect before them; and poor Mary, when she saw the Mormon encampment shut out from her sight by the rolling bluffs, and nothing before her but the bleak, barren prairie, could not divest herself of the idea that she had looked for the last time on civilized fellow-creatures, and fairly burst into tears.

In the morning the heavy wagons rolled on again across the upland prairies, to strike the trail used by the traders in passing from the south fork of the Platte to the Arkansas. They had for guide a Canadian voyageur, who had been in the service of the Indian traders, and knew the route well, and had agreed to pilot them to Fort Lancaster on the north fork of the Platte. Their course led for about thirty miles up the Boiling Spring River, whence they pursued a north-easterly course to the dividing ridge which separates the waters of the Platte and Arkansas. Their progress was slow, for the ground was saturated with wet, and exceedingly heavy for the cattle, and they scarcely advanced more than ten miles a day.

At the camp fire at night, Antoine, the Canadian guide amused them with tales of the wild life and perilous adventures of the hunters and trappers who make the mountains their home; often extorting a scream from the women by the description of some scene of Indian fight and slaughter, or beguiling them of a commiserating tear by the narrative of the sufferings and privations endured by those hardy hunters in their arduous life.

Mary listened with the greater interest, since she remembered that such was the life which had been led by one very dear to her—by one, long supposed to be dead, of whom she had never but once, since his departure, nearly fifteen years before, heard a syllable. Her imagination pictured him as the bravest and most daring of these adventurous hunters, and conjured up his figure charging through the midst of whooping savages, or stretched on the ground perishing from wounds, or cold, or famine.

Among the characters who figured in Antoine's stories, a hunter named La Bonte was made conspicuous for deeds of hardiness and daring. The first mention of the name caused the blood to rush to Mary's face: not that she for a moment imagined it was her La Bonte, for she knew the name was a common one; but, associated with feelings which she had never got the better of, it recalled a sad epoch in her former life, to which she could not look back without mingled pain and pleasure.

Once only, and about two years after his departure, had she ever received tidings of her former lover. A mountaineer had returned from the Far West to settle in his native state, and had found his way to the neighborhood of old Brand's farm. Meeting him by accident, Mary, hearing him speak of the mountain hunters, had inquired tremblingly, after La Bonte. Her informant knew him well—had trapped in company with him—and had heard at the trading fort, whence he had taken his departure for the settlements, that La Bonte had been killed on the Yellow Stone by Blackfeet; which report was confirmed by some Indians of that nation. This was all she had ever learned of the lover of her youth.

Now upon hearing the name of La Bonte so often mentioned by Antoine, a vague hope was raised in her breast that he was still alive, and she took an opportunity of questioning the Canadian closely on the subject.

"Who was this La Bonte, Antoine, who you say was so brave a mountaineer?" she asked one day.

"J'ne sais pas; he vas un beau garçon, and strong comme le diable— enfant de garce, mais he pas not care a dam for les sauvages, pe gar. He shoot de centare avec his carabine; and ride de cheval comme one Comanche. He trap heap castor (what you call beevare,) and get plenty dollare—mais he open hand vare wide—and got none too. Den, he hont vid de Blackfeet and avec de Cheyenne, and all round de montaignes he hont dam sight."

"But, Antoine, what became of him at last? and why did he not come home, when he made so many dollars?" asked poor Mary.

"Enfant de garce, mais pourquoi he come home? Pe gar, de montaigne-man, he love the montaigne and prairie more better dan he love de grandes villes—meme de Saint Louis ou de Montreal. Wagh! La Bonte, well, he one montaigne-man, wagh! He love de buffaloe and de chevreaux plus que de bœuf and de mouton, may be. Mais on-dit dat he have autre raison—dat de gal he lofe in Missouri not lofe him, and for dis he not go back. Mais now he go ondare, m' on dit. He vas go to de Californe, may be to steal de hos and de mule—pe gar, and de Espagnols rub him out, and take his hair, so he mort."

"But are you sure of this?" she asked, trembling with grief.

"Ah, now, j'ne suis pas sur, mais I tink you know dis La Bonte. Enfant de garce, maybe you de gal in Missouri he lofe, and not lofe him. Pe gar! 'fant de garce! fort beau garçon dis La Bonte, pourquoi you ne l'aimez pas? Maybe he not gone ondar. Maybe he turn op, autrefois. De trappares, dey go ondar tree, four, ten times, mais dey turn op twenty time. De sauvage not able for kill La Bonte, ni de dam Espagnols. Ah, non! ne craignez pas; pe gar, he not gone ondare encore."

Spite of the good-natured attempts of the Canadian, poor Mary burst into a flood of tears; not that the information took her unawares, for she had long believed him dead; but because the very mention of his name awoke the strongest feelings within her breast, and taught her how deep was the affection she had felt for him whose loss and violent fate she now bewailed.

As the wagons of the lone caravan roll on towards the Platte, we return to the camp where La Bonte, Killbuck, and the stranger, were sitting before the fire when last we saw them: Killbuck loquitur.

"The doins of them Mormon fools can't be beat by Spaniards, stranger. Their mummums and thummums you speak of won't 'shine' whar Injuns are about; nor pint out a trail, whar nothin crossed but rattlesnakes since fust it snow'd on old Pike's Peak. If they pack along them *profits*, as you tell of, who can make it rain hump-ribs and marrow-guts when the crowd gets out of the buffler range, they are 'some,' now, that's a fact. But this child don't believe it. I'd laugh to get a sight of these darned Mormonites, I would. They're 'no account,' I guess; and it's the 'meanest' kind of action to haul their women critters and their young 'uns to sech a starving country as the Californys."

"They are not all Mormons in the crowd," said the strange hunter; "and there's one family among them with some smartish boys and girls, I tell you. Their name's Brand."

La Bonte looked up from the lock of his rifle, which he was cleaning—but either didn't hear, or, hearing, didn't heed, for he continued his work.

"And they are going to part company," continued the stranger, "and put out alone for Platte and the South Pass."

"They'll lose their hair, I'm thinking," said Killbuck, "if the Rapahos are out thar."

"I hope not," continued the other, "for there's a girl among them worth more than that."

"Poor beaver!" said La Bonte, looking up from his work. "I'd hate to see any white gal in the hands of Injuns, and of Rapahos worse than all. Where does she come from, stranger?"

"Down below St. Louis, from Tennessee, I've heard them say."

"Tennessee," cried La Bonte—"hurrah for the old State! What's her name, stran—" At this moment Killbuck's old mule pricked her ears and snuffed the air, which action catching La Bonte's eye, he rose abruptly, without waiting a reply to his question, and exclaimed, "The old mule smells Injuns, or I'm a Spaniard!"

The hunter did the old mule justice, and she well maintained her reputation as the best "guard," in the mountain; for in two minutes an Indian stalked into the camp, dressed in a cloth capote, and in odds and ends of civilized attire.

"Rapaho," cried Killbuck, as soon as he saw him; and the Indian catching the word, struck his hand upon his breast, and exclaimed, in broken Spanish and English mixed, "Si, si, me Arapaho, white man amigo. Come from Pueblo—hunt cibola—me gun break—*no puedo matar nada: mucha hambre* (very hungry)—heap eat."

Killbuck offered his pipe to the Indian, and spoke to him in his own language, which both he and La Bonte well understood. They learned that he was married to a Mexican woman, and lived with some hunters at the Pueblo fort on the Arkansas. He volunteered the information that a war party of his people were out on the Platte trail to intercept the Indian traders on their return from the North Fork; and as some "Mormons" had just started in that direction, he said his people would make a "raise." Being muy amigo himself to the whites, he cautioned his present companions from crossing to the "divide," as the "braves," he said, were a "heap" mad, and their hearts were "big," and nothing in the shape of white skin would live before them.

"Wagh!" exclaimed Killbuck, "the Rapahos know me, I'm thinking; and small gain they've made against this child. I've knowed the time when my gun-cover couldn't hold more of their scalps."

The Indian was provided with some powder, of which he stood in need; and, after gorging as much meat as his capacious stomach would hold, he left the camp, and started into the mountain.

The next day our hunters started on their journey down the river, travelling leisurely, and stopping whenever good grass presented itself. One morning they suddenly struck a wheel trail, which left the creek banks and pursued a course at right angles to it, in the direction of the "divide." Killbuck pronounced it but a few hours old, and that of three wagons drawn by oxen.

"Wagh!" he exclaimed, "if them poor devils of Mormonites ain't going head first into the Rapaho trap, they'll be 'gone beaver' afore long."

"Ay," said the strange hunter, "these are the wagons belonging to old Brand, and he has started alone for Laramie. I hope nothing will happen to them."

"Brand!" muttered La Bonte. "I knowed that name mighty well once, years ago: and should hate the worst kind that mischief happened to any one who bore it. This trail's as fresh as paint; and it goes against me to let these simple critters help the Rapahos to their own hair. This child feels like helping 'em out of the scrape. What do you say, old hos?"

"I thinks with you, boy," answered Killbuck, "and go in for following this wagon trail, and telling the poor critters that thar's danger ahead of them. What's your talk, stranger?"

"I go with you," shortly answered the latter; and both followed after La Bonte, who was already trotting smartly on the trail.

Meanwhile the three wagons, containing the household goods of the Brand family, rumbled slowly over the rolling prairie, and toward the upland ridge of the "divide," which, studded with dwarf pine and cedar thicket, rose gradually before them. They travelled with considerable caution, for already the quick eye of Antoine had discovered recent Indian sign upon the trail, and, with mountain quickness, had at once made it out to be that of a war party; for there were no horses with them, and after one or two of the moccasin tracks, the mark of a rope which trailed upon the ground was sufficient to show him that the Indians were provided with the usual lasso of skin, with which to secure the horses stolen in the expedition. The men of the party were consequently all mounted and thoroughly armed, the wagons moved in a line abreast, and a sharp look-out was kept on all sides. The women and children were all consigned to the interior of the wagons; and the latter had also guns in readiness, to take their part in the defence, should an attack be made.

However, they had seen no Indians, and no fresh sign, for two days after they had left the Boiling Spring River, and they began to think they were well out of their neighborhood. One evening they camped on a creek called Black Horse, and, as usual, had corralled the wagons, and forted as well as circumstances would permit, when three or four Indians suddenly appeared on a bluff at a little distance, and, making signals of peaceable intentions, approached the camp. Most of the men were absent at the time, attending to the cattle or collecting fuel, and only old Brand and one of his young grandchildren, about fourteen years old, remained in camp. The Indians were hospitably received, and regaled with a smoke, after which they began to evince their curiosity by examining every article lying about, and signifying their wishes that it should be given to them. Finding their hints were not taken, they laid hold of several things which took their fancies, and, among others, of the pot which was boiling on the fire, and with which one of them was about very coolly to walk off, when old Brand, who up to this moment had retained possession of his temper, seized it out of the Indian's hand, and knocked him down. One of the others instantly began to draw the buckskin cover from his gun, and would no doubt have taken summary vengeance for the insult offered to his companion, when Mary Brand courageously stepped up to him, and, placing her left hand upon the gun which he was in the act of uncovering, with the other pointed a pistol at his breast.

Whether daunted by the bold act of the girl, or admiring her devotion to her father, the Indian drew himself back, exclaimed "Howgh!" and drew the cover again on his piece, went up to old Brand, who was all this time looking him sternly in the face, and, shaking him by the hand, motioned at the same time to the others to be peaceable.

The other whites presently coming into camp, the Indians sat quietly down by the fire, and, when the supper was ready, joined in the repast, after which they gathered their buffalo robes about them, and quietly withdrew. Meanwhile Antoine, knowing the treacherous character of the savages, advised that the greatest precaution should be taken to secure the stock; and before dark, therefore all the mules and horses were hobbled and secured within the corral, the oxen being allowed to feed at liberty—for the Indians scarcely care to trouble themselves with such cattle. A guard was also set the camp, and relieved every two hours; the fire was extinguished, lest the savages should aim, by its light, at any of the party, and all slept with rifles ready at their sides. However, the night passed quietly, and nothing disturbed the tranquillity of the camp. The prairie wolves loped hungrily around, and their mournful cry was borne upon the wind as they chased deer and antelope on the neighboring plain; but not a sign of lurking Indians was seen or heard.

In the morning, shortly after sunrise, they were in the act of yoking the oxen to the wagons, and driving in the loose animals which had been turned out to feed at daybreak, when some Indians again appeared on the bluff, and, descending it, confidently approached the camp. Antoine strongly advised their not being allowed to enter; but Brand, ignorant of Indian treachery, replied that, so long as they came as friends, they could not be deemed enemies, and allowed no obstruction to be offered to their approach. It was now observed that they were all painted, armed with bows and arrows, and divested of their buffalo robes, appearing naked to the breech-clout, their legs only being protected by deerskin leggings, reaching to the middle of the thigh. Six or seven first arrived, and others quickly followed, dropping in one after the other, until a score or more were collected round the wagons. Their demeanor, at first friendly, soon changed as their numbers increased, and they now became urgent in their demands for powder and lead, and bullying in their manner. A chief accosted Brand, and, through Antoine, informed him "that, unless the demand of his braves were acceded to, he could not be responsible for the consequences; that they were out on the 'war-trail,' and their eyes were red with blood, so that they could not distinguish between white and Yuta scalps; that the party, with all their women and wagons, were in the power of the Indian 'braves,' and therefore the white chief's best plan was to make the best terms he could;

that all they required was that they should give up their guns and ammunition 'on the prairie,' and all their mules and horses—retaining the 'medicine' buffaloes (the oxen) to draw their wagons."

By this time the oxen were yoked, and the teamsters, whip in hand, only waited the word to start. Old Brand foamed while the Indian stated his demands, but, hearing him to the end, exclaimed, "Darn the red devil! I wouldn't give him a grain of powder to save my life. Put out, boys!"— and, turning to his horse, which stood ready saddled, was about to mount, when the Indians sprang at once upon the wagons, and commenced the attack, yelling like fiends.

One jumped upon Old Brand, pulled him back as he was rising in the stirrup, and drew his bow upon him at the same moment. In an instant the old backwoodsman pulled a pistol from his belt, and, putting the muzzle to the Indian's heart, shot him dead. Another Indian, flourishing his war-club, laid the old man at his feet; while some dragged the women from the wagons, and others rushed upon the men, who made brave fight in their defence.

Mary, when she saw her father struck to the ground, sprang with a shrill cry to his assistance; for at that moment a savage, frightful as red paint could make him, was standing over his prostrate body, brandishing a glittering knife in the air, preparatory to thrusting it into the old man's breast. For the rest, all was confusion: in vain the small party of whites struggled against overpowering numbers. Their rifles cracked but once, and they were quickly disarmed; while the shrieks of the women and children, and the loud yells of the Indians, added to the scene of horror and confusion. As Mary flew to her father's side, an Indian threw his lasso at her, the noose falling over her shoulders, and jerking it tight, he uttered a delighted yell as the poor girl was thrown back violently to the ground. As she fell, another deliberately shot an arrow at her body, while the one who had thrown the lasso rushed forward, his scalping-knife flashing in his hand, to seize the bloody trophy of his savage deed. The girl rose to her knees, and looked wildly toward the spot where her father lay bathed in blood; but the Indian pulled the rope violently, dragged her some yards upon the ground, and then rushed with a yell of vengeance upon his victim. He paused, however, as at that moment a shout as fierce as his own sounded at his very ear; and looking up he saw La Bonte galloping madly down the bluff, his long hair and the fringes of his hunting-shirt and leggings flying in the wind, his right arm supporting his trusty rifle, while close behind him came Killbuck and the stranger. Dashing with loud hurrahs to the scene of action, La Bonte, as he charged down the bluff, caught sight of the girl struggling in the hands of the ferocious Indian. Loud was the war-shout of the mountaineer, as he struck his heavy spurs to the rowels in the horse's side, and bounded like lightning to the rescue. In a single stride he was upon the Indian, and thrusting the muzzle of his rifle into his very breast, he pulled the trigger, driving the savage backward by the blow itself, at the same moment that the bullet passed through his heart, and tumbled him over stone-dead.

Throwing down his rifle, La Bonte wheeled his obedient horse, and drawing a pistol from his belt, again charged the enemy, among whom Killbuck and the stranger were dealing death-giving blows. Yelling for victory, the mountaineers rushed at the Indians; and they panic-struck at the sudden attack, and thinking this was but the advanced guard of a large band, fairly turned and fled, leaving five of their number dead upon the field.

Mary, shutting her eyes to the expected death-stroke, heard the loud shout La Bonte gave in charging down the bluff, and, again looking up, saw the wild-looking mountaineer rush to her rescue, and save her from the savage by his timely blow. Her arms were still pinned by the lasso, which prevented her from rising to her feet; and La Bonte was the first to run to aid her, as soon as the fight was fairly over. He jumped from his horse, cut the skin-rope which bound her, raised her from the ground, and, upon her turning up her face to thank him, beheld his never-to-be-forgotten Mary Bland; while she, hardly believing her senses, recognised in her deliverer her former lover, and still beloved La Bonte.

"What, Mary, can it be you!" he asked, looking intently upon the trembling woman.

"La Bonte, you don't forget me!" she answered, and threw herself sobbing into the arms of the sturdy mountaineer.

There we will leave them for the present, and help Killbuck and his five companions to examine the killed and wounded. Of the former five Indians and two whites lay dead, grandchildren of old Brand, fine lads of fourteen or fifteen, who had fought with the greatest bravery, and lay pierced with arrow and lance wounds. Old Brand had received a sore buffet, but a hatful of cold water from the creek sprinkled over his face soon restored him. His sons had not escaped scot-free, and Antoine was shot through the neck, and falling, had actually been half scalped by an Indian, whom the timely arrival of La Bonte had caused to leave his work unfinished.

Silently, and with sad hearts, the survivors of the family, saw the bodies of the two boys buried on the river bank, and the spot marked with a pile of loose stones, procured from the rocky bed of the creek. The carcasses of the treacherous Indians were left to be devoured by wolves, and their bones to bleach in the sun and wind—a warning to their tribe, that such foul treachery as they had meditated had met with a merited retribution.

The next day the party continued their course to the Platte. Antoine and the stranger returned to the Arkansas, starting in the night to avoid the Indians; but Killbuck and La Bonte lent the aid of their rifles to the solitary caravan, and, under their experienced guidance, no more Indian perils were encountered. Mary no longer sat perched up in her father's Conostoga, but rode a quiet mustang by La Bonte's side; and no doubt they found a theme with which to while away the monotonous journey over the dreary plains. South Fork was passed and Laramie was reached. The Sweet Water Mountains, which hang over the "pass" to California, were long since in sight; but when the waters of the North Fork of Platte lay before their horses' feet, and the broad trail was pointed out which led to the great valley of Columbia and their promised land, the heads of the oxen were turned *down* the stream where the shallow waters flow on to join the great Missouri—and not *up*, toward the mountains where they leave their spring-heads, from which spring flow several waters—some coursing their way to the eastward, fertilizing, in their route to the Atlantic, the lands of civilized man; others westward forcing a passage through rocky canons, and flowing through a barren wilderness, inhabited by fierce and barbarous tribes.

These were the routes to choose from: and, whatever was the cause the oxen turned their yoked heads away from the rugged mountains; the teamsters joyfully cracked their ponderous whips, as the wagons rolled lightly down the Platte; and men, women, and children, waved their hats and bonnets in the air, and cried out lustily, "Hurrah for home!"

La Bonte and his faithful Mary were married soon afterwards. La Bonte gave up his wandering life, and settled in Tennessee.

MRS. DORION

THE PACIFIC FUR COMPANY, founded by John Jacob Astor, of New York, in 1810, met with extraordinary difficulties in carrying on its trading operations in the wilderness of Oregon. The country and its inhabitants were almost entirely unknown. When exploring parties started from Astoria, they found that they had to proceed through regions where the greatest privations were to be endured; and the Indians displayed the most determined hostility. To add to the misfortunes of the adventurers, war broke out between Great Britain and the United States, and the Hudson's Bay Company took possession of Astoria.

Early in the summer of 1813, a party of traders, under the command of a Mr. Reed, and accompanied by Pierre Dorion, an interpreter, with his wife and two children, started on an expedition into the Snake country. Nothing more was heard of them until April of the next year, when Mrs. Dorion, accompanied by a few friendly Indians, arrived at Walla Walla. This unfortunate woman told a story of hardships, borne with a fortitude, and surmounted with a resolution, to which we can find no parallel in the annals of female heroism. We give her narrative in her own simple and touching words:

"About the middle of August we reached the Great Snake River, and soon afterwards, following up a branch to the right hand, where there were plenty of beaver, we encamped; and there Mr. Reed built a house to winter in. After the house was built, the people spent their time in trapping beaver. About the latter end of September, Hoback, Robinson, and Rezner came to us; but they were very poor, the Indians having robbed them of every thing they had about fifteen days before. Mr. Reed gave them some clothing and traps, and they went to hunt with my husband. Landrie got a fall from his horse, lingered a while, and died of it. Delaunay was killed, when trapping: my husband told me that he saw his scalp with the Indians, and knew it from the color of the hair. The Indians about the place were very friendly to us; but when strange tribes visited us, they were troublesome, and always asked Mr. Reed for guns and ammunition: on one occasion, they drove an arrow into one of the horses, and took a capot from La Chapelle. Mr. Reed not liking the place where we first built, we left it, and built farther up the river, on the other side. After the second house was built, the people went to trap as usual, sometimes coming home every night, sometimes sleeping out for several nights together at a time. Mr. Reed and one man generally stayed at the house.

"Late one evening, about the 10th of January, a friendly Indian came running to our house, in a great fright, and told Mr. Reed that a band of the bad Snakes called the Dog-rib tribe, had burnt the first house that we had built, and that they were coming on whooping and singing the war-song. After communicating this intelligence, the Indian went off immediately, and I took up my two children, got upon a horse, and set off to where my husband was trapping; but the night was dark, the road bad, and I lost my way. The next day being cold and stormy, I did not stir. On the second day, however, I set out again; but seeing a large smoke in the direction I had to go, and thinking it might proceed from Indians, I got into the bushes again and hid myself. On the third day, late in the evening, I got in sight of the hut, where my husband and the other men were hunting; but just as I was approaching the place, I observed a man coming from the opposite side, and staggering as if unwell: I stopped where I was till he came to me. Le Clerc, wounded and faint from loss of blood, was the man. He told me that La Chapelle, Rezner, and my husband had been robbed and murdered that morning. I did not go into the hut; but putting Le Clerc and one of my children on the horse I had with me, I turned round immediately, took to the woods, and I retraced my steps back again to Mr. Reed's; Le Clerc, however, could not bear the jolting of the horse, and he fell once or twice, so that we had to remain for nearly a day in one place; but in the night he died, and I covered him over with brushwood and snow, put my children on the horse, I myself walking and leading the animal by the halter. The second day I got back again to the house. But sad was the sight! Mr. Reed and the men were all murdered, scalped, and cut to pieces. Desolation and horror stared me in the face. I turned from the shocking sight in agony and despair; took to the woods with my children and horse, and passed the cold and lonely night without food or fire. I was now at a loss what to do: the snow was deep, the weather cold, and we had nothing to eat. To undertake a long journey under such circumstances was inevitable death. Had I been alone I would have run all risks and proceeded; but the thought of my children perishing with hunger distracted me. At this moment a sad alternative crossed my mind; should I venture to the house among the dead to seek food for the living? I knew there was a good stock of fish there; but it might have been destroyed or carried off by the murderers; and, besides, they might be still lurking about and see me; yet I thought of my children. Next morning, after a sleepless night, I wrapped my children in my robe, tied my horse in a thicket, and then went to a rising ground, that overlooked the house, to see if I could observe any thing stirring about the place. I saw nothing; and, hard as the task was, I resolved to venture after dark; so I returned back to my children, and found them nearly frozen, and I was afraid to make a fire in the day time lest the smoke might be seen; yet I had no other alternative, I must make a fire or let my children perish. I made a fire and warmed them. I then rolled them up again in the robe, extinguished the fire, and set off after dark to the house; went into the store and ransacked every hole and corner, and at last found plenty of fish scattered about. I gathered, hid, and slung upon my back as much as I could carry, and returned again before dawn of day to my children. They were nearly frozen, and weak with hunger. I made a fire and warmed them, and then we shared the first food we had tasted for the last three days. Next night I went back again, and carried off another load; but when these efforts were over, I sank under the sense of my afflictions, and was for three days unable to move, and without hope. On recovering a little, however, I packed all up, loaded my horse, and putting my children on the top of the load, set out again on foot, leading the horse by the halter as before. In this sad and hopeless condition I travelled through deep snow among the woods, rocks, and rugged paths for nine days, till I and the horse could travel no more.

"Here I selected a lonely spot at the foot of a rocky precipice, in the Blue Mountains, intending there to pass the remainder of the winter. I killed my horse, and hung up the flesh on a tree for my winter food. I built a small hut with pine branches, long grass, and moss, and packed it all round with snow to keep us warm, and this was a difficult task, for I had no axe, but only a knife to cut wood. In this solitary dwelling I passed fifty-three lonely days! I then left my hut and set out with my children to cross the mountains; but I became snow blind the second day, and had to remain for three days without advancing a step; and this was unfortunate, as our provisions were almost exhausted. Having recovered my sight a little, I set out again, and got clear off the mountains, and down to the plains on the fifteenth day after leaving my winter encampment; but for six days we had scarcely any thing to eat, and for the last two days not a mouthful. Soon after we had reached the plains I perceived smoke at a distance; but being unable to carry my children farther, I wrapped them up in my robe, left them concealed, and set out alone in hopes of reaching the Indian camp, where I had seen the smoke; but I was so weak that I could hardly crawl, and had to sleep on the way. Next day, at noon, I got to the camp. It proved to belong to the Walla Wallas, and I was kindly treated by them. Immediately on my arrival the Indians set off in search of my children, and brought them to the camp the same night. Here we staid for two days, and then moved on to the river, expecting to hear something of the white people on their way either up or down."

The poor woman was well provided for by the whites at Walla Walla; but it was a long time before she recovered from the suffering and exertion of her extraordinary journey. It will be observed that in her narrative, Mrs. Dorion mentions that on several occasions she was about to yield to despair, to resign herself to her fate, and perish without further struggles. But the feelings of the mother interfered. Her children's lives were at stake, and she could not look on quietly and see them freeze or starve. She lived and struggled for their salvation, and God willed that she should be successful.

WONDERFUL FORTITUDE OF
FEMALE EMIGRANTS

IN MANY CASES, where the "weaker" sex are brought in direct rivalry of endurance with their sterner companions, they prove that they are at least equal; and when the difference of habit and occupation are taken into consideration, we are compelled to award the fresher laurels to woman.

In the summer and autumn of 1846, a party of California emigrants met with a series of disasters never before experienced by adventurers upon the western plains, and of a nature so terrible that the bare recital is painful. The party consisted of J. F. Reed, wife, and four children; Jacob Donner, wife, and seven children; William Pike, wife, and two children; William Foster, wife, and one child; Lewis Kiesburg, wife, and one child; Mrs. Murphy, a widow woman, and five children; William M'Cutchen, wife, and one child; W. H. Eddy, wife, and two children; W. Graves, wife, and eight children; Jay Fosdicks and his wife; Noah James, Patrick Dolan, Samuel Shoemaker, John Denton, C. F. Stanton, Milton Elliot, ——— Smith, Joseph Rianhard, Augustus Spizer, John Baptiste, ——— Antoine, ——— Herring, ——— Hallerin, Charles Burger, and Baylis Williams. The party was well supplied with wagons, teams, cattle, provision, arms, and ammunition.

At the camp, on the Sweet Water river, on the eastern side of the Rocky Mountains, the party was induced by the representations of one Lansford W. Hastings, to take a new route to California, and they started through an unknown region, full of hope, and of a speedy journey. But they found great difficulty in proceeding, even before they came to the Utah valley. One part of the road had to be cut through a wood, and the emigrants were occupied thirty days in travelling forty miles. On the 1st day of September, they pursued their journey around the south side of the Great Salt Lake, and through a beautiful valley, since occupied by the Mormons. There they were detained a short time, by the death of Mr. Hallerin, and an accident to a wagon. Soon after resuming their journey, the party was compelled to travel two days without finding grass or water, and many of their cattle died from exhaustion. After this perilous drive, gloomy forebodings seized upon the stoutest hearts among the emigrants.

Many families were completely ruined. They were yet in a country of hostile Indians, far from all succor, betrayed by one of their own countrymen. They could not tell what was the character of the road yet before them, since the man in whose veracity they reposed confidence, had proved himself so utterly unworthy of it. To retreat across the desert to Bridger was impossible. There was no way left to them, but to advance; and this they now regarded as perilous in the extreme. The cattle that survived were exhausted and broken down; but to remain there was to die. Feeble and dispirited, therefore, they slowly resumed their journey.

On this drive thirty-six head of working cattle were lost, and the oxen that survived were greatly injured. One of Mr. Reed's wagons was brought to camp; and two, with all they contained, were buried in the plain. George Donner lost one wagon. Kiesburg also lost a wagon. The atmosphere was so dry upon the plain, that the wood-work of all the wagons shrank to a degree that made it next to impossible to get any of them through.

Having yoked some loose cows, as a team for Mr. Reed, they broke up their camp on the morning of September 16th, and resumed their toilsome journey, with feelings which can be appreciated by those only who have travelled the road under somewhat similar circumstances. On this day they travelled six miles, encountering a very severe snow storm. About three o'clock, P.M., they met Milton Elliot and William Graves, returning from a fruitless effort to find some cattle that had got off. They informed them that they were in the immediate vicinity of a spring, at which commenced another dry drive of forty miles. They encamped for the night, and at dawn of day of September 17th, they resumed their journey, and at four o'clock, A.M., of the 18th, they arrived at water and grass, some of their cattle having perished, and the teams which survived being in a very enfeebled condition. Here the most of the little property which Mr. Reed still had, was buried, or *cached*, together with that of others. Here, Mr. Eddy proposed putting his team to Mr. Reed's wagon, and letting Mr. Pike have his wagon, so that the three families could be taken on. This was done. They remained in camp during the day of the 18th to complete these arrangements, and to recruit their exhausted cattle.

The journey was continued with scarcely any interruption or accident, until the 1st of October, when some Indians stole a yoke of oxen from Mr. Graves. Other thefts followed, and it became evident that the party would suffer severely, from the hostility of the Indians. The women were kept in continual alarm by the proximity of the savages, and the prospects of their depredations. A large number of cattle were stolen or shot by these merciless marauders.

On the morning of October 12th, the emigrants resumed their journey. One of Mr. Eddy's oxen gave out during the day, and they left him. At twelve o'clock at night they encamped at the sinks of Ogden's river. At daylight on the morning of the 13th they drove their cattle to grass, and put them under a guard. The guard came in to breakfast, and in their absence the Indians killed twenty-one head, including the whole of Mr. Eddy's team, except one ox; the whole of Wolfinger's, except one. Wolfinger wished to *cache* his goods at the sinks, but the company refused to wait. Rianhard and Spitzer, who was travelling with him, remained behind to assist him. Three days afterward the two former came up to the company at Truckee river, and said that the Indians came down from the hills upon them, and after killing Wolfinger, drove them from the wagons, which they burned, after taking the goods out.

Here Mr. Eddy *cached* every thing he had, except the clothing which he and his family had on. On this morning they partook of their last remaining mouthful of food. The Indians were upon the adjacent hills, looking down upon them, and absolutely laughing at their calamity. The lock of Mr. Eddy's rifle had been broken some days before, and the gun left. He could not obtain one, and had he been able to do so, it would have been worse than insanity for him to have encountered the Indians alone. Dejected and sullen, he took up about three pounds of loaf sugar, put some bullets in his pocket, and stringing his powder-horn upon his shoulders, took up his boy in his arms, while his afflicted Eleanor carried their still more helpless infant, and in this most miserable and forlorn plight, they set out once more on foot to make their way through the pitiless wilderness. Trackless, snow-clad mountains intercepted their progress, and seemed to present an impassable barrier to all human succor:—mountains, the passage of which, with even the accessories of emigrant wagons, and in the most pleasant season, would have been a feat of no small difficulty. Without shoes—these having been worn out by the jagged rocks—they had nothing to protect their feet but moccasins, which were also so much worn as to be of little service. Their painful and perilous way led over broken rocks, presenting acute angles, or prickly pears, which alike lacerated their feet in the most dreadful manner. Nature disputed their passage, and Heaven seemed to be offended. They struggled on, however, with their precious charge, without food or water, until 4 o'clock on the morning of the 14th, when they arrived at a spring that jetted up a column of boiling hot water, about twenty feet high. It was situated in a region that had been rent into millions of fragments by volcanic fires. The desolation was such as to impress upon the mind the idea of expiring nature convulsed with the throes and agonies of the last great and terrible day, or of an angry Deity having taken vengeance on a guilty world. Having obtained some coffee from Mrs. Donner, Mr. Eddy put it into a pot, and thus boiled it in the hot spring for the nourishment of his wife and children, refusing to partake of it himself.

About nine o'clock the party left the Geyser Spring and travelled all that day until sunset, over a road in no respect different from that of the 13th. At this time Mr. Eddy's little children were in great danger of perishing for the want of water. He applied to Patrick Brinn, who he knew had ten gallons, for a half pint to give to them. Brinn denied having any; but this Mr. Eddy knew to be untrue, for he had himself filled Brinn's cask at the sinks of Ogden's river; Brinn finally admitted that he had water, but he said he did not know how far water was yet distant from them, and he feared his own family would require it. Mr. Eddy told him with an energy he never before felt, that he would have it or have Brinn's life. He immediately turned away from Brinn, and went in quest of the water and gave some to his children.

At sunset they arrived at an exceedingly difficult sand-ridge of ten miles in width. They crossed it about four o'clock on the morning of the 15th, the company losing three yoke of cattle that died from fatigue.

Neither Mr. Eddy nor his wife had tasted food for two days and nights, nor had the children any thing except the sugar with which he left the sinks at Ogden's river. He applied to Mrs. Graves and Mrs. Brinn for a small piece of meat for his wife and children, who were very faint. They both refused. The emigrants remained in camp to rest the cattle. The Indians killed some of them during the day.

Mr. Eddy procured a gun in the morning, and started to kill some geese which he heard. In about two hours he returned with nine very fat ones. Mrs. Brinn and Mrs. Graves congratulated him, and expressed the opinion that they were very fine, and wondered what he would do with them. He invited them to help themselves, and they each took two. He gave Kiesburg one.

October 16th, early in the morning, they resumed their journey, and commenced driving up Truckee river. Nothing of importance occurred until October 19th, about ten o'clock, A.M., when they met Mr. C. F. Stanton and two Indian *vaqueros* (cow-herds) of Captain Sutter, one named Lewis, and the other Salvadore. Mr. Stanton had flour and a little dried meat, which he had procured for them.

William Pike was killed by the accidental discharge of a six-shooter in the hands of William Foster. He died in one hour: he was shot through in the back.

On the evening of October 22d, they crossed the Truckee river, the forty-ninth and last time, in eighty miles. They encamped on the top of a hill. Here nineteen oxen were shot by an Indian, who put one arrow in each ox. The cattle did not die. Mr. Eddy caught him in the act, and fired upon him as he fled. The ball struck him between the shoulders, and came out at the breast. At the crack of the rifle he sprung up about three feet, and with a terrible yell fell down a bank into a bunch of willows.

On the morning of October 23d they resumed their journey, and continued travelling without any thing of importance occurring until October 28th at dark, when they encamped upon Truckee Lake, situated at the foot of Fremont's Pass of the main chain of the Sierra Nevada. The Pass is here nine thousand eight hundred and thirty eight feet high.

On the morning of October the 29th, they again continued their journey, and went on within three miles of the top of the Pass, where they found the snow about five feet deep. This compelled them to return to a cabin, which was situated one mile in advance of their camp of the previous night. Here they remained in camp during the 30th. At dark their fellow-travellers, Stanton, Graves, the Donners and some others, came up. On the morning of October 31st the whole body again started to cross the mountain. They succeeded in getting within three miles of the top of the Pass. The snow had deepened to about ten feet. The night was bitterly cold; the wind howled through the trees, and the snow and hail descended. Finding it utterly impossible to cross, they commenced retracing their steps on the morning of November 1st, and arrived at the cabin about four o'clock.*

The emigrants now saw that they would be compelled to winter where they were, and they set to work to build cabins and collect provisions. On the 12th of November, a party, headed by Mr. Eddy, started to cross the mountains on foot, and obtain relief for the families left behind. The parting between the husbands and wives was affecting, for neither knew but that it would be final. But the snow was found to be so deep upon the mountains, that the party could not proceed, and it returned to the camp. Mr. Eddy now succeeded in killing a grizzly bear and some game, but starvation began to stare the emigrants in the face.

On the 21st of November, six women and sixteen men, including Stanton and two Indians, made another effort to cross the mountains on foot. They reached the western side of the mountain, but there Stanton refused to proceed, in consequence of not being able to get along with seven mules belonging to Captain Sutter. Mr. Eddy argued and threatened in vain; and the party was once more compelled to return to camp. A violent snow storm now set in, and it became exceedingly difficult for the emigrants to obtain wood, to protect themselves against the severity of the weather. The sufferings of the women were intense, but, according to the testimony of the survivors of this trying time, they bore it with extraordinary fortitude. The snow continued to fall until the 5th of December, and, when the clouds broke away, the emigrants found it eight feet deep. The sunshine, however, cheered them somewhat and some of the party manufactured snow-shoes to make another attempt at crossing the mountains. On the 11th, the snow again descended, and

---

* "Oregon and California," by Thornton.

the hearts of the emigrants died within them. On the 14th, Baylis Williams died of starvation. Several others of the party seemed about to meet the same fate.

On the 16th of December, the following persons started on snow-shoes to cross the mountains: Sarah Fosdick, Mary Graves, William Foster, Sarah Foster, C. F. Stanton, William Graves, Jay Fosdick, William Murphy, Patrick Dolan, Antoine, Lewis, Salvadore, Charles Burger, Harriet Pike, Lemuel Murphy, Mrs. M'Cutchen, and William Eddy. The parting between Eddy and his wife has been described by the husband as agonizing in the extreme. In the early part of the journey, two men, William Murphy and Charles Burger, were compelled by weakness to turn back.

The others pressed on, and, on the third day, they encamped on the west side of the Sierra Nevada. On the 22d of December, they consumed the last of their little stock of provisions. The next day, Mr. Eddy, while examining a bag for the purpose of throwing out something, to enable him to get along with more ease, found about half a pound of bear's meat, to which was attached a paper, on which his wife had written a note, signed, "Your own dear Eleanor," in which she requested him to save it for the last extremity, and expressed the opinion that it would be the means of saving his life. The self-sacrifice involved in the little present can scarcely be conceived by those who are enjoying plenty. While the wife knew that every morsel of food she had would be necessary to sustain her and her children, until the return of the party, she had voluntary yielded a portion in the hope that her husband might be saved. She was ready to die that he might live.

Mr. Stanton fell behind and perished soon after provisions failed. On Christmas day, the snow falling fast, the party held a council, for the purpose of determining whether to proceed. All the men but Mr. Eddy, refused to go forward. The *women* and Mr. Eddy declared they would go through or perish. It was now proposed that one person should be sacrificed to furnish food for the rest. This met with a determined opposition, and the miserable travellers continued to plod on for a few miles. They then encamped; but the wind prevented them having a fire. That night, Antoine, Mr. Graves, and Patrick Dolan, perished of hunger and cold, and Lemuel Murphy became deranged. Mr. Eddy, retaining his resources of mind, devised various ways of keeping the rest of the party alive. A fire was now built. Portions of the body of Patrick Dolan were eaten by the famished travellers, except Mr. Eddy. Lemuel Murphy died. Never were more horrors concentrated upon one spot than was witnessed at that "Camp of Death." The women, singularly enough, endured their privation with a fortitude that called forth the admiration of Mr. Eddy.

On the 29th of December, the party left the "Camp of Death," and marched slowly onward. Their Indian guides declared that they had lost the way, but they still moved forward. All their provisions were now consumed. On the morning of the 4th of January, 1847, Mr. Eddy, seeing that all would soon perish, unless food was quickly obtained, resolved to take the gun, and press forward alone. He informed the party of his purpose. The women besought him not to leave them. Mary Graves, who had more strength than the other women, resolved that she would go with him or perish. The two set forward. Soon afterwards, Eddy had the great good fortune to shoot a deer, and that night the couple made a meal upon the entrails of the animal. The next day, the rest of the party, with the exception of Jay Fosdick, who had perished during the preceding night, were relieved. The emigrants, somewhat refreshed, then pursued their journey. The Indians, Lewis and Salvadore, being threatened with death at the hands of the famished party, had, some days before, stolen away—so that there now remained five women, Mary Graves, Mrs. Pike, Mrs. M'Cutchen, Mrs. Foster, and Mrs. Fosdick, in charge of Mr. Eddy and Mr. Foster. Foster was weak, and, at times, insane; so that Mr. Eddy alone, was able to guide the females.

After the body of the deer had been consumed, the party fell upon the tracks of the two Indians. Foster overtook and killed them both. The flesh was then cut from their bones and dried. On the 10th of January, when the emigrants were almost exhausted, and even Mr. Eddy was beginning to despair, they arrived at an Indian village, where they were hospitably received and their immediate wants satisfied. The Indians accompanied them to the house of Colonel M. D. Richey, where better fare was provided than the poor Indians possessed. Mr. Eddy was immediately put to bed, being completely exhausted by the privations of his awful journey.

The government of California being informed of the imminent peril of the emigrants in the mountain camp, took measures to send out relief;

and a number of inhabitants contributed articles of clothing and provisions. Two expeditions, however, failed to cross the mountains in consequence of the depth of the snow. At length, a party of seven men, headed by Aquilla Glover and accompanied by Mr. Eddy, who, though weak, insisted on returning to ascertain the fate of his beloved wife and children, succeeded in crossing the mountains and reaching the camp. What they found there is best described by Judge Thornton, from whose graphic account of this disastrous expedition we have condensed the above.

They arrived at The Mountain Camp as the last rays of the setting sun were departing from the tops of the mountains. Every thing was as silent as the grave. A painful stillness pervaded the scene. Upon some of the party raising a shout, for the purpose of finding their cabins, by attracting the attention of the living—if, indeed, any did live—the sufferers were seen coming out of the snow-holes, from the cabins, which were completely covered, the snow presenting one unbroken level. They tottered toward their deliverers, manifesting a delirium of joy, and acting in the wildest and most extravagant manner. Some wept; some laughed. All inquired, "Have you brought any thing for me?" Many of them had a peculiarly wild expression of the eye; all looked haggard, ghastly, and horrible. The flesh was wasted from their bodies, and the skin seemed to have dried upon their bones. Their voices were weak and sepulchral; and the whole scene conveyed to the mind the idea of that shout having awakened the dead from the snows. Fourteen of their number, principally men, had already died from starvation, and many more were so reduced, that it was almost certain they would never rise from the miserable beds upon which they had lain down. The unhappy survivors were, in short, in a condition the most deplorable, and beyond the power of language to describe, or of the imagination to conceive. The annals of human suffering no where present a more appalling spectacle, than that which blasted the eyes and sickened the hearts of those brave men, whose indomitable courage and perseverance, in the face of so many dangers, hardships, and privations, snatched some of these miserable survivors from the jaws of death, and who, for having done so much, merit the lasting gratitude and respect of every man who has a heart to feel for human woe, or a hand to afford relief.

Many of the sufferers had been living for weeks upon bullocks' hides, and even this sort of food was so nearly exhausted with some, that they were about to dig up from the snow the bodies of their companions, for the purpose of prolonging their wretched lives. Mrs. Reed, who lived in Brinn's cabin, had, during a considerable length of time, supported herself and four children, by cracking and boiling again the bones from which Brinn's family had carefully scraped all the flesh. These bones she had often taken, and boiled again and again, for the purpose of extracting the least remaining portion of nutriment. Mrs. Eddy and her children had perished.

Some of the emigrants had been making preparations for death, and at morning and evening the incense of prayer and thanksgiving ascended from their cheerless and comfortless dwellings. Others there were, who cursed God, cursed the snow, and cursed the mountain, and in the wildest frenzy deplored their miserable and hard fate. Some poured bitter imprecations upon the head of L. W. Hastings, for having deceived them as to the road upon which he had conducted them; and all united in common fears of a common and inevitable death. Many of them had, in a great measure, lost all self-respect. Untold sufferings had broken their spirits, and prostrated every thing like an honorable and commendable pride. Misfortune had dried up the fountains of the heart; and the dead, whom their weakness had made it impossible to carry out, were dragged from their cabins by means of ropes, with an apathy that afforded a faint indication of the extent of the change which a few weeks of dire suffering had produced, in hearts that once sympathized with the distressed, and mourned the departed. With many of them, all principle, too, had been swept away by this tremendous torrent of accumulated and accumulating calamities. It became necessary to place a guard over the little store of provisions brought to their relief; and they stole and devoured the raw-hide strings from the snow-shoes of those who had come to deliver them. But some there were, whom no temptation could seduce, no suffering move; who were

"Among the faithless, faithful still."

Upon going down into the cabins of this Mountain Camp, the party were presented with sights of woe, and scenes of horror, the full tale of which never will be told, and never ought; sights which, although the emigrants had not yet commenced eating the dead, were so revolting, that they were compelled to withdraw, and make a fire where they would not be under the necessity of looking upon the painful spectacle.

On the morning of February 20th, John Rhodes, Daniel Tucker, and R. S. Mootrey, went to the camp of George Donner eight miles distant, taking with them a little beef. These sufferers were found with but one hide remaining. They had determined, that, upon consuming this, they would dig up from the snow the bodies of those who had died from starvation. Mr. Donner was helpless. Mrs. Donner was weak, but in good health, and might have come into the settlements with Mr. Glover's party, yet she solemnly but calmly declared her determination to remain with her husband, and perform for him the last sad offices of affection and humanity. And this she did, in full view of the fact, that she must necessarily perish by remaining behind.

On the evening of the 20th, the party that had gone down to Mr. Donner's camp in the morning, returned, bringing seven persons with them.

The next day, at noon, the party, after leaving all the provisions they could spare, commenced their return from the Mountain Camp to the settlement, with twenty-three persons, principally women and children. The results of the disastrous and horrible journey of Eddy and Foster were carefully concealed from these poor sufferers. To have acted otherwise would have been to overwhelm them with fear and despondency, and this in their condition would have proved fatal.

Mrs. Pike's child and Mrs. Kiesburg's were carried by the party. After proceeding about two miles, two of Mrs. Reed's children gave out; the one a little girl of eight years old, and the other a little boy of four. It became absolutely necessary, therefore, to return them to the Mountain Camp, or to abandon them upon the way. The mother was informed by Mr. Glover, that it was necessary to take them back. And now ensued that which is hoped none may ever be called upon to witness again. She was a wife, and affection for her husband, then in the settlement, no doubt suggested her going on. But she was a mother, also; and maternal love— the strongest of all feelings, that most powerful of all instincts—determined her, immediately, to send forward the two children who could walk, while she would go back with the two youngest, and die with them.

It was impossible for Mr. Glover to shake this resolution, although he promised, that when he arrived at Bear river valley, he would go back for them. At length she asked, "Are you a mason?" Upon receiving an answer in the affirmative, she said, "Do you promise me upon the word of a mason, that when you arrive at Bear river valley, you will return and bring out my children, if we shall not, in the mean time, meet their father going for them?" Mr. Glover replied, "I do thus promise." She then consented to go on. When the mother and children were about to separate, Patty, a little girl eight years of age, took her mother by the hand, and said, "Well, mamma, kiss me. Good-bye! I shall never see you again. I am willing to go back to our Mountain Camp and die; but I cannot consent to your going back. I shall die willingly, if I can believe that you will live to see papa. Tell him, good-bye, for his poor Patty." The mother and the little children lingered in a long embrace. Being separated, Patty turned from her mother to go back to camp. As Mr. Glover and Mr. Mootrey were taking the children back, she told them that she was willing to go back and take care of her little brother, but that she "should never see her mother again."*

Messrs. Glover and Mootrey returned after the party had encamped; but they carefully concealed from Mrs. Reed the fact that Brinn and his wife absolutely refused to permit the children to come into the cabin until many promises of immediate succor were made. On the return, the party was exposed to great privation. The *cache* of provisions was found to have been completely destroyed by a cougar. John Denton perished of cold. But a little additional provision was brought by two men from the settlements. Mrs. Reed met her husband, who had been driven from the party, for some offence, before its disasters began, and who had never expected to see his wife again. Glover's party then proceeded in safety to the settlements, where the suffering emigrants were well provided.

Messrs. Reed and M'Cutchen next headed a party that proceeded to the Mountain Camp, with supplies. Mr. Reed found his children alive, but undergoing dreadful sufferings. In some of the cabins, particularly that of Lewis Kiesburg, parts of human bodies were found prepared for eating, and there were also seen the traces of many a horrid feast.

---

* "Oregon and California," by Thornton.

Mr. Reed commenced his return to the settlements, with seventeen of the unhappy beings who had wintered in the camp. During the journey, hardships and privations were endured, to which the journey of Mr. Eddy's party alone could furnish a parallel.

The persons taken under Mr. Reed's guidance were Patrick Brinn, wife, and five children; Mrs. Graves and four children; Mary and Isaac Donner, children of Jacob Donner; Solomon Hook, a step-son of Jacob Donner, and two of his children. They reached the foot of the mountain without much difficulty; but they ascertained that their provisions would not last them more than a day and a half. Mr. Reed then sent three men forward with instructions to get supplies at a *cache* about fifteen miles from the camp. The party resumed its journey, crossed the Sierra Nevada, and after travelling about ten miles, encamped on a bleak point, on the north side of a little valley, near the head of the Yuba river. A storm set in, and continued for two days and three nights. On the morning of the third day, the clouds broke away, and the weather became more intensely cold than it had been during the journey. The sufferings of the emigrants in their bleak camp were too dreadful to be described. There was the greatest difficulty in keeping up a fire, and, during the night, the women and children who had on very thin clothing, were in great danger of freezing to death. When the storm passed away, the whole party were very weak, having been two days without taking food. None were able to travel except Solomon Hook and Patrick Brinn and family. The latter said they would remain in camp, with the disabled ones; and Mr. Reed, with his California friends, his two children, Solomon Hook, and a Mr. Miller, pressed forward for supplies. Patty, Mr. Reed's daughter, displayed wonderful powers of endurance during the first day of the journey, and frequently encouraged the men by her remarks. At night, the party was joined by Messrs. Stone and Cady, from the Mountain Camp. The next day, after proceeding a short distance, Mr. Reed found a small supply of food that had been left by the first party sent back to the *cache* for provisions. This was timely, as Mr. Reed and his companions had been four days without food. Pressing forward, they soon succeeded in reaching the settlements.

Patrick Brinn and the others left by Mr. Reed, were not relieved until Messrs. Eddy and Foster led an expedition from the settlements to their camp. A shocking spectacle was presented to the eyes of the adventurers at what they appropriately called the "Starved Camp." Patrick Brinn and his wife were found sunning themselves, and apparently unconcerned. They had consumed the two children of Jacob Donner. Mrs. Graves's body was lying there with almost all the flesh cut away from her arms and limbs. Her breasts, heart, and liver, were then being boiled on the fire. Her child sat by the side of the mangled remains, crying bitterly. After these emigrants had been supplied with food, they were left to be conducted to the settlements by three men, while Messrs. Eddy and Foster went on to the horrible Mountain Camp. There mangled remains of bodies were found strewed about the cabins, and among them sat the emaciated survivors, who had fed upon human flesh, and who then resembled demons. Kiesburg had devoured Mr. Eddy's child, even when other food was to be obtained, and the enraged father was with difficulty restrained from killing him upon the spot.

The party of Messrs. Eddy and Foster, upon their arrival at the Mountain Camp, found five living children, to wit: three of George Donner's, one of Jacob Donner's, and one of Mrs. Murphy's. They also found a man whose name is Clarke. He was a shoemaker.

Clarke had gone out with Mr. Reed, under the pretence of assisting emigrants. He was found with a pack of goods upon his back, weighing about forty-pounds, and also two guns, about to set off with his booty. This man actually carried away this property which weighed more than did a child he left behind to perish. But this is not the only instance of the property of emigrants in distress being appropriated under some pretence, or directly stolen by thieves who prowled about the camp.

In addition to these, there were in camp, Mrs. Murphy, Mr. and Mrs. Donner, and Kiesburg—the latter, it was believed, having far more strength to travel than others who had arrived in the settlements. But he would not travel, for the reason, as was suspected, that he wished to remain behind for the purpose of obtaining the property and money of the dead.

Mrs. George Donner was in good health, was somewhat corpulent, and certainly able to travel. But her husband was in a helpless condition, and she would not consent to leave him while he survived. She expressed her solemn and unalterable purpose, which no danger and peril could change, to remain, and perform for him the last sad offices of duty and affection. She manifested, however, the greatest solicitude for her children; and informed Mr. Eddy that she had fifteen hundred dollars in silver, all of which she would give to him, if he would save the lives of the children. He informed her that he would not carry out one hundred dollars for all that she had, but that he would save the children, or perish in the attempt.

The party had no provisions to leave for the sustenance of these unhappy and unfortunate beings. After remaining about two hours, Mr. Eddy informed Mrs. Donner that he was constrained by the force of circumstances to depart. It was certain that George Donner would never rise from the miserable bed upon which he had lain down, worn out by toil, and wasted by famine. It was next to absolutely certain, if Mrs. Donner did not leave her husband, and avail herself of the opportunity then presented for being conducted into the settlement, that she would perish by famine, or die a violent death at the hands of a cannibal. The instinct of a mother strongly urged her to accompany her children, that she might be able to contribute her own personal efforts and attention to save the lives of her offspring. The natural love of life, too, was without doubt then felt, urging her to fly from a scene of so many horrors and dangers. Her reason may have asked the question, "Why remain in the midst of so much peril, and encounter an inevitable death—a death of all others the most terrible—since it is certain that nothing can rescue your husband from the jaws of the all-devouring grave? and when you cannot hope to do better than beguile, with your society, presence, and converse, the solitude of the few hours that remain of a life, the flame of which is absolutely flickering, and must in a very brief period be extinguished in the darkness and gloom of death?"

A woman was probably never before placed in circumstances of greater and more peculiar trial; but her duty and affection as a wife triumphed over all her instincts and her reason. And when her husband entreated her to save her life and leave him to die alone, assuring her that she could be of no service to him, since he would not probably survive, under any circumstances, until the next morning, she bent over him, and with streaming eyes kissed his pale, emaciated, haggard, and even then, death-stricken cheeks, and said:

"No! no! dear husband, I will remain with you and here perish, rather than leave you to die alone with no one to soothe your dying sorrows, and to close your eyes when dead. Entreat me not to leave you. Life, accompanied with the reflection that I had thus left you, would possess for me more than the bitterness of death; and death would be sweet with the thought, in my last moments, that I had assuaged one pang of yours in your passage into eternity. No! no! this once, dear husband, I will disobey you! No! no! no!" she continued sobbing convulsively.

The parting scene between the parents and children is represented as being one that will never be forgotten, as long as reason remains, or memory performs its functions. My own emotions will not permit me to attempt a description, which language, indeed, has not the power to delineate. It is sufficient to say that it was affecting beyond measure; and that the last words uttered by Mrs. Donner, in tears and sobs, to Mr. Eddy, were, "O, save! save my children!"

Mr. Eddy carried Georgiana Donner, who was about six years old; Hiram Miller carried Eliza Donner, about four years old; Mr. Thompson carried Frances Ann Donner, about eight years old; William Foster carried Simon Murphy, eight years old; and Clarke carried his booty, and left a child of one of the Donners to perish.

After much toil and privation, this party reached the settlements of California. The last of the survivors of the Mountain Camp having been taken to Bear river valley. The following was the result of the inquiry as to those who perished and those who were saved.

Those who perished were:—C. F. Stanton; Mr. Graves; Mrs. Graves; Franklin Graves; Jay Fosdick; John Denton; George Donner; Mrs. Donner, his wife; Jacob Donner; Betsy Donner; Isaac Donner; Louis Donner; Samuel Donner; Charles Burger; Joseph Rianhart; Augustus Spitzer; Samuel Shoemaker; James Smith; Baylis Williams; Bertha Kiesburg; Lewis Kiesburg; Mrs. Murphy; Lemuel Murphy; Lanthron Murphy; George Foster; Catharine Pike; Eleanor Eddy; Margaret Eddy; James Eddy; Patrick Dolan; Milton Elliot; Lewis and Salvadore, Captain Sutter's vaqueros. In all (including two who died before reaching the Mountain Camp) 36.

The following survived:—William Graves; Mary Graves; Ellen Graves; Viney Graves; Nancy Graves; Jonathan Graves; Elizabeth Graves; Sarah Fosdick; Loithy Donner; Leon Donner; Francis Donner; Georgiana Donner; Eliza Donner; George Donner, jr.; Mary Donner; John Baptiste; Solomon Hook; Mrs. Wolfinger; Lewis Kiesburg; Mrs. Kiesburg; William Foster; Sarah Foster; Simon Murphy; Mary Murphy; Harriet Pike;

Miriam Pike; Patrick Brinn, Margaret Brinn; John Brinn; Edward Brinn; Patrick Brinn, jr.; Simon Brinn; James Brinn; Peter Brinn; Isabella Brinn; Eliza Williams; Noah James; James F. Reed; Virginia Reed; Patty Reed; James Reed; Thomas Reed; William H. Eddy. In all, 44.

Some of the unfortunate sufferers entirely lost their reason. Of this number was Patrick Dolan at the Camp of Death. His words were vague and unconnected. He struggled until he got out from under the blankets. He called to Mr. Eddy, saying that he was the only person of their number who could be depended upon. He then pulled off his boots, and, divesting himself of nearly all his clothing, he bade Mr. Eddy follow him, and said that he would be in the settlements in a few hours. He was with great difficulty brought under the blankets, and held there until at length he became as quiet and submissive as a child; when he soon fell asleep, and expired. Lanthron Murphy was of this number also. Mr. Foster was likewise insane; but his insanity was of a totally different character. He, in a considerable degree, realized his situation, and in some respect was capable of reasoning from cause to effect. Mr. Eddy was probably the only really sane one of that party of sixteen. With but few exceptions, all the sufferers, both those who perished and those who survived, manifested the same species of insanity as did Mr. Foster.

Throughout the horrible scenes of this disastrous expedition, the courage, devotion, and fortitude of woman were gloriously illustrated. Amidst events almost too frightful for thought, the wife was found ready to sacrifice herself for her husband, and the mother for her children. When the stoutest hearts among the men sank under accumulating miseries, women preserved an unmurmuring calmness, and an unflinching energy. The genuine strength of human creatures—the power of soul over body—was there shown to be possessed in a greater degree by woman than man—and amid the savage winter of the wilderness, among horrid feasts, when to save themselves from death, men became brutes, woman's true nobility shone forth in all its splendor. The record of this expedition will always have a thrilling interest on account of the startling incidents; but as a memorial of what woman may endure and accomplish, it will be more valuable.

MISS WASHBURN

IN THE FOLLOWING thrilling adventure of two scouts, a part was performed by a young girl, which did high honor to her spirit and resolution.

As early as the year 1790, the block-house and stockade, above the mouth of the Hockhocking river, was a frontier post for the hardy pioneers of that portion of the state from the Hockhocking to the Scioto, and from the Ohio to our northern Lakes. Then nature wore her undisturbed livery of dark and thick forests, interspersed with green and flowery prairies. Then the axe of the woodman had not been heard in the wilderness, nor the plough of the husbandman marred the business of the green prairies. Among the many rich and luxuriant valleys that of Hockhocking was pre-eminent for nature's richest gifts—and the portion of it whereon Lancaster now stands, was marked as the most luxuriant and picturesque, and became the seat of an Indian village, at a period so early, that the "memory of man runneth not parallel thereto." On the green sward of the prairie was held many a rude gambol of the Indians; and here too, was many an assemblage of the warriors of one of the most powerful tribes, taking counsel for a "war path" upon some weak or defenceless frontier post. Upon one of these war-stirring occasions, intelligence reached the little garrison above the mouth of the Hockhocking, that the Indians were gathering in force somewhere up the valley, for the purpose of striking a terrible and fatal blow on one of the few and scattered defences of the whites. A council was held by the garrison, and scouts were sent up the Hockhocking, in order to ascertain the strength of the foe, and the probable point of attack. In the month of October, and on one of the balmiest days of our Indian summer, two men could have been seen emerging out of the thick plumb and hazel bushes skirting the prairie, and stealthily climbing the eastern declivity of that most remarkable promontory, now known as Mount Pleasant, whose western summit gives a commanding view to the eye of what is doing on the prairie. This eminence was gained by our two adventurous and hardy scouts, and from this point they carefully observed the movements taking place on the prairie. Every day brought an accession of warriors to those already assembled, and every day the scouts witnessed from their eyrie, the horse-racing, leaping, running and throwing the deadly tomahawk by the warriors. The old sachems looking on with indifference—the squaws, for the most part, engaged in their usual drudgeries, and the papooses manifesting all the noisy and wayward joy of childhood. The arrival of any new party of warriors was hailed by the terrible war-whoop, which striking the mural face of Mount Pleasant, was driven back into the various indentations of the surrounding hills, producing reverberation on reverberation, and echo on echo, till it seemed as if ten thousand fiends were gathered in their orgies. Such yells might well strike terror into the bosoms of those unaccustomed to them. To our scouts these were but martial music strains which waked their watchfulness, and strung their iron frames. From their early youth had they been always on the frontier, and therefore well practised in all the subtlety, craft and cunning, as well as knowing the ferocity and bloodthirsty perseverance of the savage. They were therefore not likely to be circumvented by the cunning of their foes; and without a desperate struggle, would not fall victims to the scalping-knife.

On several occasions, small parties of warriors left the prairies and ascended the Mount; at which times the scouts would hide in the fissures of the rocks, or lying by the side of some long, prostrate tree, cover themselves with the sear and yellow leaf, and again leave their hiding-places when their uninvited visitors had disappeared. For food they depended on jerked venison, and cold corn bread, with which their knapsacks had been well stored. Fire they dared not kindle, and the report of one of their rifles would bring upon them the entire force of the Indians. For drink they depended on some rain water, which still stood in excavations of the rocks, but in a few days this stock was exhausted, and M'Clelland and White must abandon their enterprise, or find a new supply. To accomplish this hazardous affair, M'Clelland being the elder, resolved to make the attempt—with his trusty rifle in his grasp, and two canteens strung across his shoulders, he cautiously descended to the prairie, and skirting the hills on the north as much as

MISS WASHBURN—*Page 163*

possible within the hazel thickets, he struck a course for the Hockhocking river. He reached its margin, and turning an abrupt point of a hill, he found a beautiful fountain of limpid water, now known as the Cold Spring, within a few feet of the river. He filled his canteens and returned in safety to his watchful companion. It was now determined to have a fresh supply of water every day, and this duty was to be performed alternately.

On one of these occasions, after White had filled his canteens, he sat a few moments watching the limpid element, as it came gurgling out of the bosom of the earth—the light sound of footsteps caught his practised ear, and, upon turning round, he saw two squaws within a few feet of him; these upon turning the jet of the hill had thus suddenly come upon him. The elder squaw gave one of those far-reaching whoops peculiar to the Indians. White at once comprehended his perilous situation—for if the alarm should reach the camp, he and his companion must inevitably perish. Self-preservation impelled him to inflict a noiseless death upon the squaws, and in such a manner as to leave no trace behind. Ever rapid in thought, and prompt in action, he sprang upon his victims with the rapidity and power of a panther, and grasping the throat of each, with one bound he sprang into the Hockhocking, and rapidly thrust the head of the elder squaw under the water, and making strong efforts to submerge the younger, who, however, powerfully resisted. During the short struggle, the younger female addressed him in his own language, though almost in inarticulate sounds. Releasing his hold, she informed him, that ten years before, she had been made a prisoner on Grave Creek flats, and that the Indians, in her presence, butchered her mother and two sisters, and that an only remaining brother had been captured with her, who succeeded on the second night in making his escape; but what had become of him she knew not. During the narrative, White, unobserved by the girl, had let go his grasp on the elder squaw, whose body floated where it would not, probably, soon be found. He now directed the girl hastily to follow him, and with his usual energy and speed, pushed for the Mount. They had scarcely gone two hundred yards from the spring, before the alarm cry was heard some quarter of a mile down the stream. It was supposed that some warriors returning from a hunt, struck the Hockhocking just as the body of the drowned squaw floated past. White and the girl succeeded in reaching the Mount, where Mr. M'Clelland had been no indifferent spectator to the sudden commotion among the Indians, as the practising parties of warriors were seen to strike off in every direction, and before White and the girl had arrived, a party of some twenty warriors had already gained the eastern acclivity of the Mount, and were cautiously ascending, carefully keeping under cover. Soon the two scouts saw the swarthy faces of the foe, as they glided from tree to tree, and rock to rock, until the whole of the rock was surrounded, and all hope of escape cut off.

In this peril nothing was left, other than to sell their lives as dearly as they could; this they resolved to do, and advised the girl to escape to the Indians, and tell them she had been a captive to the scouts. She said, "no! death, and that in presence of my people, is to me a thousand times sweeter than captivity—furnish me with a rifle, and I will show you that I can fight as well as die. This spot I leave not! here my bones shall lie bleaching with yours! and should either of you escape, you will carry the tidings of my death to my remaining relatives." Remonstrance proved fruitless; the two scouts matured their plans for a vigorous defence—opposing craft to craft, expedient to expedient, and an unerring fire of the deadly rifle. The attack now commenced, in front, where, from the narrow back bone of the Mount, the savages had to advance in single file, but where they could avail themselves of the rock and trees. In advancing the warrior must be momentarily exposed, and two bare inches of his swarthy form was target enough for the unerring rifle of the scouts. After bravely maintaining the fight in front, and keeping the enemy in check, they discovered a new danger threatening them. The wary foe now made every preparation to attack them in flank, which could be most successively and fatally done by reaching an insulated rock lying in one of the ravines on the southern hill side. This rock once gained by the Indians, they could bring the scouts under point blank shot of the rifle; and without the possibility of escape.

Our brave scouts saw the hopelessness of their situation, which nothing could avert but brave companions and an unerring shot—them they had not. But the brave never despair. With this certain fate resting upon them, they had continued as calm, and as calculating, and as unwearied as the strongest desire of vengeance on a treacherous foe could produce. Soon M'Clelland saw a tall and swarthy figure preparing to spring from a cover so near the fatal rock, that a single bound must reach it, and all hope be destroyed. He felt that all depended on one advantageous shot, although but one inch of the warrior's body was exposed, and that at a distance of one hundred yards—he resolved to risk all—coolly he raised his rifle to his eye, carefully shading the sight with his hand, he drew a bead so sure, that he felt conscious it would do—he touched the hair trigger with his finger—the hammer came down, but in place of striking fire, it crushed his flint into a hundred fragments! Although he felt that the savage must reach the fatal rock before he could adjust another flint, he proceeded to the task with the utmost composure, casting many a furtive glance towards the fearful point. Suddenly he saw the warrior stretching every muscle for the leap—and with the agility of a deer he made the spring—instead of reaching the rock he sprung ten feet in the air, and giving one terrific yell he fell upon the earth and his dark corpse rolled fifty feet down the hill. He had evidently received a death shot from some unknown hand. A hundred voices from below re-echoed the terrible shout, and it was evident that they had lost a favorite warrior, as well as been foiled for a time in their most important movement. A very few moments proved that the advantage so mysteriously gained would be of short duration; for already the scouts caught a momentary glimpse of a swarthy warrior, cautiously advancing towards the cover so recently occupied by a fellow companion. Now, too, the attack in front was resumed with increased fury, so as to require the incessant fire of both scouts, to prevent the Indians from gaining the eminence—and in a short time M'Clelland saw the wary warrior turning a somerset, his corpse rolled down towards his companion: again a mysterious agent had interposed in their behalf. This second sacrifice cast dismay into the ranks of the assailants; and just as the sun was disappearing behind the western hills, the foe withdrew a short distance, for the purpose of devising new modes of attack. The respite came most seasonably to the scouts, who had bravely kept their position, and boldly maintained the unequal fight from the middle of the day.

Now, for the first time was the girl missing, and the scouts supposed that through terror she had escaped to her former captors, or that she had been killed during the fight. They were not long left to doubt, for in a few moments the girl was seen emerging from the rock and coming to them with a rifle in her hand. During the heat of the fight she saw a warrior fall, who had advanced some fifty yards before the main body in front. She at once resolved to possess herself of his rifle, and crouching in undergrowth she crept to the spot, and succeeded in her enterprise, being all the time exposed to the cross fire of the defenders and assailants—her practised eye had early noticed the fatal rock, and hers was the mysterious hand by which the two warriors had fallen—the last being the most wary, untiring and blood-thirsty brave of the Shawanese tribe. He it was, who ten years before had scalped the family of the girl, and had been her captor. In the west dark clouds were gathering, and in an hour the whole heavens were shrouded in them; this darkness greatly embarassed the scouts in their contemplated night retreat, for they might readily lose their way, or accidentally fall on the enemy—this being highly probable, if not inevitable. An hour's consultation decided their plans, and it was agreed that the girl, from her intimate knowledge of their localities, should lead the advance a few steps. Another advantage might be gained by this arrangement, for in case they should fall in with some out-post, the girl's knowledge of the Indian tongue, would perhaps enable her to deceive the sentinel: and so the sequel proved, for scarcely had they descended one hundred feet, when a low "whist" from the girl, warned them of present danger. The scouts sunk silently to the earth, where by previous agreement, they were to remain till another signal was given them by the girl,—whose absence for more than a quarter of an hour now began to excite the most serious apprehensions. At length she again appeared, and told them that she had succeeded in removing two sentinels who were directly in their route to a point some hundred feet distant. The descent was noiselessly resumed—the level gained, and the scouts followed their intrepid pioneer for half a mile in the most profound silence, when the barking of a small dog, within a few feet, apprised them of a new danger. The almost simultaneous click of the scouts' rifles was heard by the girl, who rapidly approached them, and stated that they were now in the midst of the Indian wigwams, and their lives depended on the most profound silence, and implicitly following her footsteps. A moment afterwards, the girl was accosted by a squaw from an opening in a wigwam. She replied in the Indian language, and without stopping pressed forward. In a short time she stopped and assured the scouts that the village was cleared, and that they were now in safety.

She knew that every pass leading out of the prairie was safely guarded by Indians, and at once resolved to adopt the bold adventure of passing through the very centre of their village as the least hazardous. The result proved the correctness of her judgment. They now kept a course for the Ohio, being guided by the Hockhocking river—and after three days march and suffering, the party arrived at the block-house in safety.

The courage, energy, and fortitude of the girl were nobly displayed throughout the perilous scenes of the fight and escape. She proved to be a sister of Neil Washburn, one of the most renowned scouts upon the frontier. She possessed her brother's spirit in the delicate frame of a woman.

The escape of the party from the Indians deranged the plan of attack upon the fort, and compelled the savages to return to their homes without having effected any thing of importance.

THE HUNTER'S WIFE

THE FOLLOWING STORY appeared in "Chamber's Edinburgh Journal," in June, 1851. We are ignorant of its original source.

Tom Cooper was a fine specimen of the North American trapper. Slightly but powerfully made, with a hardy, weather-beaten, yet handsome face, strong, indefatigable, and a crack shot, he was admirably adapted for a hunter's life. For many years he knew not what it was to have a home, but lived like the beasts he hunted—wandering from one part of the country to the other in pursuit of game. All who knew Tom were much surprised when he came, with a pretty young wife, to settle within three miles of a planter's farm. Many pitied the poor young creature, who would have to lead such a solitary life; whilst others said; "If she was fool enough to marry him it was her own look-out." For nearly four months Tom remained at home, and employed his time in making the old hut he had fixed on for their residence more comfortable. He cleared and tilled a small spot of land around it, and Susan began to hope that for her sake he would settle down quietly as a squatter. But these visions of happiness were soon dispelled, for as soon as this work was finished he recommenced his old erratic mode of life, and was often absent for week together, leaving his wife alone, yet not unprotected, for since his marriage, old Nero, a favorite hound, was always left at home as her guardian. He was a noble dog—a cross between the old Scottish deerhound and the bloodhound—and would hunt an Indian as well as a deer or bear, which Tom said, "was a proof they Ingins was a sort o' varmint, or why should the brute beast take to hunt 'em, nat'ral like—him that took no notice of white men?"

One clear, cold morning, about two years after their marriage, Susan was awakened by a loud crash, immediately succeeded by Nero's deep baying. She recollected that she had shut him in the house as usual the night before. Supposing he had winded some solitary wolf or bear prowling around the hut, and effected his escape, she took little notice of the circumstance; but a few moments after came a shrill, wild cry, which made her blood run cold. To spring from her bed, throw on her clothes, and rush from the hut, was the work of a minute. She no longer doubted what the hound was in pursuit of. Fearful thoughts shot through her brain; she called wildly on Nero, and to her joy he came dashing through the thick underwood. As the dog drew near she saw that he galloped heavily, and carried in his mouth some large dark creature. Her brain reeled; she felt a cold and sickly shudder dart through her limbs. But Susan was a hunter's daughter, and all her life had been accustomed to witness scenes of danger and of horror, and in this school had learned to subdue the natural timidity of her character. With a powerful effort she recovered herself, just as Nero dropped at her feet a little Indian child, apparently between three and four years old. She bent down over him, but there was no sound or motion; she placed her hand on his little naked chest; the heart within had ceased to beat,—he was dead! The deep marks of the dog's fangs were visible on the neck, but the body was untorn. Old Nero stood with his large bright eyes fixed on the face of his mistress, fawning on her, as if he expected to be praised for what he had done, and seemed to wonder why she looked so terrified. But Susan spurned him from her; and the fierce animal, who would have pulled down an Indian as he would a deer, crouched humbly at the young woman's feet. Susan carried the little body gently to the hut, and laid it on her own bed. Her first impulse was to seize a loaded rifle that hung over the fireplace, and shoot the hound; and yet she felt she could not do it, for in the lone life she led, the faithful animal seemed like a dear and valued friend, who loved and watched over her, as if aware of the precious charge entrusted to him. She thought also of what her husband would say, when on his return he should find his old companion dead. Susan had never seen Tom roused. To her he had ever shown nothing but kindness; yet she feared as well as loved him, for there was a fire in those dark eyes which told of deep, wild passions hidden in his breast, and she knew that the lives of a whole tribe of Indians would be light in the balance against that of his favorite hound.

Having securely fastened up Nero, Susan, with a heavy heart, proceeded to examine the ground around the hut. In several places she observed the impression of a small moccasoned foot, but not a child's. The tracks were deeply marked, unlike the usual light, elastic tread of an Indian. From this circumstance, Susan easily inferred that the woman had been carrying her child when attacked by the dog. There was nothing to show why she had come so near the hut; most probably the hopes of some petty plunder had been the inducement. Susan did not dare to wander far from home, fearing a band of Indians might be in the neighborhood. She returned sorrowfully to the hut, and employed herself in blocking up the window, or rather the hole where the window had been, for the powerful hound had in his leap dashed out the entire frame, and shattered it to pieces. When this was finished, Susan dug a grave, and in it laid the little Indian boy. She made it close to the hut, for she could not bear that wolves should devour those delicate limbs, and she knew there it would be safe. The next day Tom returned. He had been very unsuccessful, and intended setting out again in a few days in a different direction.

"Susan," he said, when he had heard her sad story, "I wish you'd lef' the child where the dog killed him. The squaw's high sartan to come back a-seekin' for the body, and 'tis a pity the poor crittur should be disapinted. Besides, the Ingins will be high sartan to put it down to us; whereas if so be as they'd found the body, 'pon the spot, maybe they'd onderstand as 'twas an accident like, for they're unkimmon cunning warmints, though they a'nt got sense like Christians."

"Why do you think the poor woman came here?" said Susan. "I never knew an Indian squaw so near the hut before."

She fancied a dark shadow flitted across her husband's brow. He made no reply; and on her repeating the question, said angrily—how should he know? 'Twas as well to ask for a bear's reasons as an Ingin's.

Tom only stayed at home long enough to mend the broken window, and plant a small spot of Indian corn, and then again set out, telling Susan not to expect him home in less than a month. "If that squaw comes this way agin," he said, "as maybe she will, jist put any broken victuals you've a-got, for the poor crittur; though maybe she wont come, for they Ingins be on kimmon skeary." Susan wondered at his taking an interest in the woman, and often thought of that dark look she had noticed, and Tom's unwillingness to speak on the subject. She never knew that on his last hunting expedition, when hiding some skins which he intended to fetch on his return, he had observed an Indian watching him, and had shot him with as little mercy as he would have shown a wolf. On Tom's return to the spot, the body was gone; and in the soft damp soil was the mark of an Indian squaw's foot, and by its side a little child's. He was sorry then for the deed he had done; he thought of the grief of the poor widow, and how it would be possible for her to live until she could reach her tribe, who were far, far distant, at the foot of the Rocky Mountains; and now to feel that through his means, too, she had lost her child, put thoughts into his mind that had never before found a place there. He thought that one God had formed the Red Man as well as the White—of the souls of the many Indians hurried into eternity by his unerring rifle; and they perhaps were more fitted for their "happy hunting-grounds" than he was for the white man's heaven. In this state of mind, every word his wife had said to him seemed to him a reproach, and he was glad again to be alone in the forest with his rifle and his hounds.

The afternoon of the third day after Tom's departure, as Susan was sitting at work, she heard something scratching and whining at the door. Nero, who was by her side, evinced no sign of anger, but ran to the door, showing his white teeth, as was his custom when pleased. Susan unbarred it, when to her astonishment, the two deerhounds her husband had taken with him walked into the hut, looking weary and soiled. At first she thought Tom might have killed a deer not far from home, and had brought her a fresh supply of venison; but no one was there. She rushed from the hut, and soon, breathless and terrified, reached the squatter's cabin. John Wilton and his three sons were just returned from the clearings, when Susan ran into their comfortable kitchen; her long black hair streaming on her shoulders, and her wild arid bloodshot eyes, gave her the appearance of a maniac. In a few unconnected words, she explained to them the cause of her terror, and implored them to set off immediately in search of her husband. It was in vain they told her of the uselessness of going at that time—of the impossibility of following a trail in the dark. She said she would go herself; she felt sure of finding him; and at last they were obliged to use force to prevent her leaving the house.

The next morning at daybreak, Wilton and his two sons were mounted, and ready to set out, intending to take Nero with them; but nothing could induce him to leave his mistress; he resisted passively for some time, until one of the young men attempted to pass a rope round his neck, to drag him away: then his forbearance vanished; he sprung on his tormentor, threw him down, and would have strangled him, if Susan had not been present. Finding it impossible to make Nero accompany them, they left without him, but had not proceeded many miles before he and his mistress were at their side. They begged Susan to return, told her of the hardships she must endure, and of the inconvenience she would be to them. It was of no avail; she had but one answer: "I am a hunter's wife, and a hunter's daughter." She told them that knowing how useful Nero would be to them in their search, she had secretly taken a horse and followed them.

The party first rode to Tom Cooper's hut, and there having dismounted, leading their horses through the forest, followed the trail, as only men long accustomed to a savage life can do. At night they lay on the ground, covered with their thick bear-skin cloaks; for Susan only they heaped up a bed of dry leaves; but she refused to occupy it, saying it was her duty to bear the same hardships they did. Ever since their departure she had shown no sign of sorrow. Although slight and delicately formed, she never appeared fatigued; her whole soul was absorbed in one longing desire—to find her husband's body; for from the first she had abandoned the hope of ever again seeing him in life. This desire supported her through every thing. Early the next morning they were again on the trail. About noon, as they were crossing a small brook, the hound suddenly dashed away from them, and was lost in the thicket. At first they fancied they might have crossed the track of a deer or wolf; but a long mournful howl soon told the sad truth, for not far from the brook lay the faithful dog on the body of his master, which was pierced to the heart by an Indian arrow.

The murderer had apparently been afraid to approach on account of the dogs, for the body was left as it had fallen—not even the rifle was gone. No sign of Indians could be discovered save one small footprint, which was instantly pronounced to be that of a squaw. Susan showed no grief at the sight of the body; she maintained the same forced calmness, and seemed comforted that it was found. Old Wilton stayed with her to remove all that now remained of her darling husband, and his two sons again set out on the trail, which soon led them into the open prairie, where it was easily traced through the tall thick grass. They continued riding that afternoon, and the next morning were again on the track, which they followed to the banks of a wide but shallow stream. There they saw the remains of a fire. One of them thrust his hand in the ashes, which were still warm. They crossed the river, and in the soft sand on the opposite bank saw again the print of a small moccasoned footsteps. Here they were at a loss; for the rank prairie grass had been consumed by one of those fearful fires so common in the prairies, and in its stead grew short sweet herbage, where even an Indian's eye could observe no trace. They were on the point of abandoning the pursuit, when Richard, the younger of the two, called his brother's attention to Nero, who had of his own accord left his mistress to accompany them, as if he now understood what they were about. The hound was trotting to and fro, with his nose to the ground, as if endeavoring to pick out a cold scent. Edward laughed at his brother, and pointed to the track of a deer that had come to drink at the river. At last he agreed to follow Nero, who was now cantering slowly across the prairie. The pace gradually increased, until, on a spot where the grass had grown more luxuriantly than elsewhere, Nero threw up his nose, gave a deep bay, and started off at a furious pace, that although well mounted, they had great difficulty in keeping up with him.

It was not long before the dog brought them to the borders of another forest, where, finding it impossible to take their horses farther, they fastened them to a tree, and set off again on foot. They lost sight of the hound, but still from time to time they heard his loud baying far away. At last they fancied it sounded nearer instead of becoming less and distinct; and of this they were soon convinced. They still went on in the direction whence the sound proceeded, until they saw Nero sitting with his forepaws against the trunk of a tree, no longer mouthing like a well-trained hound, but yelling like a fury. They looked up in a tree, but could see nothing; until at last Edward espied a large hollow about half way up the trunk. "I was right, you see," he said. "After all it is only a bear; but we may as well shoot the brute that has given us so much trouble."

They set to work immediately with their axes to fell the tree. It began to totter, when a dark object, they could not tell what in the dim twilight, crawled from its place of concealment to the extremity of a branch, and from thence sprung into the next tree. Snatching up their rifles, they both fired together; when to their astonishment, instead of a bear, a young Indian squaw, with a loud yell, fell to the ground. They ran to the spot where she lay motionless, and carried her to the borders of the wood where they had that morning dismounted. Richard lifted her on his horse, and springing himself into the saddle, carried the almost lifeless body before him. The poor creature never spoke. Several times they stopped, thinking she was dead; her pulse only told the spirit had not flown from its earthly tenement. When they reached the river which had been crossed by them before, they washed the wounds, and sprinkled water on her face. This appeared to revive her; and when Richard again lifted her in his arms to place her on his horse, he fancied he heard her utter in Iroquois, one word—"revenged!"

It was a strange sight, these two powerful men tending so carefully the being they had a few hours before sought to slay, and endeavoring to staunch the blood that flowed from the wound they had made! Yet so it was. It would have appeared to them a sin to leave the Indian woman to die; yet they felt no remorse at having inflicted the wound, and would have been better pleased had it been mortal; but they would not have murdered a wounded enemy, even an Indian warrior, still less a squaw. The party continued their journey until midnight when they stopped to rest their jaded horses. Having wrapped the squaw in their bear-skins, they lay down themselves with no covering save the clothes they wore. They were in no want of provisions, as not knowing when they might return, they had taken a good supply of bread and dried venison, not wishing to lose any precious time in seeking food whilst on the trail. The brandy, still remaining in their flasks, they preserved for the use of their captive. The evening of the following day they reached the trapper's hut, where they were not a little surprised to find Susan. She told them that although John Wilton had begged her to live with them, she could not bear to leave the spot where every thing reminded her of one to think of whom was now her only consolation, and that whilst she had Nero, she feared nothing. They needed not to tell their mournful tale—Susan already understood it but too clearly. She begged them to leave the Indian woman with her. "You have no one," she said, "to tend and watch her as I can do; besides, it is not right that I should lay such a burden on you." Although unwilling to impose on her the painful task of nursing her husband's murderess, they could not but allow she was right; and seeing how earnestly she desired it, at last consented to leave the Indian woman with her.

For many long weeks, Susan nursed her charge as tenderly as if she had been her sister. At first she lay almost motionless, and rarely spoke; then she grew delirious, and raved wildly. Susan, fortunately, could not understand what she said, but often turned shudderingly away, when the Indian woman would strive to rise from her bed, and move her arms as if drawing a bow; or yell wildly, and cower in terror beneath the clothes, reacting in her delirium the fearful scenes through which she had passed. By degrees reason returned; she gradually got better, but seemed restless and unhappy, and could not bear the sight of Nero. The first proof of returning reason she had shown was to shriek in terror when he once accidentally followed his mistress into the room where she lay. One morning Susan missed her; she searched around the hut, but she was gone, without having taken farewell of her kind benefactress.

A few years after Susan Cooper (no longer "pretty Susan," for time and grief had done their work) heard late one night a hurried knock, which was repeated several times before she could unfasten the door, each time more loudly than before. She called to ask who it was at that hour of the night. A few hurried words in Iroquois were the reply, and Susan congratulated herself on having spoken before unbarring the door. But on listening again, she distinctly heard the same voice say, "Quick— quick!" and recognised it as the Indian woman's whom she had nursed. The door was instantly opened, when the squaw rushed into the hut, seized Susan by the arm, and made signs to her to come away. She was too much excited to remember then the few words of English she had picked up when living with the white woman. Expressing her meaning by gestures with a clearness peculiar to the Indians, she dragged rather than led Susan from the hut. They had just reached the edge of the forest when the wild yells of the Indians sounded in their ears. Having gone with Susan a little way into the forest her guide left her. For nearly four hours she lay there half-dead with cold and terror, not daring to move from her place of concealment. She saw the flames of the dwelling, where so many lonely hours had been passed, rising above the trees, and heard the shrill "whoops" of the retiring Indians. Nero, who was lying by her side, suddenly rose and gave a loud growl. Silently a dark figure came gliding among the trees directly to the spot where she lay. She gave herself up for lost; but it was the Indian woman who came to her, and dropped at her feet a bag of money, the remains of her late husband's savings. The grateful creature knew where it was kept; and whilst the Indians were busied examining the rifles and other objects more interesting to them, had carried it off unobserved. Waving her arm around to show that all was now quiet, she pointed in the direction of Wilton's house, and was again lost among the trees.

Day was just breaking when Susan reached the squatter's cabin. Having heard the sad story, Wilton and two of his sons started immediately for the spot. Nothing was to be seen save a heap of ashes. The party had apparently consisted of only three or four Indians; but a powerful tribe being in the neighborhood, they saw that it would be too hazardous to follow them. From this time Susan lived with the Wiltons. She was as a daughter to the old man, and a sister to his sons, who often said: "That, as far as they were concerned, the Indians had never done a kindlier action than in burning down Susan Cooper's hut."

MRS. JORDAN'S CAPTIVITY

NARRATED BY HERSELF

"ON THE NIGHT of 22d January, 1807, we were suddenly awakened from slumber by the hideous yells of the savages, who, before we could put ourselves in a situation to oppose them, succeeded in forcing the doors of the house. They were, to the number of forty or fifty, frightfully painted, and armed with tomahawks and scalping knives. My husband met them at the door, and in their own tongue asked them what they wanted—"The scalps of your family!" was their answer. My husband entreated them to have compassion on me and his innocent children, but his entreaties availed nothing; we were dragged naked out of the house, and tied severally with cords. By order of one, who appeared to be a chief, about twenty of the Indians took charge of us, who were ordered to conduct us with all possible dispatch to their settlement, about two hundred miles distant, while the remainder were left to pillage and fire the house. We commenced our journey about midnight, through an uncultivated wilderness, at the rate of nearly seven miles an hour. If either of us, through fatigue, slacked our pace, we were most inhumanly beaten and threatened with instant death.

"After a tedious travel of more than forty miles, the savages halted in a swamp;—here for the first time, from the time of our departure, we were permitted to lie down—the Indians kindled a fire, on which they broiled some bear's flesh, of which they allowed us but a small portion.

"After they had refreshed themselves and extinguished the fire, we were again compelled to pursue our journey. We travelled until sunset, when the Indians again halted and began to prepare a covering for themselves for the night. My poor children complained much of their feet being swollen, but I was not permitted to give them any relief, nor was their father allowed to discourse with them. As night approached, we shook each other by the hand, expecting never again to witness the rising of the sun. Contrary to our expectations, however, we had a tolerable night's rest, and on the succeeding day, though naked and half starved, travelled with much more ease than on the preceding one. The Indians occasionally allowed us a little raw food, sufficient only to keep us alive;—we this day travelled, according to the reckoning of the Indians, nearly forty miles, and were, about sunset, joined by the remaining savages who were left behind; they were loaded with the spoils of my husband's property; among other articles they had a keg of spirits of which they had drank plentifully, and as they became intoxicated, they exercised the more cruelty towards us—they beat my poor children so unmercifully that they were unable to stand upon their feet the ensuing morning—the Indians attributed their inability to wilfulness, and again renewed their acts of barbarity, beating them with clubs, cutting and gashing them with their knives and scorching their naked bodies with brands of fire. Finding that their hellish plans had no other effect than to render the poor unhappy sufferers less able to travel, they came to the resolution to butcher them on the spot.

"Six holes were dug in the earth, of about five feet in depth, around each of which some dried branches of trees were placed. My husband at this moment, filled with horror at what he expected was about to take place, broke the rope with which he was bound, and attempted to escape from the hands of the unmerciful cannibals—he was, however, closely pursued, soon overtaken and brought back—as he passed me, he cast his eyes towards me and fainted—in this situation he was placed erect in one of the holes. The woods now resounded with the heart-piercing cries of my poor children—'spare, O spare my father,' was their cry—'have mercy on my poor children!' was the cry of their father; but all availed nothing—my dear children were all placed in a situation similar to that of their father—the youngest (only nine years old) broke from them and ran up to me, crying, 'don't mamma, mamma, don't let them kill me!'

"Alas, O Heavens, what could I do? In vain did I beg of them to let me take my dear child's place!—by force it was torn from me.

"Having placed the poor unfortunate victims in the manner above described, they secured them in a standing position by replacing the earth, which buried them nearly to their necks! The inhuman wretches

now began their hideous pow-wows, dancing to and fro around the
victims of their torture, which they continued about a half an hour,
when they communicated fire to the fatal piles! As the flames increased,
shrieks and dying groans of my poor family were heightened!—thank
heaven! their sufferings were of short duration;—in less than a quarter
of an hour from the time the fire was first communicated, their cries
ceased, and they sunk into the arms of their kind deliverer.

"The callous-hearted wretches having sufficiently feasted their
eyes with the agonies of the unfortunate sufferers, retired to regale
themselves with what liquor remained; they drank freely, and soon
became stupid and senseless. With one of their tomahawks I might with
ease have dispatched them all, but my only desire was to flee from them
as quick as possible. I succeeded with difficulty in liberating myself by
cutting the cord with which I was bound, on which I bent my course
for this place. A piece of bear's flesh, which I fortunately found in one
of the Indian's packs, served me for food. I travelled only by night, in
the day time concealing myself in the thick swamps or hollow trees. A
party of Indians passed within a few rods of the place of my concealment
the second day after my departure, but did not discover me; they were
undoubtedly of the same party from whom I had escaped, in pursuit of
me. Two days after, I was met by an Indian of the Shawanese nation;
without his assistance I must have again fallen into the hands of my
foes."

CAPTIVITY AND SUFFERINGS OF THE GILBERT FAMILY

BENJAMIN GILBERT WAS the owner and occupier of a farm, situated on Mahoning creek, in Penn Township, Northampton county, Pennsylvania, not far from where Fort Allen was built. The improvements he had made, were such as were of great value in a new settlement. They were, besides a convenient log-house, and log-barn, a saw-mill and commodious stone grist-mill. But from this scene of comfort, the backwoodsman, with his family, was destined to be torn away; and the improvements, erected at great cost, and with much difficulty, upon the borders of the wilderness, were scarcely completed, when they were doomed to the flames.

On the 25th day of April, 1780, about sunrise, the family were alarmed by a party of Indians, who came upon them so suddenly, that to have attempted to escape would have been useless. Their only chance of saving their lives was to surrender. Without resistance they therefore gave themselves up to their savage foes, hoping, yet scarcely expecting, to escape from death by being carried off to endure the horrors of an Indian captivity.

The Indians who made this incursion were of different tribes, who had abandoned their country upon the approach of General Sullivan's army, and fled within command of the British forts in Canada, settling promiscuously within their neighborhood, and, according to Indian custom, carrying on war, frequently invading the frontier settlements, and taking captive the surprised and defenceless inhabitants. The present party consisted of two half-breeds, descended from a Mohawk and French woman, three Cayugas, one Delaware, and five Senecas—in all eleven. The two Mohawk half-breeds, whose names were Rowland Monteur and John Monteur, seemed to have command of the party.

The prisoners taken at the house of Mr. Gilbert were, himself, his wife, his sons Joseph, Jesse and Abner, his daughters Rebecca and Elizabeth, his daughter-in-law, Sarah Gilbert, wife of his son Jesse, Thomas Peart, a son of Mrs. Gilbert by a former husband, Benjamin Gilbert, jr., a grandson, Andrew Harrigar, a German laborer in the employment of Mr. Gilbert, and Abigail Dodson, a girl about fourteen years of age, who had been sent that morning by one of the neighbors with a grist to the mill.

With these captives the Indians proceeded about half a mile to the house of Benjamin Peart, (another son of Mrs. Gilbert,) whom, with his wife and their child, about nine months old, they also captured.

The prisoners were here bound with cords, and left under a guard for half an hour, during which time the rest of the Indians employed themselves in pillaging the house, and packing up such goods as they chose to carry off, until they had got together a sufficient loading for three horses, which they took. This completed, they began their retreat, two of their number being detached to fire the buildings. From an eminence called Summer Hill, which they passed over, the captives could observe the flames and the falling in of the roofs of the houses. They cast back a sorrowful look towards their dwellings, but were not permitted to stop until they had reached the further side of the hill, where the party sat down to make a short repast; but grief prevented the prisoners from eating.

The Indians speedily put forward again—not being so far removed from the settlement as to be secure from pursuit. A little further on was a hill, called Machunk, where they halted nearly an hour, and prepared moccasons for some of the children.

Resuming their journey, they passed over another steep hill, and in a short time they reached Broad Mountain, the prisoners wearied and almost exhausted. Mrs. Gilbert, who was nearly sixty years of age, believing herself unable to make the ascent of this mountain on foot, sat down in weariness of body and in anguish of spirit, declaring she could proceed no farther. But being threatened by the Indians with instant death, if she delayed them in their journey, she was compelled to make her toilsome way up the mountain, nearly fainting at every step. Having reached the summit, the captives were permitted to rest for about an hour. The Broad Mountain is said to be seven miles across, and about ten miles from Gilbert's settlement.

Leaving Broad Mountain, they struck into Neskapeck path, which they followed the remainder of the day, crossing Quackac creek, and passing over Pismire Hill, and through the Moravian Pine Swamp, to Mahoniah Mountain, where they lodged that night. The prisoners were allowed, for beds, branches of hemlock strewed on the ground, and blankets for covering—an indulgence scarcely to have been expected from their savage captors. To prevent their escape, however, a contrivance was resorted to that completely marred the little comfort they might otherwise have enjoyed. A sapling about the thickness of a man's thigh was cut down, in which notches were made; the legs of the prisoners were then placed in notches, and another sapling placed over the first and made fast; a cord was also put about their necks and fastened to a tree; thus effectually confining them, in this stretched-out position, all night upon their backs.

Early the next morning they continued their route near the waters of terrapin ponds. The Indians that day deemed it best to separate in companies of two, each under the command of a particular Indian, spreading them to a considerable distance, in order to render a pursuit as nearly impracticable as possible. During the day, the Indian under whose direction Benjamin Gilbert and his wife were placed, frequently threatened them with instant death, whenever from fatigue they began to lag in the journey. Towards evening the parties again met and encamped. Having killed a deer, they kindled a fire and roasted the flesh, each man holding a piece of it over the coals or in the flame, by means of pointed sticks. The confinement of the prisoners was similar to that which they endured the night before.

After breakfast the next morning, a council was held concerning the division of the prisoners. An allotment being made, they were delivered to their several masters, with instructions to obey the commands of the particular Indian whose property they became. In this day's journey they passed near Fort Wyoming, on the eastern branch of the Susquehanna, about forty miles from their late habitation. The Indians were alarmed as they approached this garrison, and observed great caution, suffering not the least unnecessary noise, and stepping on the stones that lay on the path, lest any footsteps should lead to a discovery. The night was spent on the banks of a stream emptying itself into the Susquehanna, not far distant from the fort. On the following morning the prisoners were all painted, according to Indian custom, some of them with red and black, some all red, and others with black only. Those whom they painted black, without the mixture of any other color, are in most cases devoted to death; and though they are not usually killed immediately, they are seldom preserved to reach the Indian hamlets alive. In the evening of this day, they came to the Susquehanna, having had a painful and wearisome journey over a very stony and hilly country. Here the Indians were more than ordinarily careful in seeking a secluded lodging-place, that they might be as secure as possible from any scouting parties of the white people. In the night their horses strayed away from them, and it was late the next morning before they found them and were ready to proceed on their journey. Their course lay along the river. In the afternoon they came to a place where the Indians had left four negroes, with a supply of corn for their subsistence, waiting their return. These negroes had escaped from their masters, and were on their way to Niagara when first discovered by the Indians. Being challenged by the latter, they said they "were for the king," upon which they were received into protection.

It was not to the comfort of the prisoners that these negroes were added to the company. They manifested an insolence and domineering spirit which were almost intolerable, frequently insulting the captives, whipping them in mere wantonness and sport, and in all respects treating them with more severity than the Indians did themselves.

On the 1st of May, the whole company came to a place where two Indians lay dead at the side of the path. Two others had been killed there, but were removed. The captives were informed that a party of Indians had taken some white people whom they were carrying off as prisoners; the latter rose upon their captors in the night time, killed four of them, and then effected their escape. When the present company came to this place the women were sent forward, and the male captives commanded to draw near and view the dead bodies. After remaining to observe them for some time, they were ordered to a place where a tree was blown down. They were then directed to dig a grave; to effect which they sharpened a piece of sapling with a tomahawk, with which rude instrument one of them broke the ground, and the others threw out the earth with their hands; the negroes being permitted to beat them severely all the time they were thus employed. The bodies were deposited in the grave, and the prisoners marched a short distance farther, where they found the Indians who had gone forward with the women, preparing a lodging place for the night. The captives were still secured every night, in the manner already described.

The next day, towards evening, they crossed the east branch of the Susquehanna in canoes, at the same place where General Sullivan's army had crossed it in the expedition against the Indians. The horses swam the river by the side of the canoes. Their encampment that night was on the western bank of the stream; but two Indians who did not cross it, sent for Benjamin Gilbert jr. and Jesse Gilbert's wife. Not being able to assign any probable cause for this order, the remaining captives spent the night in great anxiety and uneasiness of mind. The next morning, however, their fears were dispelled by seeing their companions again, who had received no worse treatment than usual. This day, the Indians, in their march, found a scalp which they took along with them, and also some corn, on which they made a supper. They frequently killed deer, which was the only provision the party had, as the flour which they took with them from the settlement was expended.

On the 4th of May, the party was divided into two companies; the one taking a path to the westward, with whom were Thomas Peart, Joseph Gilbert, Benjamin Gilbert, jr., and Jesse Gilbert's wife; the other company travelled more to the north.

In the evening, as the company that took the northern route was about to encamp, the prisoners inquired of their captors what had become of their four companions who had been taken on the western path. The reply was, "They are killed and scalped, and you may expect the same fate to-night." Andrew Harrigar was so terrified at the threat that he resolved upon flight. As soon as it was dark, he took a kettle, with pretence of bringing some water, and made his escape under cover of the night. Pursuit was made by several of the Indians as soon as he was missing; they remained out all night in search of him. They were not able, however, to overtake him, and in the morning they returned. Harrigar endured many hardships in the woods, and at length reached the settlements, and gave the first authentic intelligence of the captives to their friends and neighbors.

After this escape, the prisoners were treated with great severity on account of it, and were often accused of being privy to the design of Harrigar. Rowland Monteur carried his resentment so far that he threw Jesse Gilbert down, and lifted his tomahawk to strike him, which

Mrs. Gilbert prevented by placing her head on that of her son, and beseeching the enraged savage to spare him. Turning round, he kicked her over, and then tied both mother and son by their necks to a tree, where they remained until his fury was a little abated; he then loosed them, and bade them pack up and go forwards. In the evening they came to one of their lodging places in one of the deserted towns of the Shipquegas, and took their lodgings in one of the wigwams still standing. The Shipquegas towns had been abandoned a short time before, upon the approach of General Sullivan's army. The party remained for three days among the deserted villages of this tribe. Besides an abundance of game here, there were plenty of potatoes and turnips remaining in the fields attached to the villages, which had not been destroyed by the invading army. Several horses were taken here, which had been left by the Shipquegas in their hasty flight. Upon resuming their march, Mrs. Gilbert was placed upon one of these horses, which seemed wild and dangerous to ride, but she was not thrown; she continued to ride him for several days.

The day they renewed their journey, they first passed through a long and dreary swamp, and then began the ascent of a rugged mountain, where there was no path. The underwood made it difficult for the women to ascend; but they were compelled to keep pace with their masters, however great the fatigue. When the mountain was crossed, the party tarried awhile for the negroes, who lagged behind with the horses that carried the baggage. The whole company being now together, they agreed to encamp in a swamp not far distant. A long reach of savannas and low grounds rendering their next day's journey very fatiguing and painful, especially to the women; and Elizabeth Peart in particular was wearied almost to fainting, by being compelled to carry her child, her husband not being permitted to carry it for her, or to lend her the least assistance; and once as she was just ready to drop from fatigue, the Indian who had charge of her, struck her, a violent blow, to impel her forward.

On the third day after their departure from the Shipquegas villages, their provisions began to fail them; and there was no game in the country through which they journeyed. At night, worn down with toil and suffering from the want of food, Mrs. Gilbert was seized with a chill. The Indians, however, gave her some flour and water boiled, which afforded her some relief. But the next day she was so weak that she could only get along by the assistance of two of her children—her horse having been taken from her.

On the 14th of May, they came to Canadosago, where they met with Benjamin Gilbert, jr., and Jesse Gilbert's wife, Sarah, two of the four captives that had been separated from the rest for the last ten days, and taken along the western path. On the same day, John Huston, jr., the younger of the Cayuga Indians, under whose care Benjamin Gilbert, sr., was placed, designing to dispatch him, painted him black; this exceedingly terrified the family; but no entreaties of theirs being likely to prevail, they resigned their cause to Him whose power can control all events. Wearied with travelling, and weak from the want of food, they made a stop to recover themselves; when the elder of the Cayugas, who had been sent forward with Abner Gilbert two days before to procure a supply of provisions, returned, assuring them that a supply was at hand.

The negroes were reduced so low with hunger, that their behavior was different from what it had been, conducting themselves with more moderation. At their quarters, in the evening, two white men came to them, one of whom was a volunteer among the British, the other had been taken prisoner some time before; these two men brought some hommony, and sugar made from the sweet maple; of this provision they made a more comfortable supper than they had eaten for many days.

In the morning the volunteer, having received information of the rough treatment the prisoners met with from the negroes, relieved them by taking the negroes under his charge They crossed a large creek which was in their way, and had to swim their horses over it. Benjamin Gilbert began to fail, when an Indian put a rope around his neck, leading him along with it; fatigue at last overpowered him, and he fell to the ground, when the Indian pulled the rope so hard that it almost choked him. His wife interceded for him, when her entreaties prevailed, and their hearts were turned from their cruel purpose.

Necessity induced two of the Indians the next day to set off on horse-back, into the Seneca country, in search of provisions. The prisoners, in the mean time, were ordered to dig up a root, something resembling a potato, which the Indians call whappanies. They tarried at this place, until towards the evening of the second day, and made a soup of wild onions and turnip tops; this they ate without bread or salt, it could not therefore afford sufficient sustenance, either for young or old; their food being so very light their strength daily wasted.

Having left this place, they crossed the Genesee river on a raft of logs, bound together by hickory withes; this appeared to be a dangerous method of ferrying them over such a river, to those who had been unaccustomed to such conveyances. They fixed their station near the Genesee banks, and procured more of the wild potato roots before mentioned, for their supper.

On the following day, one of the Indians left the company, taking with him the finest horse they had, and in some hours after returned with a large piece of meat, ordering the captives to broil it; this command they cheerfully performed, anxiously watching the kettle, fresh meat being a rarity which they had not for a long time enjoyed. The Indians, when it was sufficiently boiled, distributed to each person a piece, eating sparingly themselves. The prisoners made their repast without bread or salt, and ate with a good deal of relish what they supposed to be fresh beef, but afterwards understood it was horse flesh.

A shrill halloo which they heard, gave the prisoners some uneasiness; one of the Indians immediately rode to examine the cause, and found it was Captain Rowland Monteur, and his brother John's wife, with some other Indians, who were seeking them with provisions. The remainder of the company soon reached them, and they divided some bread, which they had brought, into small pieces, according to the number of the company. The captain and his company had brought with them cakes of hommony and Indian corn; of this they made a good meal. He appeared pleased to see the prisoners, having been absent from them several days, and ordered them all round to shake hands with him. From him they received information respecting Joseph Gilbert and Thomas Peart, who were separated from the others on the fourth of the month, and learned that they had arrived at the Indian settlements, some time before, in safety. The company staid the night at this place. One of the Indians refused to suffer any of them to come near his fire, or converse with the prisoner, who, in the distribution had fallen to him. Pounding hommony was the next day's employment; the weather being warm, made it a hard task; they boiled and prepared it for supper, the Indians sitting down to eat first, and when they had concluded their meal, they wiped the spoon on the sole of their moccasons, and then gave it to the captives.

Having resumed their journey, Elizabeth Gilbert, being obliged to ride alone, missed the path, for which the Indians repeatedly struck her. Their route still continued through rich meadows. After wandering for a time out of the direct path, they came to an Indian town, and obtained the necessary information to pursue their journey; the Indians ran out of their huts to see the prisoners, and to partake of the plunder, but no part of it suited them. Being directed to travel the back path again, for a short distance, they did so, and then struck into another, and went on until night, by which time they were very hungry, not having eaten since morning; the kettle was again set on the fire for hommony, this being their only food.

On the 21st of May, the report of a morning-gun from Niagara, which they heard, contributed to raise their hopes—they rejoiced at being so near. An Indian was dispatched, on horseback, to procure some provisions from the fort.

Elizabeth Gilbert could not walk as fast as the rest, she was therefore sent forward on foot, but was soon overtaken and left behind, the rest being obliged by the Indians to go on without regarding her. She would have been greatly perplexed, when she came to a division path, had not her husband laid a branch across the path which would have led her wrong—an affecting instance of both ingenuity and tenderness. She met several Indians, who passed by without speaking to her.

An Indian belonging to the company, who was on the horse Elizabeth Gilbert had ridden, overtook her, and endeavored to alarm her, by saying that she would be left behind, and perish in the woods: yet, notwithstanding this, his heart was so softened before he had gone any great distance from her, that he alighted from his horse and left him, that she might be able to reach the rest of the company. The more seriously she considered this, the more it appeared to her to be a convincing instance of the overruling protection of Him, who can "turn the heart of man as the husbandman turneth the water-course in his field."

As the Indians approached nearer their habitations, they frequently repeated their halloos, and after some time they received an answer in the same manner, which alarmed the company much; but they soon discovered it to proceed from a party of whites and Indians, who were on some expedition, though their pretence was that they were for

New York. Not long after parting with these, Rowland Monteur's wife came to them; she was daughter to Siangorochti, king of the Senecas, but her mother being a Cayuga, she was ranked among that nation, the children generally reckoning their descent from the mother's side. This princess was attended by the captain's brother, John, one other Indian, and a white prisoner who had been taken at Wyoming, by Rowland Monteur; she was dressed altogether in the Indian manner, shining with gold lace and silver baubles. They brought with them from the fort a supply of provisions. The captain being at a distance behind, when his wife came, the company waited for him. After the customary salutations, he addressed himself to his wife, telling her that Rebecca was her daughter, and that she must not be induced, by any consideration, to part with her; whereupon she took a silver ring off her finger, and put it upon Rebecca's, by which she was adopted as her daughter.

They feasted upon the provisions that were brought, for they had been for several days before pinched with hunger, what sustenance they could procure not being sufficient to support nature.

The next day, the Indians proceeded on their journey, and continued whooping in the most frightful manner. In this day's route, they met another company of Indians, who compelled Benjamin Gilbert, the elder, to sit on the ground, when they put several questions to him, to which he gave them the best answer he could; they then took his hat from him and went off.

Going through a small town near Niagara, an Indian woman came out of one of the huts, and struck each of the captives a blow. Not long after their departure from this place, Jesse, Rebecca, and their mother, were detained until the others had got out of their sight, when the mother was ordered to push on; and as she had to go by herself, she was much perplexed what course to take, as there was no path by which she could be directed. In this dilemma, she concluded to keep as straight forward as possible, and after some space of time, she had the satisfaction of overtaking the others. The pilot then made a short stay, that those who were behind might come up, and the captain handed some rum round, giving each a dram, except the two old folks, whom they did not consider worthy of this notice. Here the captain, who had the chief direction, painted Abner, Jesse, Rebecca, and Elizabeth Gilbert, jr., and presented each with a belt of wampum, as a token of their being received into favor, although they took from them all their hats and bonnets, except Rebecca's.

The prisoners were released from the loads they had heretofore been compelled to carry, and had it not been for the treatment they expected on their approaching the Indian towns, and the hardships after a separation, their situation would have been tolerable; but the horrors of their minds, arising from the dreadful yells of the Indians, as they approached the hamlets, is easier conceived than described, for they were no strangers to the customary cruelty exercised upon captives on entering their towns. The Indians, men, women, and children, collect together, bringing clubs and stones in order to beat them, which they usually do with great severity, by way of revenge for their relations who have been slain; this is performed immediately upon their entering the village where the warriors reside. This treatment cannot be avoided, and the blows, however cruel, must be borne without complaint, and the prisoners are sorely beaten, until their enemies are wearied with the cruel sport. Their sufferings were in this case very great, they received several wounds, and two of the women, who were on horseback, were much bruised by the falling of their horses, which were frightened by the Indians. Elizabeth, the mother, took shelter by the side of one of them, but upon observing that she met with some favor upon his account, he sent her away; she then received several violent blows, so that she was almost disabled. The blood trickled from their heads in a stream, their hair being cut close, and the clothes they had on, in rags, made their situation truly piteous. Whilst they were inflicting this revenge upon the captives, the king came, and put a stop to any farther cruelty, by telling them "It was sufficient," which they immediately attended to.

Benjamin Gilbert, and Elizabeth his wife, were ordered to Captain Rowland Monteur's house; the women belonging to it were kind to them, and gave them something to eat: Sarah Gilbert, Jesse's wife, was taken from them by three women, in order to be put in the family she was to be adopted by.

Two officers, from Niagara Fort, Captains Dace and Powel, came to see the prisoners, and prevent, as they were informed, any abuse that might be given them. Benjamin Gilbert informed these officers, that he was apprehensive they were in great danger of being murdered, upon which they promised him they would send a boat, the next day, to bring them to Niagara.

Notwithstanding the kind intention of the officers, they did not derive the expected advantage from it, the next day, for the Indians insisted on their going to the fort on foot, although the bruises they had received the day before, from the many severe blows given them, rendered their journey on foot very distressing; but Captain Monteur obstinately persisting, they dared not remonstrate, or refuse.

When they left the Indian town, several issued from their huts after them with sticks in their hands, yelling and screeching in the most dismal manner; but through the interposition of four Indian women, who had come with the captives, to prevent any further abuse they might receive, they were preserved. One of them walking between Benjamin Gilbert and his wife, led them, and desired Jesse to keep as near them as he could, the other three walked behind, and prevailed with the young Indians to desist. They had not pursued their route long, before they saw Captain John Powel, who came from his boat, and persuaded (though with some difficulty) the Indians to get into it, with the captives, which relieved them from their apprehensions of further danger. After reaching the fort, Captain Powel introduced them to Colonel Guy Johnson, and Colonel Butler, who asked the prisoners many questions, in the presence of the Indians. They presented the captain with a belt of wampum, which is a constant practice among them, when they intend a ratification of the peace. Before their connection with Europeans, these belts were made of shells, found on the coasts of New England and Virginia, which were sawed out into beads of an oblong shape, about a quarter of an inch long, which when strung together on leather strings, and these strings fastened with fine threads made of sinews, compose what is called a belt of wampum. But since the whites have gained footing amongst them, they make use of the common glass beads for this purpose.

On the 25th of May, Benjamin Gilbert, his wife Elizabeth, and their son Jesse, were surrendered to Colonel Johnson, in whose family they received much kindness. The colonel's housekeeper was particularly attentive to them, not only inviting them to her house, where she gave the old folks her best room, but administering to their necessities and endeavoring to soothe their sorrows.

A few days after they came to the fort, they had information that Benjamin Peart was by the river side, with the Indians; upon hearing this report, his mother went to see him, but every attempt to obtain his release was in vain; the Indians would by no means give him up. From this place they intended to march with their prisoners to the Genesee river, about one hundred miles distant. As the affectionate mother's solicitations proved fruitless, her son not only felt the afflicting loss of his wife and child, from whom he had been torn some time before, but the renewal of his grief on this short sight of his parent. She procured him a hat, and also some salt, which was an acceptable burden for the journey.

Benjamin Gilbert, conversing with the Indian captain who made them captives, observed that he might say what none of the other Indians could, "That he had brought in the oldest man, and the youngest child"; his reply to this was expressive: "It was not I, but the great God who brought you through, for we were determined to kill you, but were prevented."

The British officers being informed that Jesse Gilbert's wife was among the Indians, with great tenderness agreed to seek her out, and after a diligent inquiry, found that she was among the Delawares; they went to them, and endeavored to agree upon some terms for her release; the Indians brought her to the fort the next day, but would not give her up to her relations.

Early next morning, Captain Robeson generously undertook to procure her liberty, which, after much attention and solicitude, he, together with Lieutenant Hillyard, happily accomplished. They made the Indians some small presents, and gave them one hundred and fifty dollars as a ransom. When Sarah Gilbert had obtained her liberty, she altered her dress more in character for her sex, than she had been able to do whilst among the Indians, and went to her husband and parents at Colonel Johnson's, where she was joyfully received. Colonel Johnson's housekeeper continued her kind attentions to them, during their stay, and procured clothing for them from the public stores.

About the 1st of June, the Senecas, among whom Elizabeth Peart was a captive, brought her with them to the fort; as soon as the mother heard of it, she went to her, and had some conversation with her, but could not learn where she was to be sent to; she then inquired of the interpreter, and pressed on his friendship, to learn what was to become of her daughter; this request he complied with, and informed her that she was to be given away to another family of the Senecas, and adopted among them, in the place of a deceased relation. Captain Powel interested himself in her case likewise, and offered to purchase her of them, but the Indians refused to give her up; and as the mother and daughter expected they should see each other no more, their parting was very affecting.

The woman who had adopted Rebecca as her daughter, came also to the fort, and Elizabeth Gilbert made use of this opportunity to inquire concerning her daughter; the interpreter informed her that there was no probability of obtaining the enlargement of her child, as the Indians would not part with her. All she could do was to recommend her to their notice, as very weakly, and in consequence not able to endure much fatigue.

Not many days after their arrival at Niagara, a vessel came up Niagara to the fort, with orders for the prisoners to go to Montreal. In this vessel came the notorious Indian chief, Brant. Elizabeth Gilbert immediately applied to him in behalf of her children who yet remained in captivity, when he promised to use his endeavors to procure their liberty, A short time before they sailed for Montreal, they received accounts of Abner and Elizabeth Gilbert the younger, but it was understood that their possessors were not disposed to give them up. As the prospect of obtaining the release of their children was so very discouraging, it was no alleviation to their distress to be removed to Montreal, where, in all probability, they would seldom be able to gain any information respecting them; on which account, they were very solicitous to stay at Niagara, but the colonel said they could not remain there, unless the son would enter into the king's service; this could not be consented to, therefore they chose to submit to every calamity which might be permitted to befal them, and confide in the great Controller of events. After continuing ten days at Colonel Johnson's, they took boat and crossed the Niagara, in order to go on board the vessel which was to take them to Montreal.

Benjamin Gilbert had been much indisposed before they left the fort, and his disorder was increased by a rain which fell on their passage, as they were without any covering. They passed Oswagatchy, an English garrison, by the side of the river, but they were not permitted to stop here; they proceeded down the St. Lawrence, and the rain continuing, went on shore on an island in order to secure themselves from the weather. Here they made a shelter for Benjamin Gilbert, and when the rain ceased, a place was prepared for him in the boat, that he might lie down with more ease. His bodily weakness made such rapid progress, that it rendered all the care and attention of his wife necessary, and likewise called forth all her fortitude: she supported him in her arms, affording every possible relief to mitigate his extreme pains. Although in this distressed condition, he, notwithstanding, gave a satisfactory evidence of the virtue and power of a patient and holy resignation, which can disarm the king of terrors, and receive him as a welcome messenger. Thus prepared, he passed from this state of probation, the 8th of June, 1780, in the evening, leaving his wife and two children, who were with him, in all the anxiety of deep distress, although they had no doubt but that their loss was his everlasting gain. Being without a light in the boat, the darkness of the night added not a little to their malancholy situation. As there were not any others with Elizabeth Gilbert but her children, and four Frenchmen, who managed the boat, and her apprehensions alarmed her lest they should throw the corpse overboard, as they appeared to be an unfeeling company, she therefore applied to some British officers who were in a boat behind them, who dispelled her fears, and received her under their protection. In the morning they passed the garrison of Cœur de Lac, and waited for some considerable time, a small distance below it. Squire Campbell, who had the charge of the prisoners, when he heard of Benjamin Gilbert's decease, sent Jesse to the commandant of this garrison to get a coffin, in which they put the corpse, and very hastily interred him under an oak, not far from the fort. The boatmen would not allow his widow to pay the last tribute to his memory, but regardless of her affliction refused to wait.

The next day, they arrived at Montreal, where they remained for more than a year, receiving much kindness both from the British officers and soldiers and a number of the inhabitants. Being placed upon the list of the king's prisoners, daily rations were allowed them.

During the time they remained here, they applied to Colonel Campbell for such assistance as he could render them in procuring the release of the other captives from the Indians. He took down a short account of their sufferings, and forwarded the narrative to General Huldimund, at Quebec, desiring his attention to the sufferers. The general immediately issued orders that all the officers under his command should endeavor to procure the release of the prisoners, and that every garrison should furnish them with necessaries as they came down. Soon after this, Mrs. Gilbert was one day at the house of a Mrs. Scott, in Montreal, when she was informed that some persons in an adjoining room were desirous of seeing her. Her joy may be imagined when, upon entering the apartment, she beheld six of her long lost children.

A messenger was sent to inform Jesse and his wife, that Joseph Gilbert, Benjamin Peart, Elizabeth his wife, and young child, Abner and Elizabeth Gilbert, the younger, were with their mother. It must afford very pleasing reflections to any affectionate disposition, to dwell awhile on this scene, that after a captivity of nearly fourteen months, so happy a meeting should take place. Thomas Peart, who had obtained his liberty, tarried at Niagara, that he might be of service to the two yet remaining in captivity, viz. Benjamin Gilbert, jr. and Rebecca Gilbert. Abigail Dodson, the daughter of a neighboring farmer, who was taken with them, having inadvertently informed the Indians she was not of the Gilbert family, all attempts for her liberty were fruitless.

We shall now relate how Joseph Gilbert, the eldest son of the deceased, fared among the Indians. He, with Thomas Peart, Benjamin Gilbert, jr. and Jesse Gilbert's wife Sarah, were taken along the westward path, as before related; after some short continuance in this path, Thomas Peart and Joseph Gilbert were taken from the other two, and by a different route through many difficulties, they were brought to Caracadera, where they received the insults of the women and children, whose husbands had fallen in their hostile excursions.

Joseph Gilbert was separated from his companion, and removed to an Indian town, called Nundow, about seven miles from Caracadera; his residence was, for several weeks, in the king's family, whose hamlet was superior to the other small huts. The king himself brought him some hommony, and treated him with great civility, intending his adoption into his family, in place of one of his sons, who was slain when General Sullivan drove them from their habitations. As Nundow was not to be the place of his abode, his quarters were soon changed, and he was taken back to Caracadera.

The situation of Elizabeth Peart, wife of Benjamin, and her child is next related. After she and the child were parted from her husband, Abigail Dodson and the child were taken several miles in the night, to a little hut, where they staid till morning, and the day following were taken within eight miles of Niagara, where she was adopted into one of the families of Senecas; the ceremonies of adoption to her were tedious and distressing; they obliged her to sit down with a young man, an Indian, and the eldest chieftain of the family repeated a jargon of words, to her unintelligible, but which she considered as some form of marriage, and this apprehension introduced the most violent agitations, as she was fully determined, at all events, to oppose any steps of this nature; but after the old Indian concluded his speech, she was relieved from the dreadful embarrassment she had been under, as she was led away by another Indian. Abigail Dodson was given the same day to one of the families of the Cayuga nation, so that Elizabeth Peart saw her no more.

The man who led Elizabeth from the company, took her into the family for whom they adopted her, and introduced her to her parents, brothers, and sisters, in the Indian style, who received her very kindly, and made a grievous lamentation over her, according to custom. After she had been with them two days, the whole family left their habitation and went about two miles to Fort Slusher, where they staid several days. This fort is about one mile above Niagara Falls.

As she was much indisposed, the Indians were detained several days for her; but as they cared little for her, she was obliged to lie on the damp ground, which prevented her speedy recovery. As soon as her disorder abated its violence, they set off in a bark canoe for Buffalo creek; and as they went slowly, they had an opportunity of taking some fish. When they arrived at their place of intended settlement, they went on shore to build a house. A few days after they came to this new settlement, they returned with Elizabeth to Fort Slusher, when she was told her child must be taken away from her; this was truly afflicting, but all remonstrances were in vain. From Fort Slusher she travelled on foot, carrying her child to Niagara, it being eighteen miles, and in sultry weather, which rendered it a painful addition to the thoughts of parting with her tender offspring. The intent of their journey was to obtain provisions, and their stay at the fort was of several days continuance, Captain Powel offered her an asylum in his house.

The Indians took the child from her, and went with it across the river, to adopt it into the family they had assigned for it, notwithstanding Captain Powel, at his wife's request, interceded that it might not be removed from its mother; but as it was so young, they returned it to its mother after its adoption, until it should be convenient to send it to the family under whose protection it was to be placed. Obtaining the provision and other necessaries they came to Niagara to trade for, they returned to Fort Slusher on foot, from whence they embarked in their canoes.

It being near the time of planting, they used much expedition in this journey. The labor and drudgery in a family falling to the share of the women, Elizabeth had to assist the squaw in preparing the ground and planting corn. Their provisions being scant, they suffered much, and their dependence for a sufficient supply until gathering their crop, was on what they should receive from the fort, they were under the necessity of making a second journey thither.

They were two days on the road at this time. A small distance before they came to the fort, they took her child from her, and sent it to its destined family, and it was several months before she had an opportunity of seeing it again. After being taken from her husband, to lose her darling infant was a severe stroke; she lamented her condition and wept sorely, for which one of the Indians inhumanly struck her. Her Indian father seemed a little moved to see her so distressed; and in order to console her, assured her they would bring it back again, but she saw it not until the spring following. After they had disposed of their peltries, they returned to their habitation by the same route which they had come.

With a heart oppressed with sorrow, Elizabeth trod back her steps, mourning for her lost infant, for this idea presented itself continually to her mind; but as she experienced how fruitless, nay, how dangerous, solicitations in behalf of her own child were, she dried up her tears and pined in secret.

Soon after they had reached their own habitation, Elizabeth Peart was again afflicted with sickness. At first they showed some attention to her complaints, but as she did not speedily recover so as to be able to work, they discontinued every attention, and built a small hut by the side of a cornfield, placing her in it to mind the corn. In this lonely condition she saw a white man, who had been made prisoner among the Indians. He informed her that her child was released and with the white people. This information revived her drooping spirits, and a short time after she recovered of her indisposition, but her employ-ment still continued to be that of attending corn until it was ripe for gathering, which she assisted in. When the harvest was over, they permitted her to return and live with them. A time of plenty now commenced, and they lived as if they had sufficient to last the year through, faring plenteously every day.

A drunken Indian came to the cabin one day, and the old Indian woman complained of him to Elizabeth, his behaviour exceedingly terrified her; he stormed like fury, and at length struck her a violent blow, which laid her on the ground; he then began to pull her about and abuse her much, when another of the women interposed, and rescued her from further suffering. Such is the shocking effects of spirituous liquor on these people, that it totally deprives them both of sense and humanity.

A tedious winter prevented them from leaving their habitation, and deprived her of the pleasure of hearing often of her friends, who were very much scattered; but a prisoner, who had lately seen her husband, informed her of his being much indisposed at the Genesee river, which was one hundred miles distant. On receiving this intelligence, she stood in need of much consolation, but had no source of comfort except in her own bosom.

Near the return of spring, the provision failing, they were compelled to go off to the fort for a fresh supply, having but a small portion of corn, which they apportioned out once each day. Through snow and severe frost they set out for Niagara, suffering much from the excessive cold. And when they came within a few miles of the fort, which they were four days in accomplishing, they struck up a small wigwam for some of the family, with the prisoners, to live in, until the return of the warriors from the fort.

As soon as Captain Powel's wife heard that the young child's mother had come with the Indians, she desired to see her, claiming some relationship in the Indian way, as she had also been a prisoner amongst them. They granted her request, and Elizabeth was accordingly introduced, and informed that her husband was returned to the fort, and there was some expectation of his release. The same day Benjamin Peart came to see his wife, but he was not permitted to continue with her, as the Indians insisted on her going back with them to the cabin, which, as has been related, was some miles distant. She was not allowed for several days to go from the cabin, but a white family who had bought the child from the Indians to whom it had been presented, offered the party with whom Elizabeth had been confined a bottle of rum if they would bring her across the river to her child, which they did, and delighted the fond mother with this happy meeting, as she had not seen it for the space of eight months.

She was permitted to remain with the family where her child was for two days, when she returned with the Indians to their cabin. After some time she obtained a further permission to go to the fort, where she had some needle work from the white people, which afforded her a plea for often visiting it. At length Captain Powel's wife prevailed with them to suffer her to continue a few days at her house and work for her family, which was granted. At the expiration of the time, upon the coming of the Indians for her to return with them, she pleaded indisposition, and by this means they were repeatedly dissuaded from taking her with them.

As the time of planting drew nigh, she made use of a little address to retard her departure; having a small swelling on her neck, she applied a poultice, which led the Indians into a belief that it was improper to remove her, and they consented to come again for her in two weeks. Her child was given up to her soon after her arrival at the fort, where she had lodged at Captain Powel's, and her husband came frequently to visit her, which was a great satisfaction, as her trials in their separation had been many.

At the time appointed, some of the Indians came again, but she still pleaded indisposition, and had confined herself to her bed. One of the women interrogated her very closely, but did not insist upon her going back. Thus several months elapsed, she contriving delays as often as they came.

When the vessel, which was to take the other five, among whom was her husband and child, was ready to sail, the officers at Niagara concluded that she might also go with them, as they saw no reasonable objection, and they doubted not but that it was in their power to satisfy those Indians who considered her as their property.

Abner Gilbert, another of the captives, when the company had reached the Indian towns, within three miles of Niagara Fort, was, with Elizabeth Gilbert the younger, separated from the rest about the latter part of May, 1780, and were both adopted into John Huston's family, who was of the Cayuga nation. After a stay of three days, at or near the settlements of these Indians, they removed to a place near the Great Falls, which is about eighteen miles distant from the fort, and loitered there three days more; they then crossed the river, and settled near its banks, clearing a piece of land, and preparing it with a hoe for planting. Until they could gather their corn, their dependence was entirely upon the fort. After the space of three weeks they packed up their moveables, which they generally carry with them in their rambles, and went down the river to get provisions at Butlersbury, a small village built by Colonel Butler, and is on the opposite side of the river to Niagara Fort. They staid one night at the village, observing great caution that none of the white people should converse with the Indians. Next day, after transacting their business, they returned to their settlement, and continued there but about one week, when it was concluded they must go again for Butlersbury; after they had left their habitation a small distance, the head of the family met with his brother, and as they are very ceremonious in such interviews, the place of meeting was their rendezvous for that day and night. In the morning, the family, with the brother before mentioned, proceeded for Butlersbury, and reached it before dark. They went to the house of an Englishman, one John Secord, who was styled brother to the chief of the family, having lived with him some time before. After some deliberation, it was agreed that Elizabeth Gilbert should continue in this family until sent for; this was an agreeable change to her.

From the time of Elizabeth being first introduced by the Indian into the family of John Secord, who was one in whom he placed great confidence, she was under the necessity of having new clothes, as those she had brought from home were much worn. Her situation in the family where she was placed was comfortable.

After she had resided a few days with them she discovered where the young child was, that had some time before been taken from its mother, Elizabeth Peart, and herself, together with John Secord's wife, with whom she lived, and Captain Fry's wife, went to see it, in order to purchase it from the Indian woman who had it under her care; but they could not then prevail with her, though some time after Captain Fry's wife purchased it for thirteen dollars. Whilst among the Indians, it had been for a long time indisposed, and in a lingering, distressed situation; but under its present kind protectress, who treated the child as her own, it soon recruited.

Elizabeth Gilbert jr., lived very agreeably in John Secord's family rather more than a year, and became so fondly attached to her benefactors, that she usually styled the mistress of the house her mamma. During her residence here, her brother Abner and Thomas Peart came several times to visit her. The afflicting loss of her father, to whom she was affectionately endeared, and the separation from her mother, whom she had no expectation of seeing again, was a severe trial, although moderated by the kind attentions shown her by the family in which she lived.

John Secord, having some business at Niagara, took Betsy with him, where she had the satisfaction of seeing six of her relations, who had been captives, but were most of them released. This happy meeting made the trip to the fort a very agreeable one. She staid with them all night, and then returned. Not long after this visit, Colonel Butler and John Secord sent for the Indian who claimed Elizabeth as his property, and when he arrived they made overtures to purchase her, but he declared he would not sell his own flesh and blood; for thus they style those whom they have adopted. They then had recourse to presents, which, overcoming his scruples, they obtained her discharge; after which she remained two weeks at Butlersbury, and afterwards went to her mother at Montreal.

Having given a brief relation of the release and meeting of such of the captives as had returned from among the Indians, it may not be improper to return to the mother, who, with several of her children, were at Montreal. Elizabeth Gilbert suffered no opportunity to pass her, of inquiring about her relations and friends in Pennsylvania, and had the satisfaction of being informed by one who came from the southward, that the Friends of Philadelphia had been very assiduous in their endeavors to gain information where the family was, and had sent to the different meetings, desiring them to inform themselves of the situation of the captured family, and, if in their power, afford them such relief as they might need.

A person who came from Crown Point, informed her that Benjamin Gilbert, a son of the deceased by his first wife, had come thither in order to be of what service he could to the family, and had desired him to make inquiry where they were, and in what situation, and send him the earliest information possible. The next agreeable intelligence she received from Niagara, by a young woman who came from thence, who informed her that her daughter Rebecca was given up to the English by the Indians. This information must have been very pleasing, as their expectations of her release were but faint; the Indian with whom she lived considering her as her own child. It was not long after this, that Thomas Peart, Rebecca Gilbert, and their cousin Benjamin Gilbert, came to Montreal to the rest of the family. This meeting, after such scenes of sorrow as they had experienced, was more completely happy than can be expressed.

Rebecca Gilbert and Benjamin Gilbert jr. were separated from their friends and connections at a place called the Five Mile Meadows, which was said to be that distance from Niagara. The Seneca king's daughter, to whom they were allowed in the distribution of captives, took them to a small hut where her father, Siangorochti, his queen, and the rest of the family were, eleven in number. Upon the reception of the prisoners into the family, there was much sorrow and weeping, as is customary on such occasions, and the higher in favor the adopted prisoners are to be placed, the greater lamentation is made over them. After three days the family removed to a place called the Landing, on the banks of the Niagara river. Here they continued two days more, and then two of the women went with the captives to Niagara, to procure clothing from the king's store for them, and permitted them to ride on horseback to Fort Slusher, which is about eighteen miles distant from Niagara Fort. On this journey they had a sight of the great Falls of Niagara.

During a stay of six days at Fort Slusher, the British officers and others used their utmost endeavors to purchase them of the Indians; but the Indian king said he would not part with them for one thousand dollars. The Indians who claimed Elizabeth Peart, came to the fort with her at this time, and although she was very weakly and indisposed, it was an agreeable opportunity to them both, of conversing with each other, but they were not allowed to be frequently together, lest they should increase each other's discontent. Rebecca being dressed in the Indian manner, appeared very different from what she had been accustomed to; short clothes, leggings, and a gold laced hat. From Fort Niagara they went about eighteen miles above the Falls to Fort Erie, a garrison of the English, and continued their journey about four miles further, up Buffalo creek, and pitched their tent. At this place they met Rebecca's father and mother, by adoption, who had gone before on horseback. They caught some fish and made some soup of them, but Rebecca could eat none of it, as it was cooked without salt, and with all the carelessness of Indians. This spot was intended for their plantation, they therefore began to clear the land for a crop of Indian corn. While the women were thus employed, the men built a log house for their residence, and then went out a hunting.

Notwithstanding the family they lived with was of the first rank among the Indians, and the head of it styled king, they were under the necessity of laboring as well as those of lower rank, although they often had advantages of procuring more provisions than the rest. This family raised this summer about seventy-five bushels of Indian corn. As Rebecca was not able to pursue a course of equal labor with the other women, she was favored by them by often being sent into their hut to prepare something to eat; and as she dressed their provisions after the English method, and had erected an oven by the assistance of the other women, in which they baked their bread, their family fared more agreeably than the others.

Benjamin Gilbert jr., who was only eleven years of age when he was captured, was considered as the king's successor, and entirely freed from restraint, so that he even began to be delighted with his manner of life; and had it not been for the frequent counsel of his fellow captive, he would not have been anxious for an exchange.

In the waters of the lakes there are various kinds of fish, which the Indians take sometimes with spears; but whenever they can obtain hooks and lines they prefer them. A fish called ozoondah, resembling a shad in shape, but rather thicker and less bony, with which Lake Erie abounded, was often dressed for their table, and was of an agreeable taste, weighing from three to four pounds.

They drew provisions this summer from the forts, which frequently induced the Indians to repair thither. The king, his daughter, grand-daughter, and Rebecca, went together upon one of these visits to Fort Erie, where the British officers entertained them with a rich feast, and so great a profusion of wine, that the Indian king got very drunk; and as he had to manage the canoe on their return, they were repeatedly in danger of being overset among the rocks in the lake.

Rebecca and Benjamin met with much better fare than the other captives, as the family they lived with were but seldom in great want of necessaries, which were the only advantages they enjoyed beyond the rest of their tribe. Benjamin Gilbert, as a badge of his dignity, wore a silver medal pendant from his neck. The king, queen, and another of the family, together with Rebecca, and her cousin Benjamin, set off for Niagara, going as far as Fort Slusher by water, from whence they proceeded on foot, carrying their loads on their backs. Their business at the fort was to obtain provisions, which occasioned them frequently to visit it.

Rebecca indulged herself with the pleasing expectation of obtaining her release, or at least permission to remain behind among the whites; but in both these expectations she was disagreeably disappointed, having to return again with her captors; all efforts for her release being in vain. Colonel Johnson's housekeeper, whose repeated acts of kindness to this captured family have been noticed, made her some acceptable presents. As they had procured some rum to carry home with them, the chief was frequently intoxicated, and always in such unhappy fits behaved remarkably foolish. On their return, Thomas Peart, who was at Fort Niagara, procured for Rebecca a horse to carry her as far as Fort Slusher, where they took boat and got home after a stay of nine days.

Soon after their return, Rebecca and her cousin were seized with the chills and fever, which held them for near three months. During their indisposition the Indians were very kind to them; and as their strength of constitution alone could not check the progress of the disorder, the Indians procured some herbs, with which the patients were unacquainted, and made a plentiful decoction; with this they washed them, and it seemed to afform them some relief. The Indians accounted it a sovereign remedy. The decease of her father, of which Rebecca received an account, kept her in a drooping way a considerable time longer than she would otherwise have been.

As soon as she recovered her health, some of the family again went to Niagara, and Rebecca was permitted to be of the company. They staid at the fort about two weeks, and Colonel Johnson exerted himself in order to obtain her release, holding a treaty with the Indians for this purpose; but this mediation proved fruitless: she had therefore to return with many a heavy step. When they came to Lake Erie, where their canoe was, they proceeded by water. While in their boat, a number of Indians in another, came towards them, and informed them of the death of her Indian father, who had made an expedition to the frontiers of Pennsylvania, and was there wounded by the militia, and afterwards died of his wounds; on which occasion she was under the necessity of making a feint of sorrow, and weeping aloud with the rest. When they arrived at their settlement, it was the time of gathering their crop of corn, potatoes, and pumpkins, and preserving their hickory-nuts. About the beginning of the winter, some British officers came amongst them, and staid with them until spring, using every endeavor to obtain the discharge of the two captives, but without success. Rebecca and her cousin had the pleasure of seeing her brother, Abner, who came with the family amongst whom he lived, to settle near this place; and as they had not seen each other for almost twelve months, it proved very agreeable. Thomas Peart endeavored to animate his sister, by encouraging her with the hopes of speedily obtaining her liberty; but her hopes had so often failed, that she received little consolation.

An officer among the British, one Captain Latteridge, came and staid some time with them, and interested himself on behalf of the prisoners, and appeared in a fair way of obtaining their release; but being ordered to his regiment, he was prevented from further attention until his return from duty; and afterwards was commanded by Colonel Johnson to go with him to Montreal on business of importance, which effectually barred his undertaking any thing further that winter.

It afforded her many pleasing reflections when she heard that six of her relatives were freed from their difficulties, and Thomas Peart visiting her again, contributed, in some measure, to reanimate her with fresh hopes of obtaining her own freedom. They fixed upon a scheme of carrying her off privately; but when they gave time for a full reflection, it was evidently attended with too great danger, as it would undoubtedly have much enraged the Indians, and perhaps the life of every one concerned would have been forfeited by such indiscretion. During the course of this winter she suffered many hardships and severe disappointments, and being without a friend to unbosom her sorrows to, they appeared to increase by concealment; but making a virtue of necessity, she summoned up a firmness of resolution, and was supported under her discouragement beyond her own expectations.

The youth and inexperience of her cousin did not allow a sufficient confidence in him, but she had often to interest herself in an attention to, and oversight of, his conduct; and it was in some measure owing to this care, that he retained his desire to return to his people. Colonel Butler sent a string of wampum to the Indian chief, who immediately called a number of the Indians together upon this occasion, when they concluded to go down to Niagara, where they understood the design of the treaty was for the freedom of the remainder of the prisoners; for especial orders were issued by General Haldimand, at Quebec, that their liberty should be obtained. At this council-fire it was agreed that they should surrender up the prisoners. When they returned, they informed Rebecca that Butler had a desire to see her, which was the only information she could gain; this being a frequent custom among them to offer a very slight surmise of their intentions.

After this the whole family moved about six miles further up Lake Erie, where they staid about two months to gather their annual store of maple sugar, of which they made a considerable quantity. As soon as the season for this business was over, they returned to their own settlement, where they had not continued long, before an Indian came with an account that an astonishing number of young pigeons might be procured at a certain place, by felling trees that were filled with nests of young, and the distance was computed to be about fifty miles; this information delighted the several tribes; they speedily joined together, young and old, from different parts, and with great assiduity pursued their expedition, and took an abundance of the young ones, which they dried in the sun and with smoke, and filled several bags which they had taken with them for this purpose. Benjamin Gilbert was permitted to accompany them in this excursion, which must have been a curious one for whole tribes to be engaged in.

As the time approached when, according to appointment, they were to return to Niagara and deliver up the prisoners, they gave Rebecca the agreeable information, in order to allow her some time to make preparation. She made them bread for their journey with great cheerfulness. The Indians, to the number of thirty, attended on this occasion, with the two captives. They went as far as Fort Slusher in a bark canoe. It was several days before they reached Niagara Fort, as they went slowly on foot. After attending at Colonel Butler's, and conferring upon this occasion, in consideration of some valuable presents made them, they released the two last of the captives, Rebecca Gilbert and Benjamin Gilbert jr.

As speedily as they were enabled, their Indian dress was exchanged for the more customary and agreeable one of the Europeans; and on the 3rd of June, 1782, two days after their release, they sailed for Montreal. On the 22d of August, attended by a great number of the inhabitants of that place, they embarked in boats prepared for them, and took their departure for home; and on the 28th of the following month, arrived at Byberry, the place of their nativity, where Elizabeth and her children were once more favored with the agreeable opportunity of seeing and conversing with her ancient mother, together with their other nearest relatives and friends, to their mutual joy and satisfaction; under which happy circumstances we now leave them.

We have condensed the foregoing narrative from an anonymous work, entitled "Incidents of Border Life."

THE EVENTFUL SHOT

THE FOLLOWING NARRATIVE is given in the "Ohio Historical Collections." Mr. Joel Thorp, with his wife moved with an ox team, in May, 1799, from North Haven, Connecticut, to Millsford, in Ashtabula county, and they were the first settlers in that region. They soon had a small clearing on and about an old beaver dam, which was very rich and mellow. Towards the first of June, the family being short of provisions, Mr. Thorp started off alone to procure some, through the wilderness, with no guide but a pocket compass, to the nearest settlement, about twenty miles distant, in Pennsylvania. His family, consisting of Mrs. Thorp and three children, the oldest child, Basil, being but eight years of age, were before his return reduced to extremities for the want of food. They were compelled, in a measure, to dig for and subsist on roots, which yielded but little nourishment. The children in vain asked for food, promising to be satisfied with the least possible portion. The boy Basil remembered to have seen some kernels of corn in a crack of one of the logs of the cabin, and passed hours in a unsuccessful search for them. Mrs. Thorp emptied the straw out of her bed and picked it over to obtain the little wheat it contained, which she boiled and gave to her children. Her husband, it seems, had taught her to shoot at a mark, in which she acquired great skill. When all her means for procuring food were exhausted, she saw, as she stood in her cabin door, a wild turkey flying near. She took down her husband's rifle, and, on looking for ammunition, was surprised to find only sufficient for a small charge. Carefully cleaning the barrel, so as not to lose any by its sticking to the sides as it went down, she set some apart for priming, and loaded the piece with the remainder, and started in pursuit of the turkey, reflecting that on her success depended the lives of herself and children. Under the excitement of her feelings she came near defeating her object, by

211

frightening the turkey, which flew a short distance and again alighted in a potato patch. Upon this, she returned to the house and waited until the fowl had begun to wallow in the loose earth. On her second approach, she acted with great caution and coolness, creeping slyly on her hands and knees from log to log until she had gained the last obstruction between herself and the desired object. It was now a trying moment, and a crowd of emotions passed through her mind as she lifted the rifle to a level with her eye. She fired; the result was fortunate: the turkey was killed and herself and family preserved from death by her skill. Mrs. Thorp married three times. Her first husband was killed, in Canada, in the war of 1812; her second was supposed to have been murdered. Her last husband's name was Gordiner, died in Orange, November 1st, 1846.